THE GRIMKÉ SISTERS

SARAH AND ANGELINA GRIMKÉ

*THE FIRST AMERICAN WOMEN ADVOCATES
OF ABOLITION AND WOMAN'S RIGHTS*

BY

CATHERINE H. BIRNEY

"The glory of all glories is the glory of self-sacrifice"

GREENWOOD PRESS, PUBLISHERS
WESTPORT, CONNECTICUT

Originally published in 1885
by Lee and Shepard

First Greenwood Reprinting, 1969

SBN 8371-1303-2

PRINTED IN UNITED STATES OF AMERICA

PREFACE.

IT was with great diffidence, from inexperience in literary work of such length, that I engaged to write the biography which I now present to the public. But the diaries and letters placed in my hands lightened the work of composition, and it has been a labor of affection as well as of duty to pay what tribute I might to the memory of two of the noblest women of the country, whom I learned to love and venerate during a residence of nearly two years under the same roof, and who, to the end of their lives, honored me with their friendship.

C. H. B.

WASHINGTON CITY, Sept., 1885.

3

CONTENTS.

1

CHAPTER VIII.

CHAPTER IX.

CHAPTER X.

CHAPTER XI.

CHAPTER XII.

CHAPTER XIII.

CHAPTER XIV.

CHAPTER XV.

CHAPTER XVI.

CHAPTER XVII.

CHAPTER XVIII.

THE SISTERS GRIMKÉ.

CHAPTER I.

SARAH and ANGELINA GRIMKÉ were born in Charleston, South Carolina; Sarah, Nov. 26, 1792; Angelina, Feb. 20, 1805. They were the daughters of the Hon. John Fauchereau Grimké, a colonel in the revolutionary war, and judge of the Supreme Court of South Carolina. His ancestors were German on the father's side, French on the mother's; the Fauchereau family having left France in consequence of the revocation of the Edict of Nantes in 1685.

From his German father and Huguenot mother, Judge Grimké inherited not only intellectual qualities of a high order, but an abiding consciousness of his right to think for himself, a spirit of hostility to the Roman Catholic priesthood and church, and faith in the Calvinistic theology. Though he exhibited, during the course of his life, a freedom from certain social prejudices general among people of his class at Charleston, he seems to have never wavered in his adhesion to the tenets of his forefathers. That they were ever questioned in his household is not probable.

From a diary kept by him, it appears that his favorite subject of thought for many years was moral discipline, and he was fond of searching out and transcribing the opinions of various authors on this subject.

His family was wealthy and influential, and he received all the advantages which such circumstances could give. As was the custom among people of means in those days, he was sent to England for his collegiate course, and, after being graduated at Oxford, he studied law and practised for a while in London, having his rooms in the Temple. With a fine person, a cultivated mind and a generous allowance, he became a favorite in the fashionable and aristocratic society of Great Britain; nevertheless, he did not hesitate to quit the pleasant life he was leading and return home as soon as his native country seemed to need him. He speedily raised a company of cavalry in Charleston, and cast his lot with the patriots whom he found in arms against the mother-country. We have no record of his deeds, but we know that he distinguished himself at Eutaw Springs and at Yorktown, where he was attached to Lafayette's brigade.

When the war was over, Col. Grimké began the practice of law in Charleston, and rose in a few years to the front rank at the bar. He held various honorable offices before he was appointed judge of the Supreme Court of the State.

Early in life Judge Grimké married Mary Smith of Irish and English-Puritan stock. She was the great-granddaughter of the second Landgrave of South Carolina, and descended on her mother's side from that famous rebel chieftain, Sir Roger Moore, of Kildare, who would have stormed Dublin Castle with his handful of men, and whose handsome person, gallant manners, and chivalric courage made him the idol of his party and the hero of song and story. Fourteen children were born to this couple, all of whom were more or less remarkable for the traits which would naturally be expected from such ancestry, while in several of them the old Huguenot-Puritan infusion colored every mental and moral quality. This was especially notable in Sarah Moore Grimké, the sixth child, who even in her childhood continually surprised her family by her independence, her sturdy love of truth, and her clear sense of justice. Her conscientiousness was such that she never sought to conceal or even excuse anything wrong she did, but accepted submissively whatever punishment or reprimand was inflicted upon her.

Between Sarah and her brother Thomas, six years her senior, an early friendship was formed, which was ever a source of gratification to both, and which continued without a break until his death. To the influence of his high, strong nature she attributed to a great extent her early tendency to think and reason upon subjects much beyond her age. Until she was twelve years old, a great deal of her time was passed in study with this brother, her bright, active mind eagerly reaching after the kind of knowledge which in those days was considered food too strong for the intellect of a girl. She begged hard to be permitted to study Latin, and began to do so in private, but her parents, and even her brother, discouraged this, and she reluctantly gave it up.

Judge Grimké's position, character, and wealth placed his family among the leaders of the very exclusive society of Charleston. His children were accustomed to luxury and display, to the service of slaves, and to the indulgence of every selfish whim, although the father's practical common sense led him to protest against the habits to which such indulgences naturally led. He was necessarily much from home, but, when leisure permitted, his great pleasure was teaching his children and discussing various topics with them. To Sarah he paid particular attention, her superior mental qualities exciting his admiration and pride. He is said to have frequently declared that if she had been of the other sex she would have made the greatest jurist in the land.

In his own habits, Judge Grimké was prudent and singularly economical, and, in spite of discouraging surroundings, endeavored to instil lessons of simplicity into his children. An extract from one of Sarah's letters will illustrate this. Referring in 1863 to her early life, she thus writes to a friend : —

"Father was pre-eminently a man of common sense, and economy was one of his darling virtues. I suppose I inherited some of the latter quality, for from early life I have been renowned for gathering up the fragments that nothing be lost, so that it was quite a common saying in the family: ' Oh, give it to Sally; she 'll find use for it,' when anything was to be thrown away. Only once within my memory did I depart from this law of my nature. I went to our country residence to pass the summer with father. He had deposited a number of useful odds and ends in a drawer. Now little miss, being installed as housekeeper to papa, and for the first time in her life being queen — at least so she fancied — of all she surveyed, went to work searching every cranny, and prying into every drawer, and woe betide anything which did not come up to my idea of neat housekeeping. When I chanced across the drawer of scraps I at once condemned them to the flames. Such a place of disorder could not be tolerated in my dominions. I never thought of the contingency of papa's shirts, etc., wanting mending; my oversight, however, did not prevent the natural catastrophe of clothes wearing out, and one day papa brought me a garment to mend, ' Oh,' said I, tossing it carelessly aside, 'that hole is too big to darn.'

"'Certainly, my dear,' he replied, 'but you can put a piece in. Look in such a drawer, and you will find plenty to patch with.'

"But behold the drawer was empty. Happily, I had commuted the sentence of burning to that of distribution to the slaves, one of whom furnished me the piece, and mended the garment ten times better than I could have done. So I was let to go unwhipped of justice for that misdemeanor, and perhaps that was the lesson which burnt into my soul. My story does n't sound Southerny, does it? Well, here is something more. During that summer, father had me taught to spin and weave negro cloth. Don't suppose I ever did anything worth while; only it was one of his maxims: 'Never lose an opportunity of learning what is useful. If you never need the knowledge, it will be no burden to have it; and if you should, you will be thankful to have it.' So I had to use my delicate fingers now and then to shell corn, a process which sometimes blistered them, and was sent into the field to pick cotton occasionally. Perhaps I am indebted partially to this for my life-long detestation of slavery, as it brought me in close contact with these unpaid toilers."

Doubtless she had many a talk with these "unpaid toilers," and learned from them the inner workings of a system which her friends would fain have taught her to view as fair and merciful.

Children are born without prejudice, and the young children of Southern planters never felt or made any difference between their white and colored playmates. The instances are many of their revolt and indignation when first informed that there must be a difference. So that there is nothing singular in the fact that Sarah Grimké, to use her own words, early felt such an abhorrence of the whole institution of slavery, that she was sure it was born in her. Several of her brothers and sisters felt the same. But she differed from other children in the respect that her sensibilities were so acute, her heart so tender, that she made the trials of the slaves her own, and grieved that she could neither share nor mitigate them. So deeply did she feel for them that she was frequently found in some retired spot weeping, after one of the slaves had been punished. She remembered that once, when she was not more than four or five years old, she accidentally witnessed the terrible whipping of a servant woman. As soon as she could escape from the house, she rushed out sobbing, and half an hour afterwards her nurse found her on the wharf, begging a sea captain to take her away to some place where such things were not done.

She told me once that often, when she knew one of the servants was to be punished, she would shut herself up and pray earnestly that the whipping might be averted; "and sometimes," she added, "my prayers were answered in very unexpected ways."

Writing to a young friend, a few years before her death, she says: "When I was about your age, we spent six months of the year in the back country, two hundred miles from Charleston, where we would live for months without seeing a white face outside of the home circle. It was often lonely, but we had many out-door enjoyments, and were very happy. I, however, always had one terrible drawback. Slavery was a millstone about my neck, and marred my comfort from the time I can remember myself. My chief pleasure was riding on horse-

back daily. 'Hiram' was a gentle, spirited, beautiful creature. He was neither slave nor slave owner, and I loved
and enjoyed him thoroughly."

When she was quite young her father gave her a little
African girl to wait on her. To this child, the only slave
she ever owned, she became much attached, treating her
as an equal, and sharing all her privileges with her. But
the little girl died after a few years, and though her
youthful mistress was urged to take another, she refused,
saying she had no use for her, and preferred to wait on
herself. It was not until she was more than twelve years
old that, at her mother's urgent request, she consented to
have a dressing-maid.

Judge Grimké, his family and connections, were all
High-Church Episcopalians, tenacious of every dogma,
and severe upon any neglect of the religious forms of
church or household worship. Nothing but sickness ex-
cused any member of the family, servants included, from
attending morning prayers, and every Sunday the well-
appointed carriage bore those who wished to attend
church to the most fashionable one in the city. The
children attended Sabbath-school regularly, and in the
afternoon the girls who were old enough taught classes
in the colored school. Here, Sarah was the only one who
ever caused any trouble. She could never be made to
understand the wisdom which included the spelling-book,
in the hands of slaves, among the dangerous weapons,
and she constantly fretted because she could only give her
pupils oral instruction. She longed to teach them to
read, for many of them were pining for the knowledge
which the " poor white trash " rejected; but the laws of
the State not only prohibited the teaching of slaves, but
provided fines and imprisonment for those who ventured

to indulge their fancy in that way. So that, argue as she might, and as she did, the privilege of opening the store-house of learning to those thirsty souls was denied her. "But," she writes, "my great desire in this matter would not be totally suppressed, and I took an almost malicious satisfaction in teaching my little waiting-maid at night, when she was supposed to be occupied in combing and brushing my long locks. The light was put out, the key-hole screened, and flat on our stomachs before the fire, with the spelling-book under our eyes, we defied the laws of South Carolina."

But this dreadful crime was finally discovered, and poor Hetty barely escaped a whipping; and her bold young mistress had to listen to a severe lecture on the enormity of her conduct.

When Sarah was about twelve years old, two impor-tant events occurred to interrupt the even tenor of her life. Her brother Thomas was sent off to Yale College, leaving her companionless and inconsolable, until, a few weeks later, the birth of a little sister brought comfort and joy to her heart. This sister was Angelina Emily, the last child of her parents, and the pet and darling of Sarah from the moment the light dawned upon her blue eyes.

Sarah seems to have felt for this new baby not only more than the ordinary affection of a sister, but the yearning tenderness of a mother, and a mysterious affin-ity which foreshadowed the heart and soul sympathy which, notwithstanding the twelve years' difference in their ages, made them as one through life. She at once begged that she might stand godmother for her sister; but her parents, thinking this desire only a childish whim, refused. She was seriously in earnest, however, and day after day renewed her entreaties, answering her father's arguments that she was too young for such a responsibility by saying that she would be old enough when it became necessary to exercise any of the responsibility.

Seeing finally that her heart was so set upon it, her parents consented; and joyfully she stood at the baptismal font, and promised to train this baby sister in the way she should go. Many years afterwards, in describing her feelings on this occasion, she said: "I had been taught to believe in the efficacy of prayer, and I well remember, after the ceremony was over, slipping out and shutting myself up in my own room, where, with tears streaming down my cheeks, I prayed that God would make me worthy of the task I had assumed, and help me to guide and direct my precious child. Oh, how good I resolved to be, how careful in all my conduct, that my life might be blessed to her!"

Entering in such a spirit upon the duties she had taken upon herself, we cannot over-estimate her influence in forming the character and training the mind of this "precious Nina," as she so often called her. And, as we shall see, for very many years Angelina followed closely where Sarah led, treading almost in her footsteps, until the seed sown by the older sister, ripening, bore its fruit in a power and strength and individuality which gave her the leadership, and caused Sarah to fall back and gaze with wonder upon development so much beyond her thoughts or hopes.

From the first, Sarah took almost entire charge of her little god-daughter; and, as "Nina" grew out of her babyhood, Sarah continued to exercise such general supervision over her that the child learned to look up to her as to a mother, and frequently when together, and in her correspondence for many years, addressed her as "Mother."

It does not appear that Judge Grimké entertained any views differing greatly from those of intelligent men in the society about him. He was a man of wide culture, varied experience of life, and a diligent student. Therefore, as he made a companion of his bright and promising daughter, he doubtless did much to sharpen her intellect, as well as to deepen her conscientiousness and sense of religious obligation. Her brother Thomas, too, added another strong influence to her mental development. She was nearly fifteen when he returned from college, bringing with him many new ideas, most of them quite original, and which he at once set to work to study more closely, with a view to putting them into practical operation. Sarah was his confidante and his amanuensis; and, looking up to him almost as to a demi-god, she readily fell in with his opinions, and made many of them her own.

Of her mother there is little mention in the early part of her life. Mrs. Grimké appears to have been a very devout woman, of rather narrow views, and undemonstrative in her affections. She was, however, intelligent, and had a taste for reading, especially theological works. Her son Thomas speaks of her as having read Stratton's book on the priesthood, and inferring from its implications the sect to which the author belonged. The oldest of her children was only nineteen when Angelina was born. The burdens laid upon her were many and great; and we cannot wonder that she was nervous, exhausted, and irritable. The house was large, and kept in the style common in that day among wealthy Southern people. The servants were numerous, and had, no doubt, the usual idle, pilfering habits of slaves. All provisions were kept under lock and key, and given out with scrupulous exactitude, and incessant watchfulness as to details was a necessity.

As children multiplied, Mrs. Grimké appears to have lost all power of controlling either them or her servants. She was impatient with the former, and resorted with the latter to the punishments commonly inflicted by slave-owners. These severities alienated her children still more from her, and they showed her little respect or affection. It never appears to have occurred to any of them to try to relieve her of her cares; and it is probable she was more sinned against than sinning, — a sadly burdened and much-tried woman. From numerous allusions to her in the diaries and letters, the evidence of an ill-regulated household is plain, as also the feelings of the children towards her. From Angelina's diary we copy the following : —

" On 2d day I had some conversation with sister Mary on the deplorable state of our family, and to-day with Eliza. They complain very much of the servants being so rude, and doing so much as they please. But I tried to convince them that the servants were just what the family was, that they were not at all more rude and self-ish and disobliging than they themselves were. I gave one or two instances of the manner in which they treated mother and each other, and asked how they could expect the servants to behave in any other way when they had such examples continually before them, and queried in which such conduct was most culpable. Eliza always admits what I say to be true, but, as I tell her, never profits by it. . . . Sister Mary is somewhat different; she will not condemn herself. . . . She will acknowledge the sad state of the family, but seems to think mother is altogether to blame. And dear mother seems to resist all I say : she will neither acknowledge the state of the family nor her own faults, and always is angry when I

speak to her. . . . Sometimes when I look back to the first
years of my religious life, and remember how unremit-
tingly I labored with mother, though in a very wrong
spirit, being alienated from her and destitute of the spirit
of love and forbearance, my heart is very sore."

This unfortunate state of things prevailed until the
children were grown, and with more or less amelioration
after that time.   Sarah's natural tenderness, and the
sense of justice which, as she grew to womanhood, was so
conspicuous in Angelina, drew their mother nearer to
them than to her other children, though Thomas always
wrote of her affectionately and respectfully.   She, however, with her rigid orthodox beliefs, could never understand her " alien daughters," as she called them ; and she
never ceased to wonder how such strange fledglings could
have come from her nest.   It was only when they had
proved by years of self-sacrifice the earnestness of their
peculiar views that she learned to respect them ; and,
though they never succeeded in converting her from her
inherited opinions, she was towards the last years of her
life brought into something like affectionate sympathy
with them.

CHAPTER II.

It was quite the custom in the last century and the beginning of the present one for cultivated people to keep diaries, in which the incidents of each day were jotted down, accompanied by the expression of private opinions and feelings. Women, especially, found this diary a pleasant sort of confessional, a confidante to whose pages they could entrust their most secret thoughts without fear of rebuke or betrayal. Sarah Grimké's diary, covering over five hundred pages of closely written manuscript, though not begun until 1821, gives many reminiscences of her youth, and describes with painful conscientiousness her religious experiences. She also repeatedly regrets the fact that her education, though what was considered at that time a good one, was entirely superficial, embracing only that kind of knowledge which is acquired for display. What useful information she received she owed to the conversations of her father and her brother Thomas, her "beloved companion and friend."

There is no doubt that this want of proper training was to her a cause of regret during her whole life. With her, learning was always a passion ; and, in passing, I may say she never thought herself too old for study and the acquisition of knowledge. As she grew up, and saw the very different education her brothers were receiving, her am-

bition and independence were fired, and she longed to
share their advantages. But in vain she entreated permission to do so. The only answer she received was:
"You are a girl; what do you want of Latin and Greek
and philosophy ? You can never use them." And when
it was discovered that she was secretly studying law, and
was ambitious to stand side by side with her brother at
the bar, smiles and sneers rebuked her "unwomanly"
aspirations. And though she argued the point with much
spirit, unable to see why the mere fact of being a girl
should confine her to the necessity of being a "doll, a
coquette, a fashionable fool," she failed to secure a single
adherent to her strong-minded ideas. Her nature thus
denied its proper nutriment, and her most earnest desires
crushed, she sought relief in another direction. Painting,
poetry, general reading occupied her leisure time, while
she was receiving private tuition from the best masters in
Charleston.

At sixteen she was introduced into society, or, as she
phrases it, "initiated into the circles of dissipation and
folly." In her account of the life she led in those circles
she does not spare herself.

"I believe," she writes, "for the short space I was exhibited on this theatre, few have exceeded me in extravagance of every kind, and in the sinful indulgence of pride
and vanity, sentiments which, however, were strongly
mingled with a sense of their insufficiency to produce even
earthly happiness, with an eager desire for intellectual
pursuits, and a thorough contempt for the trifles I was
engaged in. Often during this period have I returned
home, sick of the frivolous beings I had been with, mortified at my own folly, and weary of the ball-room and its
gilded toys. Night after night, as I glittered now in this

gay scene, now in that, my soul has been disturbed by the query, 'Where are the talents committed to thy charge?' But the intrusive thought would be silenced by the approach of some companion, or a call to join the dance, or by the presentation of the stimulating cordial, and my remorse and my hopeless desires would be drowned for the time being. Once, in utter disgust, I made a resolution to abstain from such amusements; but it was made in self-will, and did not stand long, though I was so earnest that I gave away much of my finery. I cannot look back to those years without a blush of shame, a feeling of anguish at the utter perversion of the ends of my being. But for my tutelary god, my idolized brother, my young, passionate nature, stimulated by that love of admiration which carries many a high and noble soul down the stream of folly to the whirlpool of an unhallowed marriage, I had rushed into this lifelong misery. Happily for me, this butterfly life did not last long. My ardent nature had another channel opened for it, through which it rushed with its usual impetuosity. I was converted, and turned over to doing good."

Up to this time she was a communicant in the Episcopal church, and a regular attendant on its various services, But, as she records, her heart was never touched, her soul never stirred. She heard the same things preached week after week, — the necessity of coming to Christ and the danger of delay, — and she wondered at her insensibility. She joined in family worship, and was scrupulously exact in her private devotions; but all was done mechanically, from habit, and no quickening sense of her "awful condition" came to her until she went one night, on the invitation of a friend, to hear a Presbyterian minister, the Rev. Henry Kolloch, celebrated for his eloquence.

He preached a thrilling sermon, and Sarah was deeply moved. But the impression soon wore off, and she returned to her gay life with renewed ardor. A year after, the same minister revisited Charleston; and again she went to hear him, and again felt the "arrows of conscience," and again disregarded the solemn warning. The journal continues: —

"After this he came no more; and in the winter of 1813-14 I was led in an unusual degree into scenes of dissipation and frivolity. It seemed as if my cup of worldly pleasure was filled to the brim; and after enjoying all the city afforded, I went into the country in the spring with a fashionable acquaintance, designing to finish my wild career there."

While on this visit, she accidentally met the Rev. Dr Kolloch, and became acquainted with him. He seems to have taken a warm interest in her spiritual welfare, and his conversations made a serious impression on her which her gay friends tried to remove. But her sensitive spirit was so affected by his admonitions, and warnings of the awful consequences of persisting in a course of conduct which must eventually lead to everlasting punishment, that she was made very miserable. She trembled as he portrayed her doom, and wept bitterly; but, though she assented to the truth of his declarations, she did not feel quite prepared to give up the pomps and vanities of her life, unsatisfactory as they were. A sore conflict began in her mind, and she could take no pleasure in anything. Dr. Kolloch's parting question to her, spoken in the most solemn tones, "Can you, then, dare to hesitate?" rang continually in her ears; and the next few days and nights were passed in a turmoil of various feelings, until, exhausted, she gave up the struggle, and acknowledged herself sensible of the emptiness of worldly gratifications, and thought she was willing to resign all for Christ. She returned home sorrowful and heavy-hearted. The glory of the world was stained, and she no longer dared to participate in its vain pleasures. She felt "loaded down with iniquity," and, almost sinking under a sense of her guilt and her danger, she secluded herself from society, and put away her ornaments, "determined to purchase Heaven at any price." But she found no relief in these sacrifices; and, after enduring much trial at her ill success, she wrote to Dr. Kolloch, informing him of her state of mind.

"Over his answer," she writes, "I shed many tears; but, instead of prostrating myself in deep abasement before the Lord, and craving his pardon, I was desirous of doing something which might claim his approbation and disperse the thick cloud which seemed to hide him from me. I therefore set earnestly to work to do good according to my capacity. I fed the hungry and clothed the naked, I visited the sick and afflicted, and vainly hoped these outside works would purify a heart defiled with the pride of life, still the seat of carnal propensities and evil passions; but here, too, I failed. I went mourning on my way under the curse of a broken law; and, though I often watered my couch with my tears, and pleaded with my Maker, yet I knew nothing of the sanctifying influence of his holy spirit, and, not finding that happiness in religion I anticipated, I, by degrees, through the persuasions of companions and the inclination of my depraved heart, began to go a little more into society, and to resume my former style of dressing, though in comparative moderation."

She then states how, some time after she had thus departed from her Christian profession, Dr. Kolloch came once more, and his sad and earnest rebukes made her unutterably wretched. But she tried to stifle the voice of conscience by entering more and more into worldly amusements, until she had lost nearly all spiritual sense. Her disposition became soured by incessantly yielding to temptation, and she adds : —

" I know not where I might have been landed, had not the merciful interposition of Providence stopped my progress."

This " merciful interposition of Providence " was nothing less than the declining health of her father; and it affords, indeed, a curious comment on the old Orthodox teachings, that this young woman, devotedly attached to her father, and fully appreciating his value to his family, should have regarded his ill-health as sent by God for her especial benefit, to interrupt her worldly course, and compass her salvation.

Judge Grimké's illness continued for a year or more; and so faithfully did Sarah nurse him that when it was decided that he should go to Philadelphia to consult Dr. Physic, she was chosen to accompany him.

This first visit to the North was the most important event of Sarah's life, for the influences and impressions there received gave some shape to her vague and wayward fancies, and showed her a gleam of the light beyond the tangled path which still stretched before her.

She found lodgings for her father and herself in a Quaker family whose name is not mentioned. About their life there, little is said ; Sarah being too much occupied with the care of her dear invalid to take much interest in her new surroundings. Judge Grimké's health continued to decline. His daughter's account of the last days of his life is very touching, and shows not only how deep was her religious feeling, but how tender and yet how strong she was all through this great trial. The father and daughter, strangers in a strange land, drawn more closely together by his suffering and her necessary care, became friends indeed; their attachment increasing day by day, until, ere their final separation, they loved each other with that fervent affection which grows only with true sympathy and unbounded confidence. Sarah thus wrote of it : —

"I regard this as the greatest blessing, next to my conversion, I have ever received from God, and I think if all my future life is passed in affliction this mercy alone should make me willingly, yea, cheerfully and joyously, submit to the chastisements of the Lord."

During their stay in Philadelphia, she had hoped for her father's recovery, but when, by the doctor's advice, they went to Long Branch, and she saw how weak and ill he was, this hope forsook her, and she describes her agony as something never to be effaced from her memory. Doubtless this was intensified by her lone and friendless position. They were in a tavern, without one human being to soothe them or sympathize with them. "But," she writes, "let me here acknowledge the mercy of that Being whose everlasting arms supported me in this hour of suffering. After the first burst of grief I became calm, and felt an assurance that He in whom I trusted would never leave nor forsake me, and that I would have strength given me, even to the performance of the last sad duties. But the end was not yet; the disease fluctuated, some days arousing a gleam of hope, only to be extinguished by the next day's weakness. Alas! I was compelled to see that death was certainly, though slowly, approaching, and all feeling for my own suffering was sunk in anxiety to contribute to my father's comfort, and smooth his passage to the grave. And, blessed be God, I was not only able to minister to many of his temporal wants, but permitted to strengthen his hopes of a happy immortality. I prayed with him and read to him, and I cannot recollect hearing an impatient expression from him during his whole illness, or a wish that his sufferings might be lessened or abridged. He often tried to conceal his bodily pain, and to soothe me by every appearance of cheerful piety. Thus he lingered until the 6th of August, when he grew visibly worse. Many incoherent expressions escaped him, but even then how tenderly he spoke of me, I ever shall remember. . . . About eight o'clock I moved him to his own bed, and, sitting down, prepared to watch by him. He entreated me to lie down, and I told him when he slept I would.

" 'Oh, God,' he exclaimed with fervent energy, ' how sweet to sleep and wake in heaven ! ' This last desire was realized. He clasped one of my hands, and as I bent over him and arranged his pillow he put his arm around me. I did not stir ; apparently he slept. But the relaxed grasp, the dewy coldness, the damps of death which stood upon his forehead, all told me that he was hastening fast to Jesus. Alone, at the hour of midnight, I sat by this bed of death. My eyes were fixed on that face whose calmness seemed to say, ' I rest in peace.' A gentle pressure of the hand, and a scarcely audible respiration, alone indicated that life was not extinct ; at length that pressure ceased, and the strained ear could no longer hear a breath. I continued gazing on the lifeless form, closed his eyes and kissed him. His spirit, freed from the shackles of mortality, had sprung to its source, the bosom of his God. I passed the rest of the night alone."

And alone, the only mourner, this brave, heart-stricken

girl followed the remains of her beloved father to the grave.

When all was over she went back to Philadelphia, where she remained two or three months, and then returned to Charleston.

During the season of family mourning which followed, having nothing especial to do, Sarah became more than ever concerned about her spiritual welfare. She constantly deplored her lukewarmness, and regarded herself as standing on the edge of a precipice from which she had no power to withdraw. The subject of slavery began now also to agitate her mind. After her residence in Philadelphia, where doubtless she had to listen to some sharp reflections on the Southern institution, it seemed more than ever abhorrent to her, but it does not appear that she gave utterance to her feelings on more than one or two occasions. Even her diary contains only a slight and occasional reference to them. She saw, she says, how useless it was to discuss the subject, as even Angelina, the child of her own training, could see nothing wrong in the mere fact of slave-holding, if the slaves were kindly treated.

Her brother Thomas, to whom she might have opened her overburdened heart, and received from his affection and good sense, comfort and strength, she saw little of; besides, he was a slave-owner, and among his numerous reform theories of education, politics, and religion, he does not seem to have thought of touching slavery. He was a leading member of the bar, very busy with his literary work, had a wife and family, and resided out of the city.

Alone, therefore, Sarah brooded over her trials, and those of the slaves, "until they became like a canker, incessantly gnawing." Upon the latter she could only look as one in bonds herself, powerless to prevent or ameliorate them. Her sole consolation was teaching the objects of her compassion, within the lawful restrictions, whenever she could find the opportunity. But she began to look upon the world as a wilderness of desolation and suffering, and herself as the most miserable of sinners, fast hastening to destruction. In this frame of mind she was induced to listen to the doctrine of universal salvation, and eagerly adopted it, hoping thereby to find relief from her doubts and fears. Her mother discovered this with horror, and, trembling for her daughter's safety, she aroused herself to argue so strongly against what she termed the false and awful doctrine, that, though Sarah refused to acknowledge the force of all she said, it had its effect, and she gradually lost her hold on her new belief. But losing that, she lost all hope. " Wormwood and gall " were her portion, and, while she fulfilled the outward duties of religion, dreariness and settled despondency took possession of her mind. She writes:

" Tears never moistened my eyes; to prayer I was a stranger. With Job I dared to curse the day of my birth. One day I was tempted to say something of the kind to my mother. She was greatly shocked, and reproved me seriously. I craved a hiding-place in the grave, as a rest from the distress of my feelings, thinking that no estate could be worse than the present. Sometimes, being unable to pray, unable to command one feeling of good, either natural or spiritual, I was tempted to commit some great crime, thinking I could repent and thus restore my lost sensibility. On this I often meditated, and assuredly should have fallen into this snare had not the mercy of God still followed me."

I might go on for many pages painting this dreary picture of a misdirected life, but enough has been quoted at present to show Sarah Grimké's strong, earnest, impressionable nature, and the effects upon it of the teachings of the old theology, mingled with the narrow Southern ideas of usefulness and woman's sphere. Endowed with a superior intellect, with a most benevolent and unselfish disposition, with a cheerful, loving nature, she desired above all things to be an active, useful member of society. But every noble impulse was strangled at its birth by the iron bands of a religion that taught the crucifixion of every natural feeling as the most acceptable offering to a stern and relentless God. She was now twenty-eight years of age, and with the exception of the period devoted to her father she had as yet thought and worked only for herself. I do not mean that she neglected home duties, or her private charities and visits to the afflicted, but all these offices were performed from one especial motive and with the same end in view — to avert from herself the wrath of her Maker. This one thought filled all her mind. All else was as nothing. Family and friends, home and humanity, were of importance only as they furthered this object. It is in this spirit that she mentioned her father's illness and death, and the heroic, self-sacrificing death, by shipwreck, of her brother Benjamin, to which she could resign herself from a conviction that the stroke was sent as a chastisement to her, and was a merciful dispensation to draw his young wife nearer to God. We read not one word of solicitude for mother, or brothers, or sisters, not a single prayer for their conversion. She was too busy watching and weeping over her own short-comings to concern herself about their doom. The long diary is filled with the reiteration of her fears, her sorrows, and her prayers. Many years afterwards she thus referred to this condition of her mind : —

"I cannot without shuddering look back to that period. How dreadful did the state of my mind become! Nothing interested me; I fulfilled my duties without any feeling of satisfaction, in gloomy silence. My lips moved in prayer, my feet carried me to the holy sanctuary, but my heart was estranged from piety. I felt as if my doom was irrevocably fixed, and I was destined to that fire which is never quenched. I have never experienced any feeling so terrific as the despair of salvation. My soul still remembers the wormwood and the gall, still remembers how awful the conviction that every door of hope was closed, and that I was given over unto death."

Naturally, such a strain at last impaired her health, and, her mother becoming alarmed, she was sent in the autumn of 1820 to North Carolina, where several relatives owned plantations on the Cape Fear River. She was welcomed with great affection, especially by her aunt, the wife of her uncle James Smith, and mother of Barnwell Rhett. (This name was assumed by him on the inheritance of property from a relative of that name.)

In the village near which this aunt lived there was no place of worship except the Methodist meeting-house. Sarah attended this; and under the earnest and alarming preaching she heard there, together with association with some of the most spiritual-minded of the members, she was aroused from her apathetic state, and was enabled to join in their services with some interest. She even offered up prayer with them, and at one of their love-feasts delivered a public testimony to the truths of the gospel. Thus associated with them, she was induced to examine their principles and doctrines, but found them as faulty as all the rest she had from time to time investigated. She therefore soon decided not to become one of them. From her earliest serious impressions, she had been dissatisfied with Episcopacy, feeling its forms lifeless; but now, after having carefully considered the various other sects, and finding error in all, she concluded to remain in the church whose doctrines at least satisfied her as well as those of any other, and were those of her mother and her family.

Of the Society of Friends she knew little, and that little was unfavorable. To a remark made one day by her mother, relative to her turning Quaker, she replied, with some warmth: —

"Anything but a Quaker or a Catholic!"

Having made up her mind that the Friends were wrong, she had steadily refused, during her stay in Philadelphia, to attend their meetings or read any of their writings. Nevertheless many things about them, scarcely noticed at the time, — their quiet dress, orderly manner of life and gentle tones of voice, together with their many acts of kindness to her and her father, — came back to her after she had left them, and especially impressed her as contrasting so strongly with the slack habits and irregular discipline which made her own home so unhappy.

On the vessel which carried her from Philadelphia to Charleston, after her father's death, was a party of Friends; and in the seven days which it then required to make the voyage, an intimacy sprang up between them and Sarah which influenced her whole after-life. From one of them she had accepted a copy of Woolman's works, — evidence that there must have been religious discussions between them. And that there was talk —

probably some jesting — in the family about Quakers is shown by the little incident Sarah relates of her brother Thomas presenting her, soon after her return from North Carolina, with a volume of Quaker writings he had picked up at some sale. He placed it in her hand, saying jocosely, —

"Thee had better turn Quaker, Sally; thy long face would suit well their sober dress."

She was, as we have said, of a naturally cheerful disposition; but her false views of religion led her to believe that "by the sadness of the countenance the heart is made better," and she shed more tears, and offered up more petitions for forgiveness, over occasional irresistible merriment than I have space to record.

She accepted the book from her brother, read it, and, needing some explanation of portions of it, wrote to one of the Friends in Philadelphia whose acquaintance she had made on the vessel. A correspondence ensued, which resulted after some months in her entire conversion to Quakerism.

She had now reached, she thought, a resting-place for her weary, sore-travailed spirit; and, like a tired pilgrim, she dropped all her burdens beside this fresh stream, from whose waters she expected to drink such cooling draughts. The quiet of the little meeting-house in Charleston, the absence of ornament and ceremony, the silent worship by the few members, the affectionate *thee* and *thou*, all soothed her restless soul for a while, and a sweet calm fell upon her. But she believed that God constantly spoke to her heart, directing her by the still, small voice; and the fidelity with which she obeyed this invisible guide was not only a real detriment to her spiritual progress, but the cause of much distress to her.

When, as sometimes happened from various causes, she failed in obedience, her mental suffering was intense, and in abject humility she accepted as punishment any mortification or sorrow that came to her afterwards. As a sequence to this hallucination, she also had visions at various times, and saw and communed with spirits, and did not hesitate to acknowledge their influence and to respect their intimations. So marvellously real were her feelings on these points that her immediate friends, though greatly deploring their effect upon her, seldom ventured any remonstrance against them. Now, under the influence of her new belief, the impression of a divine call to be made upon her deepened, and soon took shape in the persuasion that it was to be a call to the ministry. Her soul recoiled at the very thought of work so solemn, and she prayed the Lord to spare her; but the more she prayed, the stronger and clearer the intimations became, until she felt that no loop-hole of escape was left her from obedience to her Master's will. From the publicity the work involved, she intuitively shrank. Her natural sensitiveness and all the prejudices of her life rebelled against it, and she could not look forward to it without fear and trembling. Every meeting now found her, she says, like a craven, dreading to hear the summons which would oblige her to rise and open her lips before the two or three gathered there. Vainly did she try to "hide herself from the Lord." The evidence came distinctly to her one morning that some words of admonition were required of her; but so appalling did the act appear to her that she trembled, hesitated, resisted, and was silent. Sorrow and remorse at once filled her soul; and, feeling that she had sinned against the Holy Ghost, she thought that God never could forgive her, and that no sacrifice

she could ever offer could atone for this first act of disobedience. Through long and dreary years it was the
spectre that never would down, but stood ready to point
its accusing finger whenever she was tempted to seek the
cause of her disappointments and sorrows.

Thus, in the very outset of her new departure, arose
apprehensions which followed her continually, robbing
her religious exercises of all peace, and bringing her such
a depth of misery that, she says, it almost destroyed her
soul. The frequent letters of her Quaker friend, though
calculated to soothe and encourage her, were all firm on
the point of implicit obedience to the movements of the
Spirit; and she found herself in a straight and narrow
path, from which she was not allowed to deviate.

To this friend, Israel Morris, Sarah seems to have con-
fessed all her shortcomings, all her fears, until, encouraged
by his sympathy, and led by her longing for a wider field
of action, she began to contemplate a removal to the
North. There were other causes which urged her to seek
another home. The inharmonious life in her family,
joined to the reproaches and ridicule constantly aimed at
her, and which stung her to the quick, naturally inspired
the desire to go where she would be rid of it all, and live
in peace. In her religious exaltation, it was easy for her
to persuade herself that she was moved to make this important change by the Lord's command. She sincerely
believed it was so, and speaks of it as an unmistakable
call, not to be disregarded, to go forth from that land, and
her work would be shown her. Naturally, Philadelphia
was the spot to which she was directed. When informed
of her desires, Israel Morris not only gave his approval,
but invited her to a home in his family. A door of shelter and safety being thus thrown open to her, she no

longer hesitated, but at once made known her intention to her relatives. There seems to have been little or no opposition offered to a step so serious ; in fact, her brothers and sisters, though much attached to her, — for her loving nature was irresistible, — evidently felt it a relief when she was gone, her strict and pious life being a constant rebuke to their worldly views and practices.

Her sister Anna, at her urgent request, accompanied her on the voyage. This sister, the widow of an Episcopal clergyman, though a defender of slavery as an institution, recognized its evil influences on the society where it existed, and gladly accepted the opportunity offered to take her young daughter away from them. It was necessary, too, that she should do something to increase her slender income, and Sarah advised opening a small school in Philadelphia, — a thing which she could not have done in Charleston without a sacrifice of her own social position and of the family pride.

There is nothing said of the parting, even from Angelina, though we know it must have been a hard trial for Sarah to leave this young sister, just budding into womanhood, and surrounded by all the snares whose alluring influences she understood so well. That she could consent to leave her thus is perhaps the strongest proof of her faith in the imperative nature of the summons to which she felt she was yielding obedience.

The exiles reached Philadelphia without accident in the latter part of May, 1821. Lodgings were found for Mrs. Frost and her child, and Sarah went at once to the residence of her friend, Israel Morris.

CHAPTER III.

It is very much to be regretted that all of Sarah Grimké's letters to Angelina, and to other members of her family at this time, were, at her own request, destroyed as received. They would not only have afforded most interesting reading, but would have thrown light on much which, without them, is necessarily obscure. Nor were there more than twenty-five or thirty of Angelina's letters preserved, and they were written between the years 1826 and 1828. We therefore have but little data by which to follow Sarah's life during the five years succeeding her return to Philadelphia, and before she again went to Charleston; or Angelina's life at home, during the same period. Sarah's diary, frequently interrupted, continues to record her religious sorrows, for these followed her even into the peaceful home at "Greenhill Farm," the name of Israel Morris's place, where she was received and treated like a near and dear relative; and it was but natural and proper that she should be so accepted by the members of Mr. Morris's family. He was literally her only friend at the North. Through his influence she had been brought into the Quaker religion, and encouraged to leave her mother and native land. She was entirely unpractised in the ways of the world, and was besides in very narrow circumstances, her only available income being the interest on $10,000, the sum left by

Judge Grimké to each of his children. The estate had
not yet been settled up. Add to all this the virtue of
hospitality, inculcated by the Quaker doctrine, and it
seems perfectly natural that Sarah should accept the offer
of her friend in the spirit in which it was made, and feel
grateful to her Heavenly Father that such a refuge was
provided for her.

The notes in her journal for that summer are rather
meagre. She attended meeting regularly, but made no formal application to be received into the Society of Friends.
It would hardly have been considered so soon; she must
first go through a season of probation. How hard this
was is told in the lamentations and prayers which she
confided to her diary. The "fearful act of disobedience"
of which she was guilty in Charleston lay as a heavy
load on her spirit, troubling her thoughts by day and her
dreams by night, until she says: "At times I am almost
led to believe I shall never know good any more."

Notwithstanding these trying spiritual exercises, the
summer seems to have passed in more peace than she had
dared to hope for. Israel Morris was a truly good man,
with a strong, genial nature, which must have had a
soothing effect upon Sarah's troubled spirit. But before
many months her thoughts began to turn back to home.
Her mother's want of spirituality, from her standpoint,
grieved her greatly. The accounts she received of the
disorder in the family added to her anxieties, and she felt
that her influence was needed to bring about harmony,
and to guide her mother on the road to Zion. She laid
the case before the Lord, and, receiving no intimation
that she would be doing a wrong thing, she decided to
return to Charleston.

Before leaving Philadelphia, however, she felt that it

was her duty to assume the full Quaker dress. She had worn plain colors from the time she began to attend meeting in her native city, but the clothes were not fashioned after the Quaker style, and she still indulged herself in occasionally wearing a becoming black dress; though when she did so, she not only felt uncomfortable herself, but knew that she made many of her friends so. "Persisting in so doing," she says, "I have since been made sensible, manifested a want of condescension entirely unbecoming a Christian, and one day conviction was so strong on this subject, that, as I was dressing, I felt as if I could not proceed, but sat down with my dress half on, and these words passed through my mind: Can it be of any consequence in the sight of God whether I wear a black dress or not? The evidence was clear that it was not, but that self-will was the cause of my continuing to do it. For this I suffered much, but was at length strengthened to cast away this idol."

Remembering the fashionable life she had once led, and her natural taste for the beautiful in all things, it must have been something of a sacrifice, even though sustained by her religious exaltation, to lay aside everything pretty and becoming, and, denying herself even so much as a flower from nature's own fields, to array herself in the scant and sober dress of drab, the untrimmed kerchief, and the poke bonnet.

Writing from Greenhill in October, she says:

"On last Fifth Day I changed my dress for the more plain one of the Quakers, not because I think making my clothes in their peculiar manner makes me any better, but because I believe it was laid upon me, seeing that my natural will revolted from the idea of assuming this garb. I trust I have made this change in a right spirit, and with a single eye to my dear Redeemer. It was accompanied by a feeling of much peace."

Late in the autumn she sailed for Charleston, and was received by the home circle with affection, though her plain dress gave occasion for some slighting remarks. These, however, no longer affected her as they once had done, and she bore them in silence. Surrounded by her family, all of whom she warmly loved, in spite of their want of sympathy with her, rooming with her "precious child," with full opportunity to counsel and direct her, and intent upon carrying out reform in the household, she was for a time almost contented. She took up her old routine, her charities, and her schools, and attended meeting regularly. But a very few weeks sufficed to make her realize her utter inability to harmonize the discordant elements in her home, or to make more than a transient impression upon her mother. Day by day she became more discouraged; everything seemed to conspire to thwart her efforts for good, which were misconstrued and misunderstood. Surrounded, too, and besieged by all the familiar influences of her old life, it became harder to sustain her peculiar views and habits, and spiritual lukewarmness gained rapidly upon her. With deep humility she acknowledged the mistake she had made in going back to Charleston, which place was evidently not the vineyard in which she could labor to any profit.

In July she was again in Philadelphia, a member now of the family of Catherine Morris, sister to Israel. Here she remained until after her admission into Friends' Society, when, feeling it her duty to make herself independent of the friends who had been so kind to her, she cast about her for something to do, and was mortified and chagrined to find there was nothing suited to her capacity.

"Oh!" she exclaims, "had I received the education I desired, had I been bred to the profession of the law, I might have been a useful member of society, and instead of myself and my property being taken care of, I might have been a protector of the helpless, a pleader for the poor and unfortunate."

The industrial avenues for women were few and narrow in those days; and for the want of some practical knowledge, the doors Sarah Grimké might have entered were closed to her, and she was finally forced to abandon her hopes of independence, and to again accept a home for the winter in Israel Morris's house, now in the city. It must not be supposed, however, that either here or at Catherine's, where she afterwards made her steady home, she was a burden or a hindrance. She was too energetic and too conscientious to be a laggard anywhere. So kind and so thoughtful was she, so helpful in sickness, so sympathetic in joy and in sorrow, that she more than earned her frugal board wherever she went. Could she only have been persuaded that it was right to yield to her naturally cheerful temper, she would have been a delightful companion at all times ; but her sadness frequently affected her friends, and even drew forth an occasional reproof. The ministry, that dreadful requirement which she felt sure the Lord would make of her, was ever before her, and in fear and trembling she awaited the moment when the command would be given, "Arise and speak."

This painful preparation went on year after year, but her advance towards her expected goal was very slow. She would occasionally nerve herself to speak a few words of admonition in a small meeting, make a short prayer, or quote a text of scripture, but her services were limited to these efforts. She often feared that she was restrained by her desire that her first attempt at exhorting should be a brilliant success, and place her at once where she would be a power in the meetings; and she prayed constantly for a clear manifestation, something she could not mistake, that she might not be tempted by the hope of relief from present suffering to move prematurely in the "awful work."

Thus she waited, trying to restrain and satisfy her impatient yearnings for some real, living work by teaching charity schools, visiting prisons, and going through the duties of monthly, quarterly, and yearly meetings. But she could not shut out from herself the doubts that would force themselves forward, that her time was not employed as it should be.

We hear nothing of her family during these years, nothing to indicate any change in their condition or in their feelings. We know, however, that Sarah kept up a frequent correspondence with her mother and with Angelina, and that chiefly through her admonitions the latter was turned from her worldly life to more serious concerns.

Like Sarah, Angelina grew up a gay, fashionable girl. Her personal beauty and qualities of mind and heart challenged the admiration of all who came in contact with her. More brilliant than Sarah, she was also more self-reliant, and, though quite as sympathetic and sensitive, she was neither so demonstrative nor so tender in her feelings as her elder sister, and her manner being more dignified and positive, she inspired, even in those nearest to her, a certain degree of awe which forbade, perhaps, the fulness of confidence which Sarah's greater gentleness always invited. Her frankness and scrupulous conscientiousness were equal to Sarah's, but she always preserved her individuality and her right to think for herself. Once convinced, she could maintain her opinion against all arguments and persuasions, no matter from whom. As an illustration of this, it is related of her that when she was about thirteen years of age the bishop of the diocese called to talk to her about being confirmed. She had, of course, been baptized when an infant, and he told her she was now old enough to take upon herself the vows then made for her. She asked the meaning of confirmation, and was referred to the prayer-book. After reading the rite over, she said : —

"I cannot be confirmed, for I cannot promise what is here required."

The bishop urged that it was a form which all went through who had been baptized in the Church, and expected to remain in it. Looking him calmly in the face, she said, in a tone whose decision could not be questioned : —

"If, with my feelings and views as they now are, I should go through that form, it would be acting a lie. I cannot do it." And no persuasions could induce her to consent.

Like Sarah, she felt much for the slaves, and was ever kind to them, thoughtful, and considerate. She, too, suffered keenly when punishments were inflicted upon them; and no one could listen without tears to the account she gave of herself, as a little girl, stealing out of the house after dark with a bottle of oil with which to anoint the wounds of some poor creature who had been torn by the lash. Earlier than Sarah, she recognized the whole injustice of the system, and refused ever to have anything to do with it. She did once own a woman, but under the following circumstances : —

" I had determined," she writes, " never to own a slave ; but, finding that my mother could not manage Kitty, I undertook to do so, if I could have her without any interference from anyone. This could not be unless she was mine, and purely from notions of duty I consented to own her. Soon after, one of my mother's servants quarrelled with her, and beat her. I determined she should not be subject to such abuse, and I went out to find her a place in some Christian family. My steps were ordered by the Lord. I succeeded in my desire, and placed her with a religious friend, where she was kindly treated."

Afterwards, when the woman had become a good Methodist, Angelina transferred the ownership to her mother, not wishing to receive the woman's wages, — to take, as she said, money which that poor creature had earned.

There is no evidence that, up to the time of her first visit to Philadelphia, in 1828, she saw anything sinful in owning slaves ; indeed, Sarah distinctly says she did not. She took the Bible as authority for the right to own them, and their cruel treatment by their masters was all that distressed her for many years.

Like most of her young companions, Angelina had great respect for the ordinary observances of religion without much devotional sense of its sacred obligations, But Sarah did not neglect her duty as godmother. Her searching inquiries and solemn warnings had their effect, and soon awakened a slumbering conscience. But its upbraidings were not accepted unquestionably by Angelina, as they had been by Sarah. They only stung her into a desire for investigation. She must know the why; and her strong self-reliance helped her judgment, and buoyed her up amid waves of doubt and anxiety that would have submerged her more timid sister.

In the first letter of hers that was preserved, written in January, 1826, we are introduced to her religious feelings, and find that they were formed by the pattern set by Sarah, save that they lacked Sarah's earnestness and sincere conviction. She acknowledges herself a poor, miserable sinner, but the tone is that of confidence that she will come out all right, and that it is n't really such a dreadful thing to be a sinner after all. In this letter, too, she mentions the death of her brother Benjamin, and in the same spirit in which Sarah wrote of it.

"I was in Beaufort," she says, "when the news of my dear Ben's fate arrived. You may well suppose it was a great shock to my feelings, but I did not for one moment doubt all was right. This blow has been dealt by the hand of mercy. We have been much comforted in this dispensation. I have felt that it was good for me, and I think I have been thankful for it."

And further on: "If this affliction will only make Mary (Benjamin's wife) a real Christian, how small will be the price of her salvation!"

Poor Ben! heroic, self-sacrificing soul, he was not a professing Christian.

In this same letter she expresses the desire to become a communicant of the Episcopal Church.

But she did not wait for Sarah's answer. Before it came, she and one of her sisters had joined the Church. This was in January. Before a month had passed she began to be dissatisfied, and grew more and more so as time went on. Why, it is not difficult to surmise. From having been accustomed to much society and genial intercourse, she found herself, from her own choice, shut out from it all, and imprisoned within the rigid formalism and narrow exclusiveness of a proud, aristocratic church society. The compensation of knowing herself a lamb of this flock was not sufficient. She starved, she says, on the cold water of Episcopacy, and, to her mother's distress, began going to the Presbyterian church, just as Sarah had done.

In April, she writes thus to her sister: —

"O, my dear mother, I have joyful news to tell you. God has given me a new heart. He has renewed a right spirit within me. This is news which has occasioned even the angels in heaven to rejoice; surely, then, as a Christian, as my sister and my mother, you will also greatly rejoice. For many years I hardened my heart, and would not listen to God's admonitions to flee from the wrath to come. Now I feel as if I could give up all for Christ, and that if I no longer live in conformity to the world, I can be saved."

She then states that this change was brought about by the preaching of Mr. McDowell, the Presbyterian minister, and that she can never be grateful enough, as his ministry had been blessed to the saving of her soul. A little further on she adds: —

" The Presbyterians, I think, enjoy so many privileges that, on this account, I would wish to be one. They have their monthly concert and prayer-meetings, Bible-classes, weekly prayer-meetings, morning and evening, and many more which spring from different circumstances. I trust, my dear mother, you will approve of what I have done. I cannot but think if I had been taking an improper step, my conscience would have warned me of it, but, far otherwise, I have gone on my way rejoicing.

" Mr. Hanckel sent me a note and a tract persuasive of my remaining in his church. The latter I think the most bigoted thing I ever read. He said he would call and see me on the subject. I trust and believe God will give me words whereby to refute his arguments. Brother Tom sanctioned my change, for his liberal mind embraces all classes of Christians in the arms of charity and love, and he thinks everyone right to sit under that minister, and choose that form, which makes the deepest impression on the heart. I feel that I have begun a great work, and must be diligent. Adieu, my dear mother. You must write soon to your daughter, and tell her all your mind on this subject."

There is something very refreshing in all this, after poor Sarah's pages of bitterness and self-reproach. At that time, at any rate, Angelina enjoyed her religion. It was to her the fulfilment of promise. Sarah experienced little of its satisfactions, and groaned and wept under its requirements, from a sense of her utter unworthiness to accept any of its blessings. And this difference between the sisters continued always. Angelina knew that humility was the chief of the Christian virtues, and often she believed she had attained to it; but there was too much self-assertion, too much of the pride of power, in her composition, to permit her to go down into the depths, and prostrate herself in the dust as Sarah did. She could turn her full gaze to the sun, and bask in its genial beams, while Sarah felt unworthy to be touched by a single ray, and looked up to its light with imploring but shaded eyes.

In November, 1827, Sarah again visited Charleston. Her heart yearned for Angelina, whose religious state excited her tenderest solicitude, and called for her wisest counsel. For that enthusiastic young convert was again running off the beaten track, and picking flaws in her new doctrines. But there was another reason why Sarah desired to absent herself from Philadelphia for a while.

I can touch but lightly on this experience of her life, for her sensitive soul quivered under any allusion to it; and though her diary contains many references to it, they are chiefly in the form of prayers for submission to her trial, and strength to bear it. But it was the key-note to the dirge which sounded ever after in her heart, mingling its mournful numbers with every joy, even after she had risen beyond her religious horrors.

For months she fought against this new snare of Satan, as she termed it, this plain design to draw her thoughts from God, and compass her destruction. The love of Christ should surely be enough for her, and any craving for earthly affection was the evidence of an unsanctified heart. In a delicate reference to this, in after years, she says: —

"It is a beautiful theory, but my experience belies it, that God can be all in all to man. There are moments, diamond points in life, when God fills the yearning soul, and supplies all our needs, through the richness of his mercy in Christ Jesus. But human hearts are created for human hearts to love and be loved by, and their claims are as true and as sacred as those of the spirit."

It was very soon after her first doubts concerning her worthiness to accept the happiness offered to her that she determined to go to Charleston and put her feelings to the test of absence and unbiased reflection. The entry in her diary of November 22d is as follows: —

"Landed this morning in Charleston, and was welcomed by my dear mother with tears of pleasure and tenderness, as she folded me once more to her bosom. My dear sisters, too, greeted me with all the warmth of affection. It is a blessing to find them all seriously disposed, and my precious Angelina one of the Master's chosen vessels. What a mercy!"

CHAPTER IV.

THE strong contrast between Sarah and Angelina Grimké was shown not only in their religious feelings, but in their manner of treating the ordinary concerns of life, and in carrying out their convictions of duty. In her humility, and in her strong reliance on the "inner light," Sarah refused to trust her own judgment, even in the merest trifles, such as the lending of a book to a friend, postponing the writing of a letter, or sweeping a room to-day, when it might be better to defer it until to-morrow. She says of this : "Perhaps to some who have been led by higher ways than I have been into a knowledge of the truth, it may appear foolish to think of seeking direction in little things, but my mind has for a long time been in a state in which I have often felt a fear how I came in or went out, and I have found it a precious thing to stop and consult the mind of truth, and be governed thereby."

The following incident, one out of many, will illustrate the sincerity of her conviction on this point.

"In this frame of mind I went to meeting, and it being a rainy day I took a large, handsome umbrella, which I had accepted from brother Henry, accepted doubtfully, therefore wrongfully, and have never felt quite easy to use it, which, however, I have done a few times. After I was in meeting, I was much tried with a wandering mind, and every now and then the umbrella would come before me, so that I sat trying to wait on my God, and he showed me that I must not only give up this little thing, but return it to brother. Glad to purchase peace, I yielded ; then the reasoner said I could put it away and not use it, but this language was spoken : 'I have shown thee what was required of thee.' It seemed to me that a little light came through a narrow passage, when my will was subdued. Now this is a marvellous thing to me, as marvellous as the dealings of the Lord with me in what may appear great things."

In a note she adds : " This little sacrifice was made. I sent the umbrella with an affectionate note to brother, and believe it gave him no offence to have it returned. And sweet has been the recompense — even peace."

Whenever she acted from her own impulses, she was very clever in finding out some disappointment or mistake, which she could claim as a punishment for her self-will.

As sympathy was the strongest quality of her moral nature, she suffered intensely when, impelled by a sense of duty, she offered a rebuke of any kind. The tenderest pity stirred her heart for wrong-doers, and though she never spared the sinner, it was always manifest that she loved him while hating his sin.

Angelina, on the other hand, was wonderfully well satisfied with her own power of distinguishing right from wrong ; this power being, she believed, the gift of the Spirit to her. She sought her object, dreading no consequences, and if disaster followed she comforted herself with the feeling that she had acted according to her best light. She was a faithful disciple of every cause she espoused, and scrupulously exact in obeying even its implied provisions. In this there was no hesitancy. No matter who was offended, or what sacrifices to herself it involved, the law, the strict letter of the law, must be carried out.

In the early years of her religious life, she frequently felt called upon to rebuke those about her. She did it unhesitatingly, and as a righteous and an inflexible judge.

In order to make these differences between the sisters more plain, differences which harmonized singularly with their unity in other respects, I shall be obliged, at the risk of wearying the reader, to make some further extracts from their diaries, before entering upon that portion of their lives in which they became so closely identified.

After Sarah's return home, in 1827, we learn more of her mother and of the family generally, and see, though with them, how far apart she really was from them. The second entry in her diary at that date shows the beginning of this.

"23d. Have been favored with strength to absent myself from family prayers. A great trial this to Angelina and myself, and something the rest cannot understand. But I have a testimony to bear against will worship, and oh, that I may be faithful to this and to all the testimonies which we as a Society are called to declare.

"26th. Am this day thirty-five years old. A serious consideration that I have passed so many years to so little profit.

"How little mother seems to know when I am sitting solemnly beside her, of the supplications which arise for her, under the view of her having ere long to give an account of the deeds done in the body."

A month later she writes : "The subject of returning

to Philadelphia has been revived before me. It seems like a fresh trial, and as if, did my Master permit, here would I stay, and in the bosom of my family be content to dwell; but if he orders it otherwise, great as will be the struggle, may I submit in humble faith."

By the following extracts it will be seen that living under the daily and hourly influence of Sarah, Angelina was slowly but surely imbibing the fresh milk of Quakerism, and was preparing for another great change on her spiritual journey.

In March, 1828, she wrote as follows to her sister, Mrs. Frost, in Philadelphia: —

" I think I can say that it was owing in a great measure to my peculiar state of mind that I did not write to you for so long. During that time it seemed as though the Lord was driving me from everything on which I had rested for happiness, in order to bring me to Christ alone. My dear little church, in which I delighted once to dwell, seemed to have Ichabod written upon its walls, and I felt as though it was a cross for me to go into it. At times I thought the Saviour meant to bring me out of it, and I could weep at the bare thought of being separated from people I loved so dearly. Like Abraham, I had gone out from my kindred into a strange land, and I have often thought that by faith I was joined to that body of Christians, for I certainly knew nothing at all about them at that time."

In the latter part of the letter she mentions the visit to her of an Episcopal minister, from near Beaufort. He asked her if she could not do something to remove the lukewarmness from the Episcopal Church, and if a real evangelical minister was sent there would she not return to it. "But," she says, "I told him I could not conscientiously belong to any church which exalted itself above all others, and excluded ministers of other denominations from its pulpit. The principle of *liberty* is what especially endears the Presbyterian church to me. Our pulpit is open to all Christians, and, as I have often heard my dear pastor remark, our communion table is the *Lord's table*, and all his children are cheerfully received at it."

About the same time Sarah says in her diary: " My dear Angelina observed to-day, ' I do not know what is the matter with me; some time ago I could talk to the poor people, but now it seems as if my lips were absolutely sealed. I cannot get the words out.' I mark with intense interest her progress in the divine life, believing she is raised up to declare the wonderful works of God to the children of men."

In the latter part of March, 1828, she makes the following entry : " On the eve of my departure from home, all before me lies in darkness save this one step, to go at this time in the *Langdon Cheeves*. This seems peremptory, and at times precious promises have been annexed to obedience, — ' Go, and I will be with thee.' "

Angelina-had been very happy during the year spent in the Presbyterian Church, all its requirements suiting her temperament exactly. Her energy and activity found full exercise in various works of charity, in visiting the prison, where she delighted to exhort the prisoners, in reading, and especially in expounding the scriptures to the sick and aged; in zealously forwarding missionary work, and in warm interest in all the social exercises of the society. She was petted by the pastor, and admired by the congregation. It was very pleasant to her to feel that she not only conformed to all her duties, but was regarded as a shining light, destined to do much to build

up the church.   She still retained most of her old friendships in the Episcopal church, which had not given up all
hope of luring her back to its fold.   Altogether, life had
gone smoothly with her, and she was well satisfied.   The
change which she now contemplated was a revolution.
It was to break up all the old habits and associations, dis-
turb life-long friendships, and, stripping her of the attractions of society and church intercourse, leave her standing
alone, a spectacle to the eyes of those who gazed, a wonder and a grief to her friends.   But all this Sarah had
warned her of, and all this she felt able to endure.   Self-
sacrifice, self-immolation, in fact, was what Sarah taught ;
and, although Angelina never learned the lesson fully, she
made a conscientious effort to understand and practise it.
She began very shortly after Sarah's arrival at home.   In
January her diary records the following offering made to
the Moloch of Quakerism : —

"To-day I have torn up my novels.   My mind has long
been troubled about them.   I did not dare either to sell
them or lend them out, and yet I had not resolution to
destroy them until this morning, when, in much mercy,
strength was granted."

Sarah in her diary thus refers to this act : "This morning my dear Angelina proposed destroying Scott's novels,
which she had purchased before she was serious.   Perhaps
I strengthened her a little, and accordingly they were cut
up.   She also gave me some elegant articles to stuff a
cushion, believing that, as we were commanded to lead
holy and unblamable lives, so we must not sanction sin in
others by giving them what we had put away ourselves."

Angelina also says, "A great deal of my finery, too, I
have put beyond the reach of anyone."

An explanation of this is given in a copy of a paper

which was put into the cushion alluded to by Sarah. The copy is in her handwriting.

" Believing that if ever the contents of this cushion, in the lapse of years, come to be inspected (when, mayhap, its present covering should be destroyed by time and service), they will excite some curiosity in those who will behold the strange assemblage of handsome lace veils, flounces, and trimmings, and caps, this may inform them that in the winter of 1827–8, Sarah M. Grimké, being on a visit to her friends in Charleston, undertook the economical task of making a rag carpet, and with the shreds thereof concluded to stuff this cushion. Having made known her intention, she solicited contributions from all the family, which they furnished liberally, and several of them having relinquished the vanities of the world to seek a better inheritance, they threw into the treasury much which they had once used to decorate the poor tabernacle of clay. Now it happened that on the 10th day of the first month that, sitting at her work and industriously cutting her scraps, her well-beloved sister Angelina proposed adding to the collection for the cushion two handsome lace veils, a lace flounce, and other laces, etc., which were accepted, and are accordingly in this medley. This has been done under feelings of duty, believing that, as we are called with a high and holy calling, and forbidden to adorn these bodies, but to wear the ornament of a meek and quiet spirit, as we have ourselves laid aside these superfluities of naughtiness, so we should not in any measure contribute to the destroying of others, knowing that we shall be called to give an account of the deeds done in the body."

This was at least consistent, and in this light cannot be condemned. From that time Angelina kept up this kind of sacrifices, which were gladly made, and for which she seems to have found ample compensation in her satisfied sense of duty.

One day she records: "I have just untrimmed my hat, and have put nothing but a band of ribbon around it, and taken the lace out of the inside. I do want, if I *am* a Christian, to look like one. I think that professors of religion ought so to dress that wherever they are seen all around may feel they are *condemning* the world and all its trifling vanities."

A little later, she writes: "My attention has lately been called to the duty of Christians dressing *quite* plain. When I was first brought to the feet of Jesus, I learned this lesson in part, but I soon forgot much of it. Now I find my views stricter and clearer than they ever were. The first thing I gave up was a cashmere mantle which cost twenty dollars. I had not felt easy with it for some months, and finally determined never to wear it again, though I had no money at the time to replace it with anything else. However, I gave it up in faith, and the Lord provided for me. This part of Scripture came very forcibly to my mind, and very sweetly, too, 'And Dagon was fallen upon his face to the ground before the ark of the Lord.' It was then clearly revealed to me that if the true ark Christ Jesus was really introduced into the temple of the heart, that every idol would fall before it."

Elsewhere she mentions that she had begun with this mantle by cutting off the border; but this compromise did not satisfy conscience.

But the work thus begun did not ripen until some time after Sarah's departure, though the preparation for it went daily and silently on.

Sarah in the meanwhile was once more quietly settled at Catherine Morris' house in Philadelphia.

But we must leave this much-tried pilgrim for a little while, and record the progress of her young disciple on the path which, through much tribulation, led her at last to her sister's side, and to that work which was even now preparing for them both.

CHAPTER V.

ANGELINA's diary, commenced in 1828, is most characteristic, and in the very beginning shows that inclination to the consideration and discussion of serious questions which in after years so distinguished her.

It is rather remarkable to find a girl of twenty-three scribbling over several pages about the analogy existing between the natural and the spiritual world, or discussing with herself the question: "Are seasons of darkness always occasioned by sin?" or giving a long list of reasons why she differs from commentators upon certain texts of scriptures. She enjoyed this kind of thinking and writing, and seems to have been unwearying in her search after authorities to sustain her views. The maxims, too, which she was fond of jotting down here and there, and which furnished the texts for long dissertations, show the serious drift of her thoughts, and their clearness and beauty.

From this time it is interesting to follow her spiritual progress, so like and yet so unlike Sarah's. She, also, early in her religious life, was impressed with the feeling that she would be called to some great work. In the winter of 1828, she writes : —

"It does appear to me, and it has appeared so ever since I had a hope, that there was a work before me to which all my other duties and trials were only preparatory. I have no idea what it is, and I may be mistaken, but it does seem that if I am obedient to the 'still small voice' in my heart, that it will lead me and cause me to glorify my Master in a more honorable work than any in which I have been yet engaged."

Knowing Sarah's convictions at this time, it is easy to imagine the long, confidential talks she must have had with Angelina, and the loving persuasion used to bring this dear sister into the same communion with herself, and it is no marvel that she succeeded. Angelina's nature was an earnest one, and she ever sought the truth, and the best in every doctrine, and this remained with her after the rest was rejected. The Presbyterian Church satisfied her better than the Episcopal, but if Sarah or anyone else could show her a brighter light to guide her, a better path leading to the same goal, she would have thought it a heinous offence against God and her own true nature to reject it. That no desire for novelty impelled her in her then contemplated change, and that she foresaw all she would have to contend with, and the sacrifices she would have to make, is evident from several passages like the following : —

"Yesterday I was thrown into great exercise of mind. The Lord more clearly than ever unfolded his design of appointing me another field of labor, and at the same time I felt released from the cross of conducting family worship. I feel that very soon all the burdens will drop from my hands, and all the cords by which I have been bound to many Christian friends will be broken asunder. Soon I shall be a stranger among those with whom I took sweet counsel, and shall have to tread the wine press alone and be forsaken of all."

A day or two after she says : —

" This morning I felt no condemnation when I went into family prayers, and did not lead as usual in the duties. I felt that my Master had stripped me of the priest's garments, and put them on my mother. May He be pleased to anoint her for these sacred duties."

Her impressions may be accounted for by the influence of Sarah's feelings regarding herself, and as there was then no other field of public usefulness open to women, especially among the Quakers, than the ministry, her mind naturally settled upon that as her prospective work. But, unlike Sarah, the anticipation inspired her with no dread, no doubt even of her ability to perform the duties, or of her entire acceptance in them. It is true she craved of the Lord guidance and help, but she was confident she would receive all she needed, and in this state of mind she was better fitted, perhaps, to wait patiently for her summons than Sarah was.

She gives a minute and very interesting account of the successive steps by which she was led to feel that she could no longer worship in the Presbyterian Church, and we see the workings of Sarah's influence through it all. But it was not until after Sarah left for Philadelphia that Angelina took any decided measures to release herself from the old bonds. All winter it had grieved her to think of leaving a church which she had called the cradle of her soul, and where she had enjoyed so many privileges. She loved everything connected with it; the pastor to whom she had looked up as her spiritual guide; the members with whom she had been so intimately associated, and the Sunday-school in which she was much beloved, and where she felt she was doing a good work. Again and again she asked herself: " How can I give them up?"

Her friends all noticed the decline of her interest in the church work and services, and commented upon it. But she shrank for a long time from any open avowal of her change of views, preferring to let her conduct tell the story. And in this she was straightforward and open enough, not hesitating to act at once upon each new light as it was given to her. First came the putting away of everything like ornament about her dress. "Even the bows on my shoes," she says, "must go," and then continues : —

"My friends tell me that I render myself ridiculous, and expose the cause of Jesus to reproach, on account of my plain dressing. They tell me it is wrong to make myself so conspicuous. But the more I ponder on the subject, the more I feel that I am called with a high and holy calling, and that I ought to be peculiar, and cannot be too zealous. I rejoice to look forward to the time when Christians will follow the apostolical injunction to 'keep their garments unspotted from the world;' and is not every conformity to it a spot on the believer's character? I think it is, and I bless the Lord that He has been pleased to bring my mind to a contemplation of this subject. I pray that He may strengthen me to keep the resolution to dress always in the following style : A hat over the face, without any bows of ribbon or lace; no frills or trimmings on any part of my dress, and materials *not* the finest."

This simplicity in dress, and the sinfulness of every self-indulgence, she also taught to her Sunday-school scholars with more or less success, as one example out of several of a similar character will show.

"Yesterday," she writes, "I met my class, and think it was a profitable meeting to all. One of them has entertained a hope for about a year. She asked me if I thought it wrong to plant geraniums? I told her *I* had no time for such things. She then said that she had once taken great pleasure in cultivating them, but lately she had felt so much condemnation that she had given it up entirely. Another professed to have some little hope in the Saviour, and remarked that I had changed her views with regard to dress very much, that she had taken off her rings and flounces, and hoped never to wear them again. Her hat also distressed her. It was almost new, and she could not afford to get another. I told her if she would send it to me I would try to change it. Two others came who felt a little, but are still asleep. A good work is evidently begun. May it be carried triumphantly on."

Towards spring she began to absent herself from the weekly prayer-meetings, to stop her active charities, and to withdraw herself more from the family and social circle. In April she writes in her diary : —

"My mind is composed, and I cannot but feel astonished at the total change which has passed over me in the last six months. I once delighted in going to meeting four and five times every week, but now my Master says, ' Be still,' and I would rather be at home ; for I find that every stream from which I used to drink the waters of salvation is dry, and that I have been led to the fountain itself. And is it possible, I would ask myself to-night, is it possible that I have this day paid my last visit to the Presbyterian Church ? that I have taught my interesting class for the last time ? Is it right that I should separate myself from a people whom I have loved so tenderly, and who have been the helpers of my joy ? Is it right to give up instructing those dear children, whom I have so often carried in the arms of faith and love to the throne of grace ? Reason would sternly answer, *No*, but the Spirit whispers, ' Come out from among them ! ' I am sure if I refuse the call of my Master to the Society of Friends, I shall be a dead member in the Presbyterian Church. I have read none of their books for fear of being convinced of their principles, but the Lord has taught me Himself, and I feel that He who is Head over all things, has called me to follow Him into the little silent meeting which is in this city."

And into the little silent meeting she went, — little, indeed, as the only regular attendants were two old men ; and silent, chiefly because between these two there was a bitter feud, and the communion of spirit was naturally preferred to vocal intercession.

When Angelina became aware of this state of feeling, and saw that the two old Quakers always left the meeting-house without shaking hands, as it was the custom to do, she became much troubled, and for several weeks much of the comfort of attending meeting was destroyed. " The more I thought of it," she writes to Sarah, " the clearer became the conviction that I must write to J. K. (the one with whom she was best acquainted). This I did, after asking counsel of the Lord, for full well did I know that I should expose myself to the anger and rudeness of J. K., by touching on a point which I believed was already sore from the prickings of conscience. His reply was even harsher than I expected ; but, though it did wound my feelings, it convinced me that he needed just what I wrote, and that the pure witness within him condemned him. My letter, I think, was written in conformity to the direction given by Paul to Timothy, ' Rebuke not an *elder*, but entreat him as a father,' and in a spirit of love and tenderness. His answer spoke a spirit too proud to brook even the meekest remonstrance, and he tried to justify his conduct by saying that D. L. was a thief and a slave-holder, and had cheated him out of a large sum of money, etc. I answered him, expressing my belief that, let D. L.'s moral character be what it might, the Christian ought to be gentle and courteous to all men; and that we were bound to love our enemies, which was not at all inconsistent with the obligation to bear a decided testimony against al that we believed contrary to the precepts of the Bible. He sent me another letter, in which he declared D. L. was to him as a 'heathen and a publican,' and I was a 'busybody in other men's matters.' Here I think the matter will end. I feel that I have done what was required of me, and I am willing he should think of me as he does, so long as I enjoy the testimony of a good conscience."

We cannot wonder that Angelina drew upon herself, as Sarah had done, the arrows of ridicule; and that taunts and sneers followed her, as she walked alone in her simple dress to her humble place of worship. But we marvel that one situated as she was, — young, naturally gay and brilliant, the centre of a large circle of fashionable friends, the ewe lamb of an influential religious society, — should have unflinchingly maintained her position under persecutions and trials that would have made many an older disciple succumb. That they were martyrdom to her proud spirit there can be no doubt; but, sustained by the inner light, the conviction that she was right, she could put every temptation behind her, and resist even the prayers and tears of her mother.

Her withdrawal from the Presbyterian Church caused

the most intense excitement in the community, and every effort was made to reclaim her.

The Rev. Mr. McDowell, her pastor, visited her, and remonstrated with her in the most feeling manner, assuring her of his profound pity, as she was evidently under a delusion of the arch-adversary. Members of the congregation made repeated calls upon her, urging every argument they could think of to convince her she was deceived. Some expressed a fear that her mind was a little unbalanced, and shook their heads over the possible result; others declared that she was committing a great impropriety to shut herself up every Sunday with two old men. This, Angelina informed them, was a mistake, as the windows and doors were wide open, and the gate also. Others of her friends assured her with tears in their eyes that they would pray to the Lord to bring her back to the path of duty she had forsaken.

The superintendent of the Sunday-school came also to plead with her, in the name of the children she was abandoning. Some of the scholars themselves came and implored her not to leave them.

" But," she writes, " none of these things turn me a hair's breadth, for I have the witness in myself that I have done as the Master commanded. Some tell me this is a judgment on me for sin committed; and some say it is a chastisement to Mr. McDowell for going away last summer."

(During the prevalence of an epidemic the summer before, the Presbyterian pastor had been much blamed for deserting his flock and fleeing to the sea-shore until all danger was past.)

By all this it will be seen that Angelina was regarded as too precious a jewel in the crown of the Church to be relinquished without a struggle.

But satisfied as was her conscience, Angelina's natural feelings could not be immediately stifled. Though not so sensitive or so affectionate as Sarah, she was quite as proud, and valued as greatly the good opinion of her family and friends. She could not feel herself an outcast, an object of pity and derision, without being deeply affected by it. Her health gave way under the pressure, and a change of scene and climate was recommended. Sarah at once urged that she join her in Philadelphia; and, this meeting the approbation of her mother, she sailed for the North in July (1828).

In Sarah's diary, about this time, we find the following entry: —

"13th. My beloved Angelina arrived yesterday. Peace has, I believe, been the covering of our minds; and in thinking of her today, and trying to feel whether I should advise her not to adopt immediately the garb of a Quaker, the language presented itself, 'Touch not mine anointed, and do my prophets no harm.' So I dared not meddle with her."

The summer was a peaceful and delightful one to Angelina. She was the guest of Catherine Morris, and was treated like a daughter by all the kind Quaker circle. The novelty of her surroundings, the fresh scenes and new ideas constantly presented before her, opened up a field of thought whose boundaries only she had until then touched, but which she soon began eagerly and conscientiously to explore. Two extracts from letters written by her at that time will show how strict she was in her Quaker principles, and also that the persuasion that she was to be given some great work to do was becoming even more firmly grounded.

To Sarah, who was absent from her for a short time, she writes: —

"Dear Mother: My mind begins to be much exercised. I scarcely want to converse at all, and believe it best I should be much alone. Sister Anna is very kind in leaving me to myself. She appears to feel much for me, but I do not feel at liberty to ask her what occasions the tears which at times flow as she throws her arms around me. I sometimes think she sees more than I do about myself. I often tremble when I think of the future, and fear that I am not entirely resigned to my Master's will. Read the first chapter of Jeremiah; it rests much on my mind, and distresses me; and though I would wish to put far off the evil day, yet I am urged continually to pray that the Lord would cut short the work of preparation."

Her sister Anna (Mrs. Frost) was one of those who thought Angelina was under a terrible delusion, and mourned over her wasted energies. But it is certainly singular that the chapter to which she refers, taken in connection with the work with which she afterwards became identified, should have made the impression on her mind which it evidently did, as she repeatedly alludes to it. This letter is the last in which she addresses Sarah as *mother*. Their Quaker friends all objected to the habit, and it was dropped.

In another letter she describes a visit she made to a friend in the country, and says: —

"I have already had reason to feel my great need of watchfulness here. Yesterday the nurse gave me a cap to tuck and trim for the baby. My hands actually trembled as I worked on it, and yet I had not faithfulness enough to refuse to do it. This text was repeatedly presented to me, 'Happy is he who condemneth not himself in that thing which he alloweth.' While working, my heart was lifted up to the Father of mercies for strength to bear my testimony against such vanities; and when I put the cap into Clara's hands, I begged her not to give me any more such work to do, as I felt it a duty to bear my testimony against dress, and believed it sinful in me to assist anyone in doing what I was convinced was sinful, and assured her of my willingness to do any plain work. She laughed at my scruples, but my agitated mind was calmed, and I was satisfied to be thought foolish for Christ's sake. Thomas (Clara's husband) and I had a long talk about Quakers yesterday. I tried to convince him that they do not reject the Bible, explained the reason of their not calling it the word of God, and got him to acknowledge that in several texts I repeated the word was the Spirit. We conversed on the ordinances. He did not argue much for them, but was immovable in his opinions. He thinks if all Quakers were like *me*, he could like them, but believes I have carried all the good of Presbyterianism into the Society, therefore they cannot be judged of by me."

On the 11th of November Sarah writes: "Parted with my dearly beloved sister Angelina this afternoon. We have been one another's consolation and strength in the Lord, mingling sweetly in exercise, and bearing one another's burdens."

The first entry in Angelina's diary after her return to Charleston is as follows: "Once more in the bosom of my family. My prayer is that our coming together may be for the better, not for the worse."

Considering the agitation which had been going on at the North for several years concerning slavery, we must suppose that Angelina and Sarah Grimké heard it frequently discussed, and had its features brought before them in a stronger light than that in which they had previously viewed them. In Sarah's mind, absorbed as it was at that time by her own sorrows and by the deeply-rooted conviction of her prospective and dreaded call to the ministry, there appears to have been no room for any other subject, if we except the strife then going on in the Quaker Church, and which called forth all her sympathy for the Orthodox portion, and her strong denunciation of the Hicksites. But upon Angelina every word she heard against the institution which she had always abhorred, but accepted as a necessary evil, made an indelible impression, which deepened when she was again face to face with its odious lineaments. This begins to show itself soon after her return home, as will be seen by the following extract: —

"Since my arrival I have enjoyed a continuation of that rest from exercise of mind which began last spring, until to-night. My soul is sorrowful, and my heart bleeds. I am ready to exclaim, When shall I be released from this land of slavery! But if my suffering for these poor creatures can at all ameliorate their condition, surely I ought to be quite willing, and I can now bless the Lord that my labor is not all in vain, though much remains to be done yet."

The secluded and inactive life she now led confirmed the opinion of her Presbyterian friends that she was a backslider in the divine life.

I must reserve for another chapter the recital of Angelina's efforts to open the eyes of the members of her household to the unchristian life they were leading, and the sins they were multiplying on their heads by their treatments of those they held in bondage.

CHAPTER VI.

MANY things about the home life which habit had prevented Angelina from remarking before, now, since her
visit among Friends, struck her as sinful, and inconsistent
with a Christian profession. Only a few days after her
return, she thus writes in her diary : —

"I am much tried at times at the manner in which I
am obliged to live here in so much luxury and ease, and
raised so far above the poor, and spending so much on
my board. I want to live in plainness and simplicity
and economy, for so should every Christian do. I am at
a loss how to act, for if I live with mother, which seems
the proper place for me, I must live in this way in a great
degree. It is true I can always take the plainest food,
and this I do generally, believing that whether at home
or abroad I ought to eat nothing I think too sumptuous
for a *servant* of Jesus Christ. For this reason, when I
took tea at a minister's house a few evenings since, I did
not touch the richest cakes, nor the fruit and nuts handed
after tea; and when paying a visit the other morning, I
refused cake and wine, although I felt fatigued, and
would have liked something plain to eat. But it is not
only the food I eat at mother's, but the whole style of
living is a direct departure from the simplicity that is in
Christ. The Lord's poor tell me they do not like to come
to such a fine house to see me ; and if they come, instead

of being able to read a lesson of frugality, and deadness
to the world, they must go away lamenting over the inconsistency of a sister professor. One thing is very hard
to bear — I feel obliged to pay five dollars a week for
board, though I disapprove of this extravagance, and am
actually accessory in maintaining this style of living,
when I know it is wrong, and am thereby prevented from
giving to the poor as liberally as I would like."

She and Sarah had for several years, when at home,
paid board regularly to their mother, and this was probably one thing which irritated the other members of the
family, several of whom were living in idleness on their
mother, doing nothing and paying nothing. The brothers
at least could not but feel the implied rebuke. As we
have seen, she was not at all backward in expressing her
disapprobation, when she found her silent testimony was
disregarded or misunderstood; and her language was generally rather forcible. This, of course, was trying to
those who did not see the necessity of living according
to her standard, and very trying to Angelina, whose convictions were clear, and whose interest in her relatives
was as tender as it was sincere. Scarcely a day passed
that something did not occur to wound her feelings, shock
her religious prejudices, or arouse her righteous indignation. Slavery was always the cause of the latter, and for
the others ample reason was to be found in what she
styled the vain lusts of the world, and in the coldness and
irritability of some members of the family. Unre-
strained self-indulgence, joined to high-strung and undis-
ciplined tempers, made of what should have been a
united, bright, and charming home circle, a place of constant discord, jealousy, and unhappiness.

Sarah had borne this state of things better than Angelina could, her extreme gentleness and kindness disarming all unkind feelings in others. But even she was forced to flee from it at last. The record is a most painful one, and it gives another evidence of Angelina's sense of her own power, and of her reliance on divine help, that she should for one moment have contemplated effecting any change. But the respite from those dissensions, and the rest thus given to her spirit by her visit North, softened the bitter feelings she had once entertained, and when she returned home it was with sentiments of affection for everyone, and especially for her mother, from whom she had been grievously estranged. She prayed that she might not do or say anything to alienate them further from her; but when she fully realized, as she had never yet done, the sad condition of things, she could not keep silent. She felt it her duty to speak, and she did so, kindly and affectionately, but unsparingly. She relates many incidents proving this, and showing also how badly her reproofs were received. The mistake she made, and which in after years she freely acknowledged, was in excess of zeal. But Angelina was a born radical, and if a thing was wrong, it was wrong, and she could not see why it should not be righted at once. Temporizing with a wrong, or compromising with it in any way, were things outside of her reasoning, and she never would admit that they were justifiable under any circumstances. It was, of course, difficult to apply this principle in the desired reform of her mother's inherited and life-long prejudices. Hence the incessant chafing and irritation which daily made Angelina feel more keenly her isolated position, and caused her to turn with increasing longing to the North, where her beloved sister and many dear friends were in sympathy with her.

To illustrate what I have said, one or two examples
will be sufficient. She was much troubled because her
mother had the drawing-room repainted and handsomely
papered. Mrs. Grimké doubtless selected a paper in harmony with the house and furniture, and had no suspicion
that she was thereby committing a sin. But Angelina
thought it entirely too fine, and felt that she could never
sit in the room. When the work was at last finished, and
some friends were invited to tea, and afterwards repaired
to the newly-decorated apartment, Angelina did not accompany them, but remained below, reading alone, much
disturbed during the evening by the talking and laughing
up stairs. Her mother did not notice her absence, or
ascribed it to some other cause ; but Angelina explained
it to her some time afterwards, when, she says, a way
seemed to open for it.

"I spoke to her of how great a trial it was to me to see
her living in the luxury she did, and explained to her that
it was not, as she seemed to think, because I did not wish
to see brother John and sister Sally that I was tried at
their dining here every week, but it was the parade and
profusion which was displayed when they came. I spoke
also of the drawing-room, and remarked it was as much
my feeling about *that* which had prevented my coming
into the room when M. A. and others drank tea here, as
my objection to fashionable company. She said it was very
hard that she could not give her children what food she
chose, or have a room papered, without being found fault
with ; that, indeed, she was weary of being continually
blamed about everything she did, and she wished she
could be let alone, for she saw no sin in these things. 'I
trust,' I said, 'that I do not speak to thee, mother, in the
spirit thou art now speaking to me ; nothing but my con-

viction that I am bound to bear my testimony to the truth could induce me to find fault with thee. In doing so, I am acting with eternity in view. I am acting in reference to that awful hour when I shall stand at thy death-bed, or thou by mine.' Interrupting me, she said if *I* was so constantly found fault with, I would not bear it either; for her part, she was quite discouraged. ' Oh, mother,' said I, ' there is something in thee so alienated from the love of Christ that thou canst not bear to be found fault with.' ' Yes,' she said, ' you and Sally always say *I* speak in a wrong spirit, but both of you in a right one.' She then went on to say how much I was changed, about slavery, for instance, for when I was first serious I thought it was right, and never condemned it. I replied that I acted according to the light I had. ' Well, then,' she continued, ' you are not to expect everyone to think like Quakers.' I remarked that true believers had but one leader, who would, if they followed Him, guide them into all truth, and teach them the same things. She again spoke of my turning Quaker, and said it was because I was a Quaker that I disapproved of a great many things that nobody but Quakers could see any harm in. I was much roused at this, and said with a good deal of energy, ' Dear mother, what but the *power* of God could ever have made *me* change my sentiments?' Some very painful conversation followed about Kitty. I did not hesitate to say that no one with *Christian* feelings could have treated her as she was treated before I took her; her condition was a disgrace to the name of Christian. She reminded me that *I* had advised the very method that had been adopted with her. This stung me to the quick. ' Not after I professed Christianity,' I eagerly replied, ' and that I should have done so before, only proved the

wretched manner of my education.' But mother is perfectly blind as to the miserable manner in which she
brought us up. During the latter part of the conversation I was greatly excited, for so acute have been my sufferings on account of slavery, and so strong my feelings
of indignation in looking upon its oppressions and degra-
dations, that I cannot command my feelings in speaking
of what my own eyes have seen, and thus, I believe, I lost
the satisfaction I should otherwise have felt for speaking
the truth.''

Though constantly disregarded, taunted, and thwarted,
Angelina faithfully persevered in her efforts at reform, at
the same time as faithfully striving after more meekness
and singleness of purpose herself.

After a while, she obtained two concessions from which
she hoped much : one, that the servants should come to
her in the library every day for religious instruction; the
other, that her mother would sit with her in silence every
evening for half an hour before tea.

The servants came as directed, and Angelina made her
instructions so interesting that soon some of the neighbors' servants asked to be admitted, and then her mother
and one or two of her sisters joined the meetings; and
though no very marked fruit of her labors appeared for
some time, she persevered, with a firm faith that the seed
she was sowing would not all be scattered to the winds.

The proposal to her mother to sit in silence for a while
with her every evening was in accordance with the
Quaker practices. She thought they would both find it
profitable, and that it would be the means of forming a
bond of union between them. The mother's assent to
this was certainly an amiable concession to her daughter's
views, enhanced by the regularity with which she kept

the appointment, although the dark, silent room must have been at times a trifle wearisome. Angelina always sat on a low seat beside her, with her head in her mother's lap, and very rarely was the silence broken. The practice was kept up until the mosquitoes obliged them to discontinue it. That it did not prove entirely satisfactory, we judge from several entries in the diary like the following : —

"I still sit in silence with dear mother, but feel very sensibly that she takes no interest at all in it; still, I do not like to relinquish the habit, believing it may yet be blessed. Eliza came this evening, as she has several times before. It was a season of great deadness, and yet I am glad to sit even thus, for where there is communion there will be some union."

Her position was certainly a difficult and a painful one ; for, apart from other troubles, her eyes were now fully open to all the iniquities of the slave system, and she could neither stay in nor go out without having some of its miserable features forced upon her notice. In the view of her after-work, it is interesting to note the beginning of her strong feelings on the subject, as well as her faithful crusades against it in her own family. In April, 1829, she writes as follows in her diary : —

"Whilst returning from meeting this morning, I saw before me a colored woman who in much distress was vindicating herself to two white boys, one about eighteen, the other fifteen, who walked on each side of her. The dreadful apprehension that they were leading her to the workhouse crossed my mind, and I would have avoided her if I could. As I approached, the younger said to her, 'I will have you tied up.' My knees smote together, and my heart sank within me. As I passed them, she ex-

claimed, 'Missis!' But I felt all I had to do was to
suffer the pain of seeing her. My lips were sealed, and
my soul earnestly craved a willingness to bear the exercise which was laid on me. How long, O Lord, how long
wilt thou suffer the foot of the oppressor to stand on the
neck of the slave! None but those who know from
experience what it is to live in a land of bondage can
form any idea of what is endured by those whose eyes are
open to the enormities of slavery, and whose hearts are
tender enough to feel for these miserable creatures. For
two or three months after my return here it seemed to
me that all the cruelty and unkindness which I had from
my infancy seen practised towards them came back to my
mind as though it was only yesterday. And as to the
house of correction, it seemed as though its doors were
unbarred to me, and the wretched, lacerated inmates of
its cold, dark cells were presented to my view. Night
and day they were before me, and yet my hands were
bound as with chains of iron. I could do nothing but
weep over the scenes of horror which passed in review
before my mind. Sometimes I felt as though I was
willing to fly from Carolina, be the consequences what
they might. At others, it seemed as though the very exercises I was suffering under were preparing me for future
usefulness to them; and this, — *hope*, I can scarcely call it,
for my very soul trembled at the solemn thought of such a
work being placed in my feeble and unworthy hands, —
this idea was the means of reconciling me to suffer, and
causing me to feel something of a willingness to pass
through any trials, if I could only be the means of exposing the cruelty and injustice which was practised in the
institution of oppression, and of bringing to light the
hidden things of darkness, of revealing the secrets of

iniquity and abolishing its present regulations, — above all, of exposing the awful sin of professors of religion sending their slaves to such a place of cruelty, and having them whipped so that when they come out they can scarcely walk, or having them put upon the treadmill until they are lamed for days afterwards. These are not things I have heard; no, my own eyes have looked upon them and wept over them. Such was the opinion I formed of the workhouse that for many months whilst I was a teacher in the Sunday-school, having a scholar in my class who was the daughter of the master of it, I had frequent occasion to go to it to mark her lessons, and no one can imagine my feelings in walking down that street. It seemed as though I was walking on the very confines of hell; and this winter, being obliged to pass it to pay a visit to a friend, I suffered so much that I could not get over it for days, and wondered how any real Christian could live near such a place."

It may appear to some who read this biography that Angelina's expressions of feeling were over-strained. But it was not so. Her nervous organization was exceedingly delicate, and became more so after she began to give her best thoughts to the cause of humanity. In her own realization, at least, of the suffering of others there was no exaggeration.

Not long after making the above record of her feelings on this subject, she narrates the following incident: —

"I have been suffering for the last two days on account of Henry's boy having run away, because he was threatened with a whipping. Oh, who can paint the horrors of slavery! And yet, so hard is the natural heart that I am constantly told that the situation of slaves is very good, much better than that of their owners. How strange that anyone should believe such an absurdity, or try to make others believe it! No wonder poor John ran away at the threat of a flogging, when he has told me more than once that when H. last whipped him he was in pain for a week afterwards. I don't know how the boy must have felt, but I know that that night was one of agony to me; for it was not only dreadful to hear the blows, but the oaths and curses H. uttered went like daggers to my heart. And this was done, too, in the house of one who is regarded as a light in the church. O Jesus, where is thy meek and merciful disposition to be found now? Are the marks of discipleship changed, or who are thy true disciples? Last night I lay awake weeping over the condition of John, and it seemed as though that was all I could do. But at last I was directed to go to H. and tenderly remonstrate with him. I sought strength, and was willing to do so, if the impression continued. To-day, was somewhat released from this exercise, though still suffering, and almost thought it would not be required. But at dusk it returned; and, having occasion to go into H.'s room for something, I broached the subject as guardedly and mildly as possible, first passing my arm around him, and leaning my head on his shoulder. He very openly acknowledged that he meant to give John such a whipping as would cure him of ever doing the same thing again, and that he deserved to be whipped until he could not stand. I said that would be treating him worse than he would treat his horse. He now became excited, and replied that he considered his horse no comparison better than John, and would *not* treat *it* so. By this time my heart was full, and I felt so much overcome as to be compelled to seat myself, or rather to fall into a chair before him, but I don't think he observed this. The conversation proceeded. I pleaded the cause of humanity. He grew very angry, and said I had no business to be meddling with him, that he never did so with me. I said if I had ever done anything to offend him I was very sorry for it, but I had tried to do everything to please him. He said I had come from the North expressly to be miserable myself and make everyone in the house so, and that I had much better go and live at the North. I told him that I was not ignorant that both C. and himself would be very glad if I did, and that as soon as I felt released from Carolina I would go; but that I had believed it my duty to return this winter, though I knew I was coming back to suffer. He again accused me of meddling with his private affairs, which he said I had no right to do. I told him I could not but lift up my voice against his manner of treating John. He said rather than suffer the continual condemnation of his conduct by me, he would leave mother's house. I appealed to the witness in his own bosom as to the truth of what I urged. To my surprise he readily acknowledged that he felt something within him which fully met all I asserted, and that I had harrowed his feelings and made him wretched. Much more passed. I alluded to his neglect of me, and testified that I had experienced no feeling but that of love towards him and all the family, and a desire to do all I could to oblige them; and I left the room in tears. I retired to bless my Saviour for the strength he had granted, and to implore his continued support."

"7th. Surely my heart ought to be lifted to my blessed Master in emotions of gratitude and praise. His boy came home last night a short time after our conversation, and instead of punishing him, as I am certain he intended to do, he merely told him to go about his business. I was amazed last night after all my sufferings were over, and I was made willing to leave all things in my Father's hands, to see John in the house. This was a renewed proof to me how necessary it is for us to watch for the right *time* in which to do things. If I had not spoken just when I did, I could not have done so before John's return. He has escaped entirely. . . . Oh, how earnestly two nights ago did I pray for a release from this land of slavery, and how my heart still pants after it! And yet, I think, I trust it is in submission to my Heavenly Father's will. I feel comfortable to-night; my relief from suffering about John is so great that other trials seem too light to name."

" 8th. My heart sings aloud for joy. I feel the sweet testimony of a good conscience, the reward of obedience in speaking to H. Dear boy, he has good, tender feelings naturally, but a false education has nearly destroyed them, and his own perverted judgment as to what is manly and what is necessary in the government of slaves has done the rest. Lord, open thou his eyes."

On the 13th of March she says: " To-day, for the first time, I ironed my clothes, and felt as though it was an acceptable sacrifice. This seemed part of the preparation for my removal to the North. I felt fearful lest this object was a stronger incentive to me than the desire to glorify my divine Master."

There was doubtless some truth in the charge brought against her by her brothers, that her face was a perpetual condemnation of them. Referring to a call she received from some friends, she says : —

" An emptiness and vapidness pervaded all they said about religion. I was silent most of the time, and fear what I did say sprang from a feeling of too great indignation. Just before they went away, I joined in a joke; much condemnation was felt, for the language to me constantly is, ' I have called *thee* with a *high* and *holy* calling,' and it seems as though solemnity ought always to pervade my mind too much to allow *me* ever to joke, but my natural vivacity is hard to bridle and subdue."

The bond between Sarah and Angelina was growing stronger every day, their separation in matters of religion from the other members of the family serving more than anything else to draw them closely and lovingly together. Every letter from Sarah was hailed as a messenger of peace and joy, and to her Angelina turned for counsel and sympathy. It is very pleasant to read such words as the following, and know that they expressed the inmost feelings of Angelina's heart : —

" Thou art, dearest, my best beloved, and often does my heart expand with gratitude to the Giver of all good for the gift of such a friend, who has been the helper of my joy and the lifter up of my hands when they were ready to hang down in hopeless despair. Often do I look back to those days of conflict and suffering through which I passed last winter, when thou alone seemed to know of the deep baptisms wherewith I was baptized, and to be qualified to speak the words of encouragement and reproof which I believe were blessed to my poor soul.

" I received another long letter from thee this afternoon. I cannot tell thee what a consolation thy letters are to her who feels like an exile, a stranger in the place of her nativity, ' as unknown, and yet well known,' and one of the very least where she was once among the greatest."

In one of her letters, written soon after her return home, she thus speaks of her Quaker dress : —

" I thought I should find it so trying to dress like a

Quaker here; but it has been made so easy that if it is a cross I do not feel the weight of it. . . . It appears to me that at present I am to be little and unknown, and that the most that is required of me is that I bear a decided testimony against dress. I am literally as a wonder unto many, but though I am as a gazing-stock — perhaps a laughing-stock — in the midst of them, yet I scarcely feel it, so sensible am I of the presence and approbation of Him for whose sake I count it a high privilege to endure scorn and derision. I begin to feel that it is a solemn thing even to dress like a Quaker, as by so doing I profess a belief in the purest principles of the Bible, and warrant the expectation in others that my life will exhibit to all around those principles drawn out in living characters."

There is a pride of conscience in all this, strongly contrasting with Sarah's want of self-confidence when travelling the same path. If Angelina suffered for her religion, no one suspected it, and for this very reason she was enabled to exert a stronger influence upon those about her than Sarah ever could have done. She herself saw the great points of difference between them, and frequently alluded to them. On one page of her diary she writes: —

"I have been reading dear sister's diary the last two days, and find she has suffered great conflict of mind, particularly about her call to the ministry, and I am led to look at the contrast between our feelings on the subject. I clearly saw winter before last that my having been appointed to this work was the great reason why I was called out of the Presbyterian Society, but I don't think my will has ever rebelled against it.

"So far from murmuring against the appointment, I have felt exceedingly impatient at not being permitted to enter upon my work at once; and this is probably an evidence that I am not prepared for it. But it is hard for me to *be* and to *do* nothing. My restless, ambitious temper, so different from dear sister's, craves high duties and high attainments, and I have at times thought that this ambition was a motive to me to do my duty and submit my will. The hope of attaining to great eminence in the divine life has often prompted me to give up in little things, to bend to existing circumstances, to be willing for the time to be trampled upon. These are my temptations. For a long time it seemed to me I did everything from a hope of applause. I could not even write in my diary without a feeling that I was doing it in the hope that it would one day meet the eye of the public. Last winter I wrote more freely in it, and am still permitted to do so. Very often, when thinking of my useless state at present, something of disappointment is felt that I am as nothing, and this language has been presented with force, ' Seekest thou great things for thyself, seek them not.' "

CHAPTER VII.

AT this time of her life, ere a single sorrow had thrown its shadow across her heart, and all her tears were shed for other's woes, we see very distinctly Angelina's peculiar characteristics. Her conscientiousness and her pride are especially conspicuous. The former, with its attendant sacrifices at the shrine of religious principle, had the effect of silencing criticism after a while, and inspiring a respect which touched upon veneration. One of her sisters, in referring to this, says: —

"Though we considered her views entirely irrational, yet so absolute was her sense of duty, her superiority to public sentiment, and her moral courage, that she seemed to us almost like one inspired, and we all came to look upon her with a feeling of awe."

Of her pride — "that stumbling block," as she calls it, to Christian meekness — she herself writes: —

"My pride is my bane. In examining myself, I blush to confess this fault, so great do I find its proportions. I am all pride, and I fear I am even proud of my pride."

But hers was not the pride that includes personal vanity or the desire for the applause of the multitude, for of these two elements few ever had less; neither was there any haughtiness in it, only the dignity which comes from the conscious possession of rare advantages, joined to the desire to use them to the glory of something better than self. Still it was pride, and, in her eyes, sinful, and called for all her efforts to subdue its manifestations. It especially troubled her whenever she entered into any argument or discussion, both of which she was rather fond of inviting. She knew full well her intellectual power, and thoroughly enjoyed its exercise.

I regret that space does not permit me to copy her discussion with the Rev. Mr. McDowell on Presbyterianism; her answers to the questions given her when arraigned before the Sessions for having left the Church; her conversation on Orthodoxy with some Hicksites who called on her, and her arguments on silent worship. They all show remarkable reasoning power, great lucidity of thought, and great faculty of expression for so young a woman.

But, interesting as is the whole history of Angelina's last year in Charleston, I may not dwell longer upon it, but hasten towards that period when the reason for all this mental and spiritual preparation was made manifest in the work in which she became as a "light upon the hill top," and, which, as long as it lasted, filled the measure of her desires full to the brim.

As it is important to show just what her views and feelings about slavery were at this time, and as they can be better narrated in her own words than in mine, I shall quote from her diary and a few letters all that relates to the subject.

In May, 1829, we find this short sentence in her diary : —

"May it not be laid down as an axiom, that that system must be radically wrong which can only be supported by transgressing the laws of God."

"3d Mo. 20th. Could I think I was in the least advancing the glory of God by staying here, I think I would be satisfied, but I am doing nothing. Though ' the fields are white for harvest, yet am I standing idle in the market place.' I am often tempted to ask, Why am I kept in such a situation, a poor unworthy worm, feeding on luxuries my soul abhors, tended by slaves, who (I think) I would rather serve than be served by, and whose bondage I deeply deplore? Oh! why am I kept in Carolina? But the answer seems to be : ' I have set thee as a sign to the people.' Lord, give me patience to stand still."

" 29th. At times slavery is a heavy burden to my heart. Last night I was led to speak of this subject, of all others the sorest on which to touch a Carolinian. The depravity of slaves was spoken of with contempt, and one said they were fitted to hold no other place than the one they do. I asked what had made them so depraved? Was it not because of their degraded situations, and was it not white people who had placed them and kept them in this situation, and were *they* not to blame for it? Was it not a fact that the minds of slaves were totally uncultivated, and their souls no more cared for by their owners than if they had none? Was it not true that, in order to restrain them from vice, coercion was employed instead of the moral restraint which, if proper instruction had been given them, would have guarded them against evil? ' I wish,' exclaimed one, ' that you would never speak on the subject.' ' And why?' I asked. ' Because you speak in such a serious way,' she replied. ' Truth cuts deep into the heart,' I said, and this is no doubt the reason why no one likes to hear me express my sentiments, but I did feel it my duty to bear a decided testimony against an institution which I believe altogether contrary to the spirit of the Gospel; for it was a system which nourished

the worst passions of the human heart, a system which
sanctioned the daily trampling under foot of the feelings
of our fellow creatures. 'But,' said one, 'it is exceedingly imprudent in you to speak as you do.' I replied I
was not speaking before servants, I was speaking only to
owners, whom I wished to know my sentiments; this wrong
had long enough been covered up, and I was not afraid
or ashamed to have any one know my sentiments — they
were drawn from the Bible. I also took occasion to speak
very plainly to sister Mary about the bad feeling she had
towards negroes, and told her, though she wished to get
rid of them, and would be glad to see them *shipped*, as
she called it, that this wish did not spring from pure
Christian benevolence. My heart was very heavy after
this conversation."

"3d Mo. 31st. Yesterday was a day of suffering. My
soul was exceedingly sorrowful, and out of the depths of
it, I cried unto the Lord that He would make a way for
me to escape from this land of slavery. Is there any suffering so great as that of seeing the rights and feelings of
our fellow creatures trodden under foot, without being
able to rescue them from bondage? How clear it is to
my mind that slaves can be controlled only by one of two
principles,— fear or love. As to moral restraint, they know
nothing of it, for they are not taught to act from principle.
I feel as though I had nothing to do in this thing, but by
my manner to bear a decided testimony against such an
abuse of power. The suffering of mind through which
I have passed has necessarily rendered me silent and
solemn. The language seems to be, 'It behooves thee to
suffer these things,' and this morning I think I saw very
plainly that this was a part of the preparation for the awful work of the ministry."

"4th Mo. 4th. Does not this no less positive than comprehensive law under the Gospel dispensation entirely exclude slavery : ' Do unto others as you would be done by ? ' After arguing for some time, one evening, with an individual, I proposed the question : ' Would'st thou be willing to be a slave thyself ? ' He eagerly answered ' No ! ' ' Then,' said I, ' thou hast no right to enslave the negro, for the Master expressly says : " Do unto others as thou wouldst they should do unto thee." ' Again I put the query : ' Suppose thou wast obliged to free thy slaves, or take their place, which wouldst thou do ? ' Of course he said he would free them. ' But why,' I asked, ' if thou really believest what thou contendest for, namely, that their situation is as good as thine ? ' But these questions were too close, and he did not know what to say."

"4th Mo. 23d. Friend K. drank tea here last night. It seems to me that whenever mother can get anyone to argue with her on the subject of slavery, she always introduces it; but last night she was mistaken, for, to my surprise, Friend K. acknowledged that notwithstanding all that could be said for it, there was something in her heart which told her it was wrong, and she admitted all I said. Since my last argument on this subject, it has appeared to me in another light. I remarked that a Carolina mistress was literally a slave-driver, and that I thought it degrading to the female character. The mistress is as great a slave to her servants, in some respects, as they are to her. One thing which annoys me very much is the constant orders that are given. Really, when I go into mother's room to read to her, I am continually interrupted by a variety of orders which might easily be avoided, were it not for the domineering spirit which is, it seems to me, inherent in a Carolinian ; and they are such fine ladies that if a shutter is to be hooked, or a chair moved, or their work handed to them, a servant must be summoned to do it for them. Oh! I do very much desire to cultivate feelings of forbearance, but I feel at the same time that it is my duty to bear an open and decided testimony against such a violation of the divine command."

"28th. It seems this morning as if the language was spoken with regard to dear mother: *Thy* work is done. My mind has been mostly released from exercises, and it seems as though I had nothing to do now but to bear and forbear with her. I can truly say I have not shunned to ' declare unto her the whole counsel of God, but she would none of my reproofs.' I stretched out my hands to her, speaking the truth in *love*, but she has not regarded. Perhaps He has seen fit not to work by me lest I should be exalted above measure."

"5th Mo. 6th. Today has been one of much trial of mind, and my soul has groaned under the burden of slavery. Is it too harsh to say that a person must be destitute of Christian feelings to be willing to be served by slaves, who are actuated by no sentiment but that of fear? Are not these unfortunate creatures expected to act on principles directly opposite to our natural feelings and daily experience? They are required to do more for others than for themselves, and all without thanks or reward."

"12th. It appears to me that there is a real want of natural affection among many families in Carolina, and I have thought that one great cause of it is the independence which members of families feel here. Instead of being taught to do for themselves and each other, they are brought up to be waited on by slaves, and become unami-

able, proud, and selfish. I have many times felt exceedingly tried, when, in the flowings of love towards mother,
I have offered to do little things for her, and she has refused to allow me, saying it was Stephen's or William's
duty, and she preferred one of them should do it. The
other night, being refused in this way, I said : —

" 'Mother, it seems to me thou would'st at any time
rather have a servant do little things for thee, than me.'
She replied it was their business. 'Well,' said I, 'mother,
I do not think it ever was designed that parents and children should be independent of each other. Our Heavenly
Father intended that we should be dependent on each
other, not on servants.' From time to time ability is
granted me to labor against slavery. I may be mistaken,
but I do not think it is any longer without sin in mother,
for I think she feels very sensibly that it is not right,
though she never will acknowledge it."

" *Night.* Left the parlor on account of some unpleasant occurrence, and retired to weep in solitude over the
evils of slavery. The language was forcibly revived :
' Woe unto you, for you bind heavy burdens, grievous to
be borne, on men's shoulders, and will not move them
yourselves with one of your fingers.' I do not think I
pass a single day without apprehension as to something
painful about the servants."

" 15th. Had a long conversation with Selina last evening about servants, and expressed very freely my opinion
of Henry's feelings towards them, and his treatment of
John. She admitted all I said, and seemed to feel for
slaves, until I said I thought they had as much right to
freedom as I had. Of course she would not admit this,
but I was glad an opportunity was offered for me to tell
her that my life was one of such continual and painful

exercise on account of the manner in which our servants were treated, that, were it not for mother, I would not stay a day longer in Carolina, and were it not for the belief that Henry would treat his servants worse if we were not here, that both Eliza and I would leave the house. Dear girl; she seemed to feel a good deal at these strictures on her husband, but bore with me very patiently."

"18th. Oh, Lord! grant that my going forth out of this land may be in such a time and such a way, let what may happen after I leave my mother's house, I may never have to reproach myself for doing so. Of late my mind has been much engrossed with the subject of slavery. I have felt not only the necessity of feeling that it is sinful, but of being able to prove from Scripture that it is not warranted by God."

"30th. Slavery is a system of abject selfishness, and yet I believe I have seen some of the best of it. In its worst form, tyranny is added to it, and power cruelly treads under foot the rights of man, and trammels not only the body, but the mind of the poor negro. Experience has convinced me that a person may own a slave, with a single eye to the glory of God. But as the eye is kept single, it will soon become full of light on this momentous subject; the arm of power will be broken; the voice of authority will tremble, and strength will be granted to obey the command : 'Touch not the unclean thing.' "

" *Night.* Sometimes I think that the children of Israel could not have looked towards the land of Canaan with keener longing than I do to the North. I do not expect to go there and be exempt from trial, far from it; and yet it looks like a promised land, a pleasant land, because it is a land of freedom; and it seems to me that I would rather bear much deeper spiritual exercises than, day after day, and month after month, to endure the countless evils which incessantly flow from slavery. 'Oh, to grace how great a debtor for my sentiments on this subject. Surely I may measurably adopt the language of Paul, when with holy triumph he exclaimed: ' By the grace of God I am what I am.' ' "

A few weeks later, we read: " If I could believe that I contributed to dear mother's happiness, surely duty, yea, inclination, would lead me to continue here ; but I do not. Yesterday morning I read her some papers on slavery, which had just come by the L. C. (vessel). It was greatly against her will, but it seemed to me I must do it, and that this was the last effort which would be required of me. She was really angry, but I did not feel condemned."

" *Night*. Have sought a season of retirement, in order to ponder all these things in my heart, for I feel greatly burdened, and think I must open this subject to dear mother to-morrow, perhaps. I earnestly desire to do the Lord's will."

" 12th. This morning I read parts of dear sister's letters to mother, on the subject of my going to the North. She did not oppose, though she regretted it. My mind is in a calm, almost an indifferent, state about it, simply acquiescing in what I believe to be the divine will concerning me."

Had we all of Sarah's letters written to Angelina, we should doubtless see that she fully sympathized with her in her anti-slavery sentiments; but Sarah's diary shows her thoughts to have been almost wholly absorbed by her disappointed hopes, and her trials in the ministry. As positive evidences of her continued interest in slavery, we have only the fact that, in 1829, Angelina mentions, in her diary, receiving anti-slavery documents from her sister, and the statements of friends that she retained her interest in the subject which had, in her earlier years, caused her so much sorrow.

It is astonishing how ignorant of passing events, even of importance, a person may remain who is shut up as Sarah Grimké was, in an organization hedged in by restrictions which would prevent her from gaining such knowledge. She mingled in no society outside of her church; her time was so fully occupied with her various charitable and religious duties, that she frequently laments the necessity of neglecting reading and writing, which, she says, " I love so well."

When a few friends met together, their conversation was chiefly of religious or benevolent matters, and it is probable that Sarah even read no newspaper but the *Friends' Journal.*

That this narrow and busy life was led even after Angelina joined her we judge from what Angelina writes to her brother Thomas, thanking him for sending them his literary correspondence to read. She says : " It is very kind in thee to send us thy private correspondence. We enjoy it so much that I am sure thou would'st feel compensated for the trouble if thou could'st see us. We mingle almost entirely with a Society which appears to know but little of what is going on outside of its own immediate precincts. It is therefore a great treat when we have access to information more diffuse, or that which introduces our minds in some measure into the general interest which seems to be exciting the religious world."

The fact, however, remains, that in 1829 Sarah sent to Angelina various anti-slavery publications, from which the latter drew strength and encouragement for her own

arguments.   Angelina also mentions reading carefully
Woolman's works, which she found very helpful.   But it
is evident that neither she nor Sarah looked forward at
all to any identification of themselves with the active
opponents of slavery.   For them, at that time, there
seemed to be nothing more to do than to express their
opinions on the subject in private, and to get as far away
from the sight of its evils as possible.   As Sarah had
done this, so now Angelina felt that the time had come
when she too must go.

She had done what she could, and had failed in making
the impression she had hoped to make.   Why should she
linger longer where her feelings were daily tortured, and
where there was not one to sympathize with her or aid
her, where she could neither give nor receive any good?
Still there was a great struggle in her mind about leaving
her mother.   She thus writes of it:

" Though I am favored to feel this is the right time for
me to go, yet I cannot but be pained at the thought of
leaving mother, for I am sure I shall leave her to suffer.
It has appeared very plain to me that I never would have
been taken from her again if she had been willing to
listen to my remonstrances, and to yield to the requisi-
tions of duty, as shown her by the light within.   And I
do not think dear sister or I will ever see her again until
she is willing to give up slavery."

" 10th Mo. 4th.   Last night E. T. took tea here.   As
soon as she began to extol the North and speak against
slavery, mother left the room.   She cannot bear these
two subjects.   My mind continues distressingly exercised
and anxious that mother's eyes should be open to all the
iniquities of the system she upholds.   Much hope has
lately been experienced, and it seems as though the lan-

guage to me was: 'Thou hast done what was given thee to do ; now go and leave the rest to *me*."

Two weeks later, she writes as follows:

" *Night*. This morning I had a very satisfactory conversation with dear mother, and feel considerably relieved from painful exercise. I found her views far more correct than I had supposed, and I do believe that, through suffering, the great work will yet be accomplished. She remarked that, though she had found it very hard to bear many things which sister and I had from time to time said to her, yet she believed that the Lord had raised us up to teach her, and that her fervent prayer was that, if we were right and she was wrong, she might see it. I remarked that if she was *willing*, she would, I was sure, see still more than she now did ; and I drew a contrast between what she once approved and now believed right. ' Yes,' she said, ' I see very differently ; for when I look back and remember what I used to do, and think nothing of it, I shrink back with horror. Much more passed, and we parted in love."

Two weeks later Angelina left Charleston, never to return. The description of the parting with her mother is very affecting, but we have not room for it here. It shows, however, that Mrs. Grimké had the true heart of a mother, and loved her daughter most tenderly. She shed bitter tears as she folded her to her bosom for the last time, murmuring amid her sobs : " Joseph is not, and Simeon is not, and ye will take Benjamin away also!" The mother and daughter never saw each other again.

CHAPTER VIII.

ANGELINA arrived in Philadelphia in the latter part of October, 1829, and made her home with Sarah in the family of Catherine Morris.

Over the next four or five years I must pass very briefly, although they were marked by many interesting incidents and some deep sorrows, and much that the sisters wrote during that time I would like to notice, if space permitted.

We see Sarah still regarding herself as the vilest of sinners, against whom it seemed at times as if every door of mercy was closed, and still haunted by her horror of horrors, the ministry. Her preparation continued, but brought her apparently no nearer the long-expected and dreaded end. She was still unrecognized by the Church. First-day meetings were looked forward to without pleasure, while the Quarterly and Yearly meetings were seasons of actual suffering. Of one of the latter she says, —

"I think no criminal under sentence of death can look more fearfully to the day of execution than I do towards our Yearly Meeting."

Still she would nerve herself from time to time to arise when the Spirit moved her, and say a few words, but deriving no satisfaction from the exercise, except that of obedience to the divine will.

Doubtless she would have grown out of all this timidity, and would have acquitted herself more acceptably in meeting, if she had met with consideration and kindness from the elders and influential members of the Society. But, for reasons not clearly explained, her efforts do not seem to have been generally regarded with favor; and so sensibly did she feel this that she trembled in every limb when obliged even to offer a prayer in the presence of one of the dignitaries. It is probable that her ultra views on various needed reforms in the society, and declining — as she and Angelina both did — to conform to all its peculiar usages, gave offence. For instance, the sisters never could bring themselves to use certain ungrammatical forms of speech, such as *thee* for *thou*, and would wear bonnets of a shape and material better adapted to protect them from the cold than those prescribed by Quaker style. It was also discovered that they indulged in vocal prayer in their private devotions, which was directly contrary to established usage. These things were regarded as quiet protests against customs which all members of the Society were expected to respect. As to the *principles* of Quakerism, the sisters were more scrupulous in obeying them than many of the elders themselves. Sarah frequently mentions the coldness and indifference with which she was treated by those from whom she had a right to look for tender sympathy and friendly counsel, and feelingly records the kindness and encouragement offered to her by many of the less conspicuous brothers and sisters. It is no doubt that to this treatment by those in authority was due the gradual waning of her interest in Quakerism, although she is far from acknowledging it.

One obstacle in the way of her success as a preacher was her manner of speaking. Though a clear, forcible thinker and writer, she lacked the gift of eloquence which so distinguished Angelina, and being, besides, exceedingly self-conscious, it was difficult for her to express herself satisfactorily in words.   Her speech was sometimes slow and hesitating; at others, when feeling very deeply, or at all embarrassed, rapid and a little confused, as though she was in a hurry to get through.   This irregularity laid her open to the charge which was frequently brought against her, that she prepared and committed her offerings to memory before coming to meeting, an almost unpardonable offence according to the views of those making the accusation.   That her earnest denial of this should be treated lightly was an additional wrong which Sarah never entirely succeeded in forgiving.   In reference to this she says: —

" The suffering passed through in meeting, on account of the ministry, feeling as if I were condemned already whenever I arise; the severe reproofs administered by an elder to whom I did a little look for kindness; the cutting charge of preparing what I had to say out of meeting, and going there to preach, instead of to worship, like poor Mary Cox, was almost too much for me.   It cost me hours of anguish; but Jesus allayed the storm and gave me peace; for in looking at my poor services I can truly say it is not so, although my mind is often brought under exercise on account of this work, and many are the sleepless hours I pass in prayer for preservation in it, feeling it indeed an awful thing to be a channel of communication between God and His people."

Referring to the charge again, some time later, she says: —

" There are times when I greatly fear my best life will perish in this conflict.   I have felt lately as if I were ready to give up all, and to question all I have known and done."

As contrasting with the very different opinions she held a few years later, the following lines from her diary, about the beginning of 1830, are interesting : —

"There are seasons when my heart is so filled with apostolic love that I feel as if I could freely part with all I hold most dear, to be instrumental to the salvation of souls, especially those of the members of my own religious society; and the language often prevails, 'I am not sent but to the lost sheep of the house of Israel.' Yet woman's preaching mocks at all my reasoning. I cannot see it to be right, and I am moving on in faith alone, feeling that 'Woe is me, if I preach not the Gospel.' To see is no part of my business, but I marvel not at the unbelief of others; every natural feeling is against it."

About this time, Angelina was admitted as a member of Friends' Society, and began her preparation for the ministry. But her active spirit needed stronger food to satisfy its cravings. It was not enough for her to accept the few duties assigned to her; she must make others for herself. Her restless energy, which was only her ambition to be practically useful, refused to let her sit with folded hands waiting for the Lord's work. She was too strong to be idle, too conscious of the value of the talents committed to her charge, to be willing to lay them away for safe keeping in a Quaker napkin, spotless as it might be. She never loved the Society of Friends as Sarah did. She chafed under its restrictions, questioned its authority, and rebelled against the constant admonition to "be still." On one page of her diary, dated a short time before her admission to Friends' Society, she says : —

"I have passed through some trying feelings of late about becoming a member of Friends' Society. Perhaps it is Satan who has been doing all he could to prevent my joining, by showing me the inconsistencies of the people, and persuading me that *I* am too good to be one of them. I have been led to doubt if it was right for me ever to have worn the dress of a Quaker, for I despised the very form in my heart, and have felt it a disgrace to have adopted it, so empty have the people seemed to me, and sometimes it has seemed impossible that I should ever be willing to join them. My heart has been full of rebellion, and I have even dared to think it hard that I should have to bear the burdens of a people I did not, could not, love."

Angelina's devotion to Sarah led her to resent the treatment of the latter by the elders, and came near producing a breach between Catherine Morris and the sisters.

Nevertheless, she did join the Society, impelled thereto, we are forced to believe, more by love and consideration for Sarah than by religious conviction. But she constantly complains of her "leanness and barrenness of spirit," of "doubts and distressing fears" as to the Lord's remembrance of her for good, and grieves that she is such a useless member of the Church, the "activity of nature," she says, "finding it very hard to stand and *wait*."

Her restlessness, no doubt, gave Sarah some trouble, for there are several entries in her diary like the following : —

"O Lord, be pleased, I beseech Thee, to preserve my precious sister from moving in her own will, or under the deceitful reasonings of Satan. Strengthen her, I beseech Thee, to be *still*."

But though Angelina tried for a time to submit passively to the slow training marked out for her, she found no satisfaction in it. She looked to the ministry as her ultimate field of labor, but she must be doing something in the meanwhile, something outside of the missionary work which satisfied Sarah's conscience. But what should that be? The same difficulties which had humiliated and frightened Sarah into a life of quiet routine now faced Angelina. But she looked at them bravely, measured herself with them, and resolved to conquer them. The field of education was the only one which seemed to promise the active usefulness she craved; and she at once set about fitting herself to be a teacher. She was now twenty-six years old, but no ambitious girl of fifteen ever entered upon school duties with more zest than she exhibited in preparing a course of study for herself. History, arithmetic, algebra, and geometry were begun, with her sister Anna as a fellow-student, and much time was devoted to reading biography and travels. All this, however, was evening work. Her days were almost wholly given up to charities and the appointed meetings assigned to her by the society, into all of which she infused so much energy that Catherine and Sarah both began to fear that she was in danger of losing some of her spirituality. She says herself that she was so much interested in some of her work that the days were not long enough for her.

There is no allusion in the diary or letters of either of the sisters, in 1829 or 1830, to the many stirring events of the anti-slavery movement which occurred after the final abolition of slavery in New York, in 1827, and which foreshadowed the earnest struggle for political supremacy between the slave power and the free spirit of the nation. The daily records of their lives and thoughts exhibit them in the enjoyment of their quiet home with Catherine Morris, visiting prisons, hospitals, and alms-houses, and mourning over no sorrow or sins but their own. Angelina was leading a life of benevolent effort, too busy to admit of the pleasures of society, and her Quaker associations did not favor contact with the world's people, or promote knowledge of the active movements in the larger reforms of the day. As to Sarah, she was still suffering keenly under the great sorrow of her life.

At this time, Angelina was a most attractive young woman. Tall and graceful, with a shapely head covered with chestnut ringlets, a delicate complexion and features, and clear blue eyes, which could dance with merriment or flash with indignation, and withal a dignified, yet gentle and courteous bearing, it is not surprising that she should have had many admirers of the opposite sex, even in the limited society to which she was confined. Nor can we wonder that, with a heart so susceptible to all the finer emotions, she should have preferred the companionship of one to that of all others. But though for more than two years this friendship — for it never became an engagement — absorbed all her thoughts, to the exclusion even of her studies, I must conclude from the plain evidence in the case that it was only a warm *friendship*, at least on her side, not the strong, enduring love, based upon entire sympathy, which afterwards blessed her life. It owed its origin to her admiration for intellectuality in men, and its continuance to her womanly pity; for the object of her preference suffered much from ill-health, which at last gave way altogether in the latter part of 1832, when he died.

To the various emotions naturally aroused during this long experience, and to the depression of spirits which followed the final issue, we may perhaps partially ascribe Angelina's indifference to the excited state of feeling throughout the country on the subject of that institution which "owned no law but human will."

In November, 1831, Sarah Grimké once more, and for the last time, visited Charleston.

In December, the slave insurrection in Jamaica — tenfold more destructive to life and property than the insurrection of Nat Turner, in Virginia, of the preceding August — startled the world; but even this is scarcely referred to in the correspondence between the two sisters. But that Angelina, at least, was interested in matters outside of her religion, we gather from a postscript to one of her letters. "Tell me," she says, "something about politics."

This refers to nullification, that ill-judged and premature attempt at secession made by the Calhoun wing of the slave power, which was then the most exciting topic in South Carolina. Thomas Grimké was one of the few eminent lawyers in the State who, from the first, denounced and resisted the treasonable doctrine, — he so termed it in an open letter of remonstrance addressed to Calhoun, McDuffie, Governor Hayne, and Barnwell Rhett, his cousin and legal pupil, who was afterwards attorney-general of the State.[1] Mr. Grimké represented at that time the city of Charleston in the State Senate; and in a two days' argument he so triumphantly exposed the sophistries and false pretences of the nullifiers, that his constituents, enraged by it, gathered a mob, and with threats of personal violence attacked his house. But this descendant of the Huguenots had been seasonably warned; and, sending his family to the country, he illuminated his front windows, threw open his doors, and seated himself quietly on the porch to await his visitors. The howling

---

[1] Mr. Grimké told Carolina that, if she persisted in her disloyalty, she would stand as a blasted tree in the midst of her sister States.

horde came on, but when the man they sought boldly advanced to meet them, and announced himself ready to be mobbed for the cause he had denounced, their courage faltered; they tried to hoot, balked, broke ranks, and straggled away.

A few words just here about this "beloved brother Thomas," who was always held in reverence by every member of his family, will not be out of place. As before stated, he was a graduate of Yale College, and rose to eminence at the bar and in the politics of his State. But he was a man of peculiar views on many subjects, and while his intellectual ability was everywhere acknowledged, his judgment was often impugned and his opinions severely criticised. He gained a wide reputation on account of his brilliant addresses, especially those of Peace, Temperance, and Education. He was a prominent member of the American Peace Society, and did not believe that even defensive warfare was justifiable. He was a fine classical scholar, but held that both the classics and the higher mathematics should not be made obligatory studies in a collegiate education, as being comparatively useless to the great majority of American young men. A High Church Episcopalian, and very religious, he strongly urged the necessity of establishing a Bible class for religious instruction in every school. He also attempted to make a reform in orthography by dropping out all superfluous letters, but abandoned this after publishing a small volume of essays, in which he used his amended words, which, as he gave no prefatory explanation, were misunderstood and ridiculed. In all these subjects he was much interested, and succeeded in interesting his sisters, delegating to them the supervision and correction of his addresses and essays published in Philadelphia. Strange, indeed, is it, that this very religious, liberal-minded, and conscientious man was a large slave-owner, and yet the oppressed and persecuted Cherokees of Georgia and Alabama had no more earnest advocate than he! And to this "Indian question" both Sarah and Angelina gave their cordial sympathy.

The correspondence between them and Thomas was a remarkable one. It embraced the following subjects: Peace, Temperance, the Classics, the Priesthood, the Jewish Dispensation, Was the Eagle the Babylonian and Persian Standard? Catholicism, and the universality of human sacrifice, with short discussions on minor controversial topics. Into all of these Angelina especially entered with great and evident relish, and her long letters, covering page after page of foolscap, would certainly have wearied the patience of any one less interested than Thomas was in the subjects of which they treated. That which claimed Sarah's particular interest was Peace, and she held to her brother's views to the end of her life. She especially indorsed the sentiment expressed in his written reply to the question, what he would do if he were mayor of Charleston and a pirate ship should attack the city?

"I would," he answered, "call together the Sunday-school children and lead them in procession to meet the pirates, who would be at once subdued by the sight."

In answer to a letter written by Sarah soon after her arrival in Charleston, Angelina says: —

"I am not at all surprised at the account thou hast given of Carolina, and yet am not alarmed, as I believe the time of retribution has not yet fully come, and I cannot but hope that those most dear to us will have fled from her borders before the day of judgment arrives."

This refers to nullification, which was threatening to end in bloodshed; but there is in the sentence also an evident allusion to slavery.

In her next letter she describes the interest she feels in the infant school, of which she had become a teacher, and does not know which is the most absorbing, — that, or the Arch Street prison. Before closing, she says : —

"No doubt thou art suffering a double portion now, for in a land of slavery there is very much daily — yea, almost hourly, — to try the better feelings, besides that suffering which thou art so constantly enduring."

Catherine Morris must have acted the part of a good mother to both Sarah and Angelina, for they frequently refer to their peaceful home with her. In one of her letters Angelina says, —

"I never valued the advantages I enjoy so much as I do now ; no, nor my home, either, dear sister. Many a time of late has my heart been filled with gratitude in looking at the peaceful shelter provided for me in a strange land. It is just such a home as I would desire were I to have a choice, and I often ask why my restless heart is not quite happy in the land of ease which has been assigned me, for I do believe I shall, in after life, look back upon this winter as one of peculiar favor, a time granted for the improvement of my mind and my heart."

Again : "Very often do I contrast the sweet, unbroken quiet of the home I now enjoy with the uncongenial one I was taken from."

In one of her letters she asks : "Dearest, does our precious mother seem to have any idea of leaving Carolina? Such seems to be the distressing excitement there from various causes, that I think it cannot be quite safe to remain there. What does brother Thomas think will be the issue of the political contest? I find the fate of the poor Indians is now inevitable."

Towards the close of the winter there are two paragraphs in her letters which show that she did at least read the daily papers. In one she asks: " Didst thou know that great efforts are making in the House of Delegates in Virginia to abolish slavery?"

The other one is as follows: —

"Read the enclosed, and give it to brother Thomas from me. Do you know how this subject has been agitated in the Virginia legislature?"

The question naturally arises: if a little, why not more? If she could refer to the subject of the Virginia debates, why should she not in some of her letters give expression to her own views, or answer some expressions from Sarah? The *Quaker Society*, is the only answer we can find; the Society whose rules and customs at that time tended to repress individuality in its members, and independence of thought or action; which forbade its young men and maidens to look admiringly on any fair face or manly form not framed in a long-eared cap, or surmounted by the regulation broad-brim; which did not accord to a member the right even to publish a newspaper article, without having first submitted it to a committee of its Solons.

From the beginning, the Quaker Church bore its testimony against the abolition excitement. Most Friends were in favor of the Colonization Society; the rest were gradualists. Their commercial interests were as closely interwoven with those of the South as were the interests of any other class of the Northern people, and it took them years to admit, if not to discover, that there was any new light on the subject of human rights.

" The mills of the gods grind slowly; " and perhaps it was all the better in the end, for the cause they advocated so grandly, that Sarah and Angelina Grimké should have gone through this long period of silence and repression, during which their moral and intellectual forces gathered power for the conflict — the great work which both had so singularly and for so many years seen was before them, though its nature was for a long time hidden.

Angelina's experience in the infant school, interesting as it was to her, was discouraging so far as her success as a teacher went; and she soon gave it up and made inquiries concerning some school in which she could prepare herself to teach. Catherine Beecher's then famous seminary at Hartford was recommended, and a correspondence was opened. Several letters passed between Catherine and her would-be pupil, which so aroused Catherine's interest, that she went on to Philadelphia chiefly to make a personal acquaintance with the very mature young woman who at the age of twenty-seven declared she knew nothing and wanted to go to school again. In one of her letters to Sarah, early in the spring of 1832, Angelina says, —

" Catherine Beecher has actually paid her promised visit. She regretted not seeing thee, and seemed much pleased with me. The day after she arrived she went to meeting with me, and I think was more tired of it than any person I ever saw. It was a long, silent meeting, except a few words from J. L."

When Catherine Beecher took her leave of Angelina, she cordially invited her to visit Hartford, and examine for herself the system of education there pursued.

Sarah returned to Philadelphia in March, 1832, cutting short her visit at the earnest entreaty of Angelina, who was then looking forward to her first Yearly Meeting, and desired her sister's encouraging presence with her. Writing to Sarah, she says: "I have much desired that we might at that time mingle in sympathy and love. Truly we have known, might I not say, the *agony* of separation."

Soon after Sarah's return, Angelina went to live with Mrs. Frost, in order to give that sister the benefit of her board. This separation was a great trial to both sisters, and only consented to from a sense of duty.

CHAPTER IX.

In July, 1832, Angelina, accompanied by a friend, set out to make her promised visit to Hartford. Her journal, kept day by day, shows her to have been at this time in a most cheerful frame of mind, which fitted her to enjoy not only the beautiful scenery on her journey, but the society of the various people she met. At times she is almost like a young girl just out of school; and we can hardly wonder that she felt so, after the monotonous life she had led so long, and the uniform character of the people with whom she had associated. She visited New Haven, with its great college, and then went to Hartford, where a week was pleasantly spent in attendance on Catherine Beecher's classes, and in visiting Lydia Sigourney, and others, to whom she had brought letters. After examining Angelina, Catherine gave her the gratifying opinion that she could be prepared to teach in six months, and she at once began to try her hand at drawing maps, and to take part in many of the exercises of the school. She could, however, make no definite arrangement until her return to Philadelphia; but she was full of enthusiasm, and utilized to the very utmost the advantages of conversation with Catherine and Harriet Beecher. She was evidently quite charmed with Harriet's bright intellect and pleasant manner, and refers particularly to a very satisfactory conversation held with her about Quakers. The people of this Society were so little known in New England at that period, that Angelina and her friend, in their peculiar dress, were objects of great curiosity wherever they went.   Catherine Beecher accompanied them back to New York, and saw them safely on their way to Philadelphia.   But when Angelina mentioned to Friends her desire to return to Hartford and become a teacher, she was answered with the most decided disapprobation. Several unsatisfactory reasons were given — "going among strangers " — "leaving her sisters," — " abandoning her charities," &c., the real one probably being the fear to trust their impressionable young member to Presbyterian influence.   And so she must content herself to sink down in the old ruts, and plod on in work which was daily becoming more insufficient to her intellectual and spiritual needs.   Her chief pleasure was her correspondence with her brother Thomas, with whom she discussed controversial Bible questions, and various moral reforms, including prison discipline; but only once does she seem to have touched the question of slavery, which absorbed the public mind to such a degree that there was scarcely a household throughout the length and breadth of the land, that did not feel its influence in some way.

In 1832 the most intense excitement prevailed throughout the South, especially in South Carolina, where Mr. Calhoun had just thrown down the gauntlet to the Federal government.   In this Angelina expresses some interest, though chiefly from a religious point of view, as she regards all the important events then taking place as "signs of the times," and congratulates herself and her brother that they live in " such an important and interesting era, when the laws of Christianity are interwoven with the system of education, and with even the discipline of prisons and houses of refuge." In one of her letters we find the following : —

" I may be deceived, but the cloud which has arisen in the South will, I fear, spread over all our heavens, though it looks now so small. It will come down upon us in a storm which will beat our government to pieces; for, beautiful as it may appear, it is, nevertheless, not built upon the foundation of the apostles and the prophets, Jesus Christ himself being the chief corner-stone. We may boast of this temple of liberty, but oh, my brother, it is not of God."

In this letter she speaks of being much interested in " Ramsey's Civil and Ecclesiastical Polity of the Jews," and mentions that they were studying together, in the family, " Townsend's Old Testament, chronologically arranged, with notes, a work in twenty-eight volumes." She adds : —

" Will not the study of the Bible produce a thirst for the purest and most valuable literature, as, to understand it, we must study the history of nations, natural history, philosophy, and geography."

In another letter she says : —

" I am glad of thy opinions, but I cannot see that Carolina will escape. Slavery is too great a sin for justice always to sleep over, and this is, I believe, the true cause of the declining state of Carolina; this the root of bitterness which is to trouble our republic. I am not moved by fear to these reflections, but by a calm and deliberate consideration of the state of the Church, and while I believe convulsions and distress are coming upon this country, I am comforted in believing that *my* kingdom is not of this world, nor thine either, I trust, beloved brother."

To this letter Sarah adds a postscript, and says: "My fears respecting you are often prevalent, but I endeavor not to be too anxious. The Lord is omnipotent, and although I fear His sword is unsheathed against America, I believe He will remember His own elect, and shield them. . . . Do the planters approve or aid the Colonization Society? There have been some severe pieces published in our papers about it."

At this time — that is, during the summer of 1832 — Sarah lived a more than usually retired life, and her diary only records her increased depression of spirits, and her continued painful experiences in meeting. She would gladly have turned her back upon it all, and sought a home elsewhere at the North, or have returned to Charleston, but she dared not move without divine approbation, and this never seemed sufficiently clear to satisfy her.

"Surely," she says, "though I cannot understand why it is so, there must be wisdom in the decree which forbids my seeking another home. Most gladly would I have remained in Charleston, but my Father's will was not so."

And again she says, —

"But while the desire to escape present conflict has turned my mind there [to Charleston] with longing towards my precious mother, all the answer I can hear from the sanctuary is, 'Stay here;' and Satan adds, 'to suffer.'" According to Sarah's own views, she had thus far made little or no progress towards the great end and aim of her labors and sacrifices, — the securing of her eternal salvation; and the amount of misery she managed to manufacture for herself out of this thought, and her many fancied transgressions, is sad in the extreme. Years afterwards, in a letter to a young friend, she says, —

"I have suffered the very torments of the fabled hell,

because my conscience was sore to the touch all over. I would fain have you spared such long, dark years of anguish."

And to another friend, concerning this portion of her life, she writes, —

"Much of my suffering arose from a morbid conscience, — a conscience which magnified infirmities into crimes, and transformed our blessed Father in heaven into a stern judge, who punishes to the uttermost every real or imaginary departure from what we apprehend to be his requirements. Deceived by the false theological views in which I was educated, I was continually lashed by the scorpion whip of a perverted conscience."

During the winter of 1832–33, the time of both sisters was much taken up in nursing a sick woman, whose friendless position stirred Angelina's sense of duty, and she had her removed to Mrs. Frost's house. She and Sarah took upon themselves all the offices of nurse, even the most menial. They read to her, and tried to cheer her during the day, sat up with her at night, and in every way devoted themselves to the poor consumptive, until death came to her relief. Such a sacrifice to a sense of duty was all the more admirable, as the invalid was unusually exacting and unreasonable, and felt apparently little appreciation of the trouble she gave. Angelina, being in the same house, was more with her than Sarah, and she could scarcely have shown her greater attention if the tenderest ties had existed between her and her charge.

This was only one among the many similar acts of self-abnegation which were dotted all along Angelina's path through life; she never went out of her way to avoid them, but would travel any distance to take them up, if duty pointed her to them; and in accepting them she never seemed to think she was doing more than just what she ought to do, although they were generally of the kind which bring no honor or reward, except that sense of duty fulfilled which spreads over hearts like hers such sweet content.

From many passages in the diaries, it is evident that, as the agitating questions of the time were forced upon the notice of Sarah and Angelina, their thoughts were diverted from the narrow channel to which they had so long been confined ; and, in proportion as their interest in these matters increased, the cords which bound them to their religious society loosened. Angelina, as we have before remarked, never stood in the same attitude as Sarah towards the Society. To the latter, it was as the oracle of her fate, whose decrees she dared not question, much less disobey. It represented to her mind the divine will and purposes, which were wisdom entirely, and could only fail through the pride or disobedience of sinners like herself. Angelina, on the contrary, regarded it as made up of human beings with human intellects, full of weakness, and liable to err in the interpretation of the Lord's will, and, while praying for guidance and strength, believed it wise to follow her own judgment to a great extent. She could not be restrained from reasoning for herself, and would often have acted more independently, but for her affection for Sarah. The scales, however, were slowly falling from Sarah's eyes, though it was long before she saw the new light as anything but a snare of Satan, who she felt sure was bound to have her, in spite of all her struggles. Against the growing coolness towards her Society she did struggle and pray in deepest contrition. At one time she writes, —

" Satan is tempting me strongly with increased dissatisfaction with Friends; but I know if I am to be of any
use it is in my own Society."

And again : " I beseech thee, O God, to fill my heart
with love for the Society of Friends. I shall be ruined
if I listen to Satan."

But all this was of no avail. Angelina was growing in
knowledge, and was imparting to Sarah what she learned.
The evidence is meagre, but there is enough to show that
the ruling topics claimed much of their attention during
that summer, and that Angelina, especially, drew upon
herself more than one reproof from Catherine Morris for
the interest she manifested in " matters entirely outside
of the Society." In the spring, she writes in a letter to
Thomas : —

" The following proposition was made at a Colonization
meeting in this city : is it strictly true? ' No two nations,
brought together under similar circumstances with those
under which the Africans have been brought into this country, have amalgamated.' Are not the people in the West
Indies principally mulatto? And how is it in South
America? Did they not amalgamate there? Did not
the Helots, a great many of whom were Persians, etc.,
taken in battle, amalgamate with the Grecians, and rise to
equal privileges in the State? I ask for information.
Please tell me, also, whether slavery is not an infringement of the Constitution of the United States. You
Southerners have no idea of the excitement existing at
the North on the subjects of abolition and colonization."

This shows only the dawning of interest in the mighty
subject. The evidence is full and conclusive that at this
time neither Sarah nor Angelina had formed any decided
opinions concerning either of the societies mentioned

above, or contemplated taking any active part whatever in the cause of freedom.

In February, 1834, occurred the famous debate at Lane Seminary, near Cincinnati, presided over by Dr. Lyman Beecher, which, for earnestness, ability, and eloquence, has probably never been surpassed in this country. A colonization society, composed in great part of Southern students, had been formed in 1832 in the seminary, but went to pieces during the debate, which lasted eighteen evenings, and produced a profound sensation throughout the Presbyterian Church, and even outside of it. President Beecher took no part in it, standing too much in awe of the trustees of the institution to countenance it even by his presence, although he had promised to do so.

The speakers were all students, young men remarkable for their sincerity and their energy, and several of them excelling as orators. Among the latter were Henry B. Stanton and Theodore D. Weld, both possessing great powers of reasoning and natural gifts of eloquence. Of Theodore D. Weld it was said, that when he lectured on temperance, so powerfully did he affect his audiences, that many a liquor dealer went home and emptied out the contents of his barrels. Those who remember him in his best days can well believe this, while others who have had the privilege of hearing him only in his " parlor talks " can have no difficulty in understanding the impression he must have made on mixed audiences in those times when his great heart, filled from boyhood with sorrow for the oppressed, found such food for its sympathies.[1]

---

[1] An incident of the childhood of this zealous champion of human rights, related in a letter I have, shows how early he took his stand by the side of the weak and defenceless. When he was about six years old, and going to school in Connecticut, a little

It is no disparagement to the many able and eloquent advocates of the anti-slavery cause, between 1833 and 1836, to say that public opinion placed Weld at the head of them all. In him were combined reason and imagination, wide and accurate knowledge, manly courage, a tender and sympathetic nature, a remarkable faculty of expression, and a fervent enthusiasm which made him the best platform orator of his time. As a lecturer on education, temperance, and abolition, he drew crowded houses and made many converts. The late Secretary Stanton was one of these, and often mentioned Mr. Weld as the most eloquent speaker he had ever heard; and Wendell Phillips, in a recent letter, says of him: "In the first years of the anti-slavery cause, he was our foremost advocate."

Of Henry B. Stanton, a newspaper reporter once said in excuse for not reporting one of his great anti-slavery speeches, that he could not attempt to report a whirlwind or a thunderstorm.

With such leaders, and with followers no less earnest

---

colored boy was admitted as a pupil. Weld had never seen a black person before, and was grieved to find that the color of his skin caused him to be despised by the other boys, and put off on a seat by himself. The teacher heard him his lessons separately, and generally sent him back to his lonely seat with a cuff or a jeer. After witnessing this injustice for a day or two, little Weld went to the teacher and asked to have his own seat changed. "Why, where do you want to sit?" asked the teacher. "By Jerry," replied Weld. The master burst out laughing, and exclaimed: "Why, are you a nigger too?" and, "Theodore Weld is a nigger!" resounded through the school. "I never shall forget," says Mr. Weld, "the tumult in my little bosom that day. I went, however, and sat with Jerry, and played with Jerry, and we were great friends; and in a week I had permission to say my lessons with Jerry, and I have been an abolitionist ever since, and never had any prejudices to overcome."

if less brilliant, it is not surprising that the Lane Seminary debate arrested such general attention, and afterwards assumed so much importance in the anti-slavery
struggle. The trustees, fearing its effect upon their
Southern patrons, ordered that both societies should be
dissolved, and no more meetings held. The anti-slavery
students replied to this order by withdrawing in a body
from the institution. Some went over to Oberlin; others,
— and among them the two I have named — entered the
field as lecturers and workers in the cause they had so ardently espoused.

In September, 1834, Sarah and Angelina were gratified
by a visit from their brother Thomas, who was on his way
to Cincinnati, to deliver an address on Education before
the College of Professional Teachers, and also to visit his
brother Frederic, residing in Columbus, whom he had not
seen for sixteen years. As Angelina had not seen him
since her departure from Charleston in 1829, the few days
of his society she now enjoyed were very precious, and
made peculiarly so by after-events. The cholera was
then for the second time epidemic in the West, but those
who knew enough about it to be prudent felt no fear, and
the sisters bade farewell to their brother, cheered by his
promise to see them again on his way home. He delivered his address in Cincinnati, started for Columbus,
arrived within twelve miles of it, when, at a wayside tavern, he was seized with cholera. His brother, then holding a term of the Supreme Court, was sent for. He at
once adjourned court and hastened to Thomas with a
physician. He was already speechless, but was able to
turn upon Frederic a look of recognition, then pressed
his hand, and died.

Angelina, writing of her brother's death, says: "The

world has lost an eminent reformer in the cause of Christian education, an eloquent advocate of peace, and one who was remarkably ready for every good work. I never saw a man who combined such brilliant talents, such diversity and profundity of knowledge, with such humility of heart and such simplicity and gentleness of manner. He was a great and good man, a pillar of the church and state, and his memory is blessed."

In a letter written in 1837, referring to her brother's visit to Philadelphia, Sarah says: "We often conversed on the subject of slavery, and never did I hear from his lips an approval of it. He had never examined the subject; he regarded it as a duty to do it, and he intended devoting the powers of his mind to it the next year of his life, and asked us to get ready for him all the abolition works worth studying. But God took him away. My own views were dark and confused. Had I had my present light, I might have helped him."

Angelina bore her testimony to the same effect. Referring to Thomas in a letter to a member of her family many years after his death, she says:

"He was deeply interested in *every* reform, and saw very clearly that the anti-slavery agitation which began in 1832 would shake our country to its foundation. He told me in Philadelphia that he knew slavery would be the all-absorbing subject here, and that he intended to devote a whole year to its investigation; and, in order that he might do so impartially, he requested me to subscribe for every periodical and paper, and to buy and forward to him any books, that might be published by the Anti-Slavery and Colonization societies. I asked whether he believed colonization could abolish slavery. IIe said: 'No, never!' but observed: 'I help that only on account of its reflex influence upon slavery here. If we can build up an intelligent, industrious community of colored people in Africa, it will do a great deal towards destroying slavery in the United States.' "

The loss of her brother almost crushed Sarah, although she expresses only submission to the Lord's will. It had the effect of closing her heart and mind once more to everything but religion, and again she gave herself fully and entirely to her evangelical preparation. She expresses herself as longing to preach the everlasting Gospel, and prays that she may soon be called to be a minister, and be instrumental in turning her fellow sinners away from the wrath to come. Later, in the early part of 1835, after having re-perused her brother's works, she solemnly dedicated herself to the cause of peace, persuading herself that Thomas had left it as a legacy to her and Angelina. She resolved to use all her best endeavors to promote its advancement, and daily prayed for a blessing on her exertions and for the success of the cause. This at least served to divert her thoughts from herself, and no doubt helped her to the belief which now came to her, that at last Satan was conquered, and she was accepted of God.

If she could only have been comforted also with the knowledge that her labors in the ministry were recognized, her satisfaction would have been complete, but more than ever was she tormented by the slights and sneers of the elders, and by her own conviction that she was a useless vessel. There is scarcely a page of her diary that does not tell of some humiliation, some disappointment connected with her services in meeting.

CHAPTER X.

ALTHOUGH the Quakers were the first, as a religious society, to recognize the iniquity of slavery, and to wash their hands of it, so far as to free all the slaves they owned; few of them saw the further duty of discouraging it by ceasing all commercial intercourse with slave-holders. They nearly all continued to trade with the South, and to use the products of slave-labor. After the appearance in this country of Elizabeth Heyrick's pamphlet, in which she so strongly urged upon abolitionists the duty of abstinence from all slave products, the number was increased of those who declined any and every participation in the guilt of the slave-holder, and exerted themselves to convert others to the same views; but the majority of selfish and inconsiderate people is always large, and it refused to see the good results which could be reasonably expected from such a system of self-denial. As the older members, also, of Friends' Society were opposed to all exciting discussions, and to popular movements generally, while the younger ones could not smother a natural interest in the great reforms of the day; it followed that, although all were opposed to slavery in the abstract, there was no fixed principle of action among them. In their ranks were all sorts: gradualists and immediatists, advocates of unconditional emancipation, and colonizationists, thus making it impossible to discuss the main question

without excitement.   Therefore all discussion was discouraged and even forbidden.

The Society never counted among its members many
colored persons.   There were, however, a few in Philadelphia, all educated, and belonging to the best of their
class.   Among them was a most excellent woman, Sarah
Douglass, to whom Sarah and Angelina Grimké became
much attached, and with whom Sarah kept up a correspondence for nearly thirty years.

The first letter of this correspondence which we have,
was written in March, 1835, and shows that Sarah had
known very little about her colored brethren in Philadelphia, and it also shows her inclination towards colonization.   She mentions having been cheered by an account
of several literary and benevolent societies among the
colored residents, expresses warm sympathy with them,
and gives them some good, practical advice about helping
themselves.   She then says : —

"I went about three weeks ago to an anti-slavery meeting, and heard with much interest an address from
Robert Gordon.   It was feeling, temperate, and judi-
cious; but *one* word struck my ear unpleasantly.   He
said, 'And yet it is *audaciously* asked: What has the
North to do with slavery?'   The word 'audaciously,'
while I am ready to admit its justice, seemed to me inconsistent with the spirit of the Gospel; although we
may abhor the system of slavery, I want us to remember
that the guilt of the oppressor demands Christian pity
and Christian prayer.

"My sister went last evening to hear George Thompson.   She is deeply interested in this subject, and was
much pleased with his discourse.   Do not the colored
people believe that the Colonization Society may prove a

blessing to Africa, that it may be the means of liberating some slaves, and that, by sending a portion of them there, they may introduce civilization and Christianity into this benighted region? That the Colonization Society can ever be the means of breaking the yoke in America appears to me utterly impossible, but when I look at poor heathen Africa, I cannot but believe its efforts will be a blessing to her."

In the next letter, written in April, she descants on the universal prejudice against color, — " a prejudice," she says, "which will in days to come excite as much astonishment as the facts now do that Christians — some of them I verily believe, sincere lovers of God — put to death nineteen persons and one dog for the crime of witchcraft."

And yet, singularly enough, she does not, at this time, notice the inconsistency of a separate seat for colored people in all the churches. In the Quaker meeting this was especially humiliating, as it was placed either directly under the stairs, or off in a corner, was called the " negro seat," and was regularly guarded to prevent either colored people from passing beyond it, or white people from making a mistake and occupying it. Two years later, Sarah and Angelina both denounced it ; but before that, though they may have privately deplored it, they seem to have accepted it as a necessary conformity to the existing feeling against the blacks.

The decision of Friends' Society concerning discussion Sarah Grimké seems to have accepted, for, as we have said, there is no expression of her views on emancipation in letters or diary. But Angelina felt that her obligations to humanity were greater than her obligations to the Society of Friends ; and as she listened to the eloquent speeches of George Thompson and others, her life-long interest in the slave was stimulated, and it aroused in her a desire to work for him in some way, to do something that would practically help his cause.

On one of several loose leaves of a diary which Angelina kept at this time, we find the following under date, " 5th Mo. 12th, 1835 : Five months have elapsed since I wrote in this diary, since which time time I have become deeply interested in the subject of abolition. I had long regarded this cause as utterly hopeless, but since I have examined anti-slavery principles, I find them so full of the power of truth, that I am confident not many years will roll by before the horrible traffic in human beings will be destroyed in this land of Gospel privileges. My soul has measurably stood in the stead of the poor slave, and my earnest prayers have been poured out that the Lord would be pleased to permit me to be instrumental of good to these degraded, oppressed, and suffering fellow-creatures. Truly, I often feel ready to go to prison or to death in this cause of justice, mercy, and love; and I do fully believe if I am called to return to Carolina, it will not be long before I shall suffer persecution of some kind or other."

Her fast-increasing enthusiasm alarmed her cautious sister, and drew from her frequent and serious remonstrances. But that she also travelled rapidly towards the final rending of the bonds which had hitherto held her, we find from a letter to Sarah Douglass, written in the spring of 1835. Speaking of Jay's book of Colonization, which had just appeared, she says: —

" The work is written for the most part in a spirit of Christian candor and benevolence. There is here and there a touch of satire or sarcasm I would rather should have been spared. The subject is one of solemn impor-

tance to our country, and while I do desire that every
righteous means may be employed to give to America a
clear and convincing view of the fearful load of guilt
that rests upon her for trading in the souls of men, yet I
do want the friends of emancipation to take no unhallowed weapons to sever the manacles of the slave. I
rejoice in the hope that all the prominent friends of abolition are peace men. My sister sends her love to thee.
Her mind is deeply engaged in the cause of immediate,
unconditional emancipation. I believe she does often
pray for it."

In July, 1835, Angelina went to visit a friend in
Shrewsbury, New Jersey. In this quiet retreat she had
ample time for reflection, and for the study of abolition.
She could, she says, think of nothing else; and the question continually before her was, "What can I do?
What can I do?" But the more she thought, the more
perplexed she became. The certainty that any independent action, whatever, would not only offend her Society,
but grieve her sister, stood in the way of reaching any
conclusion, and kept her in a state of unrest which plainly
showed itself in her letters to Sarah.

Doubtless she did consider Sarah's advice, for she still
looked up to her with filial regard, but before she could
do more than consider it, an event occurred which made
the turning point in her career, and emancipated her forever from the restrictions to which she had so unwillingly
assented.

The difficulty which abolitionists found in holding
meetings in Boston, to be addressed by George Thompson, of England, brought out in July an Appeal to the
citizens of Boston from Mr. Garrison. This reached Angelina's hands, and so touched her feelings, so aroused all

her anti-slavery enthusiasm, that she could no longer keep quiet. She must give expression to her sympathy with the great cause. She wrote to the author — a brave thing for her to do — but we doubt if she could have refrained even if she could have fully realized the storm of reproach which the act brought down upon her. On account of its length, I cannot copy this letter entire, but a few extracts will give an idea of its general tone and spirit. It is dated Philadelphia, 8th Month 30th, 1835, and begins thus : —

"RESPECTED FRIEND : It seems as if I was compelled at this time to address thee, notwithstanding all my reasonings against intruding on thy valuable time, and the uselessness of so insignificant a person as myself offering thee the sentiments of sympathy at this alarming crisis.

"I can hardly express to thee the deep and solemn interest with which I have viewed the violent proceedings of the last few weeks. Although I expected opposition, I was not prepared for it so soon — it took me by surprise — and I greatly feared abolitionists would be driven back in the first outset, and thrown into confusion. . . . Under these feelings I was urged to read thy Appeal to the citizens of Boston. Judge, then, what were my feelings on finding that my fears were utterly groundless, and that thou stoodest firm in the midst of the storm, determined to suffer and to die, rather than yield one inch. . . The ground upon which you stand is holy ground; never, never surrender it."

She then goes on to encourage him to persevere in his work, reminding him of the persecutions of reformers in

past times, and that religious persecution always began
with mobs.

"If," she says, "persecution is the means which God
has ordained for the accomplishment of this great end,
Emancipation ; then, in dependence upon Him for
strength to bear it, I feel as if I could say, *Let It Come!*
for it is my deep, solemn, deliberate conviction that *this is
a cause worth dying for.* I say so, from what I have seen,
heard, and known in a land of slavery, where rests the
darkness of Egypt, and where is found the sin of Sodom.
Yes! *Let it come — let us suffer,* rather than insurrections
should arise."

This letter Mr. Garrison published in the *Liberator,* to
the surprise of Angelina, and the great displeasure and
grief of her Quaker friends. But she who had just coun-
selled another to suffer and die rather than abate an inch
of his principles was not likely to quail before the
strongly expressed censure of her Society, which was at
once communicated to her. Only over her sister's tender
disapproval did she shed any tears. Her letter of explanation to Sarah shows the sweetness and the firmness of
her character so conspicuously, that I offer no apology for
copying a portion of it. It is dated Shrewsbury, Sept.
27th, 1335, and enters at once upon the subject : —

"MY BELOVED SISTER : I feel constrained in all the tenderness of a sister's love to address thee, though I hardly
know what to say, seeing that I stand utterly condemned
by the standard which thou hast set up to judge me by —
the opinion of my friends. This thou seemest to feel an
infallible criterion. If it is, I have not so learned Christ,
for He says, 'he that loveth father or mother more than
me is not worthy of me,' etc. I do most fully believe

that had I done what I have done in a church capacity, I should justly incur their censure, because they disapprove of any intermeddling with the question, but what I did was done in a private capacity, on my own responsibility. Now, my precious sister, I feel willing to be condemned by all but thyself, *without* a hearing; but to thee I owe the sacred duty of vindication, though hardly one ray of hope dawns on my mind that I shall be acquitted even by *thee.* If I know mine own heart, I desire *not* to be acquitted; if I have erred, or if this trial of my faith is needful for me by Him who knoweth with what food to feed His poor dependent ones, thou hast been with me in heights and in depths, in joy and in sorrow, therefore to thee I speak. Thou knowest what I have passed through on the subject of slavery; thou knowest I am an exile from the home of my birth because of slavery — therefore, to thee I speak.

"Previous to my writing that letter, I believe four weeks elapsed, during which time, though I passed through close and constant exercise, I did not read anything on the subject of abolition, except the pieces in the Friends' paper and the *Pennsylvanian* relative to the insurrections and the bonfires in Charleston. I was afraid to read. After this, I perused the Appeal. I confess I could not read it without tears, so much did its spirit harmonize with my own feelings. This introduced my mind into deep sympathy with Wm. Lloyd Garrison. I found in that piece the spirit of my Master; my heart was drawn out in prayer for him, and I felt as if I would like to write to him, but forebore until this day four weeks ago, when it seemed to me I *must* write to him. I put it by and sat down to read, but I could not read. I then thought that perhaps writing would relieve *my own mind*, without it being required of me to send what I wrote. I wrote the letter and laid it aside, desiring to be preserved from sending it if *it* was *wrong* to do so. On Second Day night, on my bended knees, I implored Divine direction, and next morning, after again praying over it, I felt easy to send it, and, after committing it to the office, felt anxiety removed, and as though I had nothing more to do with it. Thou knowest what has followed. I think on Fifth Day I was brought as low as I ever was. After that my Heavenly Father was pleased in great mercy to open the windows of heaven, and pour out upon my grief-bound, sin-sick soul, the showers of His grace, and in prayer at the footstool of mercy I found that relief which human hearts denied me. A little light seemed to arise. I remembered how often, in deep and solemn prayer, I had told my Heavenly Father I was willing to suffer anything if I could only aid the great cause of emancipation, and the query arose whether *this* suffering was not the peculiar kind required of *me*. Since then I have been permitted to enjoy a portion of that peace which human hands cannot rob me of, though great sadness covers my mind; for I feel as though my character had sustained a deep injury in the opinion of those I love and value most — how justly, they will best know at a future day. Silent submission is my portion, and in the everlasting strength of my Master, I humbly trust I shall be enabled to bear whatever is put upon me.

"I have now said *all* I have to say, and I leave this text with thee: 'Judge not by appearance, but judge righteous judgment;' and again, 'Judge nothing before the time.' Farewell. In the love of the blessed Gospel of God's Son, I remain, thy afflicted sister.

"A. E. G."

The entry in Sarah's diary respecting this incident is as follows. The date is two days before that of Angelina's letter to her.

"The suffering which my precious sister has brought upon herself by her connection with the anti-slavery cause, which has been a sorrow of heart to me, is another proof how dangerous it is to slight the clear convictions of truth. But, like myself, she listened to the voice of the tempter. Oh! that she may learn obedience by the things that she suffers. Of myself I can say, the Lord brought me up out of the horrible pit, and my prayer for her is that she may be willing to bear the present chastisement *patiently*."

In Angelina's diary, she describes very touchingly some of her trials in this matter. Writing in September, 1835, after recording in similar language to that used in her letter to Sarah the state of feelings under which she wrote and sent the letter to Garrison, she says : —

"I had some idea it might be published, but did not feel at liberty to say it must not be, for I had no idea that, if it was, my name would be attached to it. As three weeks passed and I heard nothing of it, I concluded it had been broken open in the office and destroyed. To my great surprise, last Fourth Day, Friend B. came to tell me a letter of mine had been published in the *Liberator*. He was most exceeding tried at my having written it, and also at its publication. He wished me to re-examine the letter, and write to Wm. Lloyd Garrison, expressing disapproval of its publication, and altering some portions of it. His visit was, I believe, prompted by the affection he bears me, but he appeared utterly incapable of understanding the depth of feeling under which that letter was written. The editor's remarks were deeply trying to him.

Friend B. seemed to think they were the ravings of a fanatic, and that the bare mention of my precious brother's name was a disgrace to his character, when coupled with mine in such a cause and such a paper, or rather in a cause advocated in such a way. I was so astonished and tried that I hardly knew what to say. I declined, however, to write to W. L. G., and said I felt willing to bear any suffering, if it was only made instrumental of good. I felt my great unworthiness of being used in such a work, but remembered that God hath chosen the weak things of this world to confound the wise. But I was truly miserable, believing my character was altogether gone among my dearest, most valued friends. I was indeed brought to the brink of despair, as the vilest of sinners. A little light dawned at last, as I remembered how often I had told the Lord if He would only prepare me to be, and make me, instrumental in the great work of emancipation, I would be willing to bear any suffering, and the question arose, whether this was not the peculiar kind allotted to me. Oh, the extreme pain of extravagant praise! to be held up as a saint in a public newspaper, before thousands of people, when I felt I was the chief of sinners. Blushing, and confusion of face were mine, and I thought the walls of a prison would have been preferable to such an exposure. Then, again, to have my name, not so much *my* name as the name of Grimké, associated with that of the despised Garrison, seemed like bringing disgrace upon my *family*, not myself alone. I felt as though the name had been tarnished in the eyes of thousands who had before loved and revered it. I cannot describe the anguish of my soul. Nevertheless, I could not blame the publication of the letter, nor would I have recalled it if I could.

" My greatest trial is the continued opposition of my precious sister Sarah. She thinks I have been given over to blindness of mind, and that I do not know light from darkness, right from wrong. Her grief is that I cannot see it was wrong in me ever to have written the letter at all, and she seems to think I deserve all the suffering I have brought upon myself."

We approach now the most interesting period in the lives of the two sisters. A new era was about to dawn upon them; their quiet, peaceful routine was to be disturbed; a path was opening for them, very different from the one which had hitherto been indicated, and for which their long and painful probation had eminently prepared them. Angelina was the first to see it, the first to venture upon it, and for a time she travelled it alone, unsustained by her beloved sister, and feeling herself condemned by all her nearest friends.

CHAPTER XI.

ALL through the winter of 1835–36, demonstrations
of violence continued to be made against the friends of
emancipation throughout the country.   The reign of
terror inaugurated in 1832 threatened to crush out the
grandest principles of our Constitution.   Freedom of
press and speech became by-words, and personal liberty
was in constant danger.   A man or woman needed only
to be pointed out as an abolitionist to be insulted and
assaulted.   No anti-slavery meetings could be held unin-
terrupted by the worst elements of rowdyism, instigated
by men in high position.   In vain the authorities were
appealed to for protection; they declared their inability
to afford it.   The few newspapers that dared to express
disapproval of such disregard of the doctrine of equal
rights were punished by the withdrawal of subscriptions
and advertisements, while the majority of the public
press teemed with the vilest slanders against the noble
men and women who, in spite of mobs and social ostracism, continued to sow anti-slavery truths so diligently
that new converts were made every day, and the very
means taken to impose upon public opinion enlightened
it more and more.[1]

---

[1] Apropos of sowing anti-slavery truths, I remember seeing at
the first anti-slavery fair I attended,—in 1853, I think,—a sampler

During this winter we find nothing especial to narrate concerning Sarah and Angelina. Sarah's diary continues to record her trials in meeting, and her religious sufferings, notwithstanding her recently expressed belief that her eternal salvation was secured. Angelina kept no diary at this time, and wrote few letters, but we see from an occasional allusion in these that her mind was busy, and that her warmest interest was enlisted in the cause of abolition.

She read everything she could get on the subject, wrote some effective articles for the anti-slavery papers, and pondered night and day over the question of what more she could do. One practical thing she did was to write to the widow of her brother Thomas, proposing to purchase from her the woman whom she (Angelina) in her girlhood had refused to own, and who afterwards became the property of her brother. This woman was now the mother of several children, and Angelina, jointly with Mrs. Frost, proposed to purchase them all, bring them to Philadelphia, and emancipate them. But no notice was taken of the application, either by their sister-in-law or their sister Eliza, to whom Angelina repeatedly wrote on the subject.

Learning from their mother that she was about to make her will, Angelina and Sarah wrote to her, asking that her slaves be included in their portions. To this she assented, but managed to dispose of all but four before she died. These were left to her two anti-slavery daughters,

---

made in 1836 by a little girl, a pupil in a school where evidently great pains were taken to propagate anti-slavery principles. On the sampler was neatly worked the words : " May the points of our needles prick the slave-holders' consciences."

who at once freed them, at the same time purchasing the husband of one of them and freeing him.

As she continued to study anti-slavery doctrines, one thing became very plain to Angelina — that the friends of emancipation, in order to clear their skirts of all participation in the slave-owner's sin, must cease to use the products of slave labor. To this view she tried to bring all with whom she discussed the main subject, and so important did it appear to her, that she thought of writing to some of the anti-slavery friends in New York about it, but her courage failed. After what she had gone through because of the publication of her letter to Mr. Garrison, she shrank from the risk of having another communication made public. But her mind was deeply exercised on this point, and when — in the spring — she and Sarah went to attend Yearly Meeting in Providence, R. I., an opportunity offered for her to express her views to a prominent member of the New York Society, whom she met on the boat. She begged this lady to talk to Gerrit Smith, recently converted from colonization, and others, about it, and to offer them, in her name, one hundred dollars towards setting up a free cotton factory. This was the beginning of a society formed by those willing to pledge themselves to the use of free-labor products only. In 1826 Benjamin Lundy had procured the establishment, in Baltimore, of a free-labor produce store; and subsequently he had formed several societies on the same principle. Evan Lewis had established one in Philadelphia about 1826, and it was still in existence.

The sisters had been so long and so closely tied to Philadelphia and their duties there, that the relief of the visit to Providence was very great. Sarah mentions it in this characteristic way: —

"The Friend of sinners opened a door of escape for me out of that city of bonds and afflictions." In Providence she records how much more freedom she felt in the exercise of her ministerial gift than she did at home.

Angelina sympathized with these sentiments, feeling, as she expresses it, that her release from Philadelphia was signed when she left for Providence. She found it delightful to be able to read what she pleased without being criticised, and to talk about slavery freely. While in Providence she was refreshed by calls upon her of several abolitionists, among them a cotton manufacturer and his son, Quakers, with whom she had a long talk, not knowing their business. She discussed the use of slave-labor, and descanted on the impossibility of any man being clean-handed enough to work in the anti-slavery cause so long as he was making his fortune by dealing in slave-labor products. These two gentlemen afterwards became her warm friends.

An Anti-slavery Society meeting was held in Providence while Angelina was there, but she did not feel at liberty to attend it, though she mentions seeing Garrison, Henry B. Stanton, Osborne, "and others," but does not say that she made their acquaintance; probably not, as she was visiting orthodox Quakers who all disapproved of these men, and Angelina's modesty would never have allowed her to seek their notice.

Leaving Providence, the sisters attended two Quarterly Meetings in adjacent towns, where, Angelina states, the subject of slavery was brought up, "and," she says, "gospel liberty prevailed to such an extent, that even poor *I* was enabled to open my lips in a few words." She neglected to say that these few words introduced the subject to the meetings, and produced such deep feeling that many hitherto wavering ones went away strengthened and encouraged.

They also attended Yearly Meeting at Newport, where many friends were made ; and where Angelina's conversations on the subject which absorbed all her thoughts produced such an impression that she was strongly urged to remain in New England, and become an anti-slavery missionary in the Society of Friends. But she did not feel that she could stay, as, she says, it was shown her very clearly that Shrewsbury was her right place for the summer, though why, she knew not. The reason was plainly revealed a little later.

She returned to Shrewsbury refreshed and strengthened, and feeling that her various experiences had helped her to see more clearly where her duty and her work lay. But she was saddened by the conviction that if she gave herself up, as she felt she must, to the anti-slavery cause, she would be cast loose from her peaceful home, and from very many dear friends, to whom she was bound by the strongest ties of gratitude and affection. She thus writes to a friend : —

"Didst thou ever feel as if thou hadst no home on earth, except in the bosom of Jesus? I feel so now."

For several weeks after her return to Shrewsbury, Angelina tried to withdraw her mind from the subject which her sister thought was taking too strong hold on it, and interfering with her spiritual needs and exercises. Out of deference to these views, she resumed her studies, and tried to become interested in a "History of the United States on Peace Principles," which she had thought some time before of writing. Then she began the composition of a little book on the "Beauty and Duty of Forgiveness, as Illustrated by the Story of Joseph," but gave that up to commence a sacred history. In this she did become much interested for a time, but her mind was too heavily burdened to permit her to remain tranquil long. Still the question was ever before her : " Is there nothing that I can do ? " She tried to be cheerful, but felt at all times much more like shedding tears. And her suffering was greater that it was borne alone. The friend, Mrs. Parker, whom she was visiting, was a comparative stranger, whose views she had not yet ascertained, and whom she feared to trouble with her perplexities. Of Sarah, so closely associated with Catherine Morris, she could not make an entire confidant, and no other friend was near. Catherine, and some others in Philadelphia, anxious about her evident and growing indifference to her Society duties, tried to persuade her to open a school with one who had long been a highly-prized friend, but Angelina very decidedly refused to listen to the project.

" As to S. W.'s proposal," she writes, " I cannot think of acceding to it, because I have seen so clearly that my pen, at least, must be employed in the great reformations of the day, and if I engaged in a school, my time would not be my own. No money that could be given could induce me to bind my body and mind and soul so completely in Philadelphia. There is no lack of light as to the right decision about this."

For this reply she received a letter of remonstrance from Sarah, to which she thus answered : —

" I think I am as afraid as thou canst be of my doing anything to hurt my usefulness in our Society, if that is the field designed for me to labor in. But, Is it ? is often a query of deep interest and solemnity to my mind. I feel no openness among Friends. My spirit is oppressed and heavy laden, and shut up in prison. What am I to do? The only relief I experience is in writing letters and pieces for the peace and anti-slavery causes, and this makes me think that my influence is to reach beyond our own limits. My mind is fully made up not to spend next winter in Philadelphia, if I can help it. I feel strangely released, and am sure I know not what is to become of me. I am perfectly blind as to the future."

But light was coming, and her sorrowful questionings were soon to be answered.

It was not long before Mrs. Parker saw that her guest's cheerfulness was assumed, and only thinly veiled some great trouble. As they became more intimate, she questioned her affectionately, and soon drew from her the whole story of her sorrows and her perplexities, and her great need of a friend to feel for her and advise her. Mrs. Parker became this friend, and, though differing from her on some essential points, did much to help and strengthen her. For many days slavery was the only topic discussed between them, and then one morning Angelina entered the breakfast-room with a beaming countenance, and said: —

"It has all come to me; God has shown me what I can do; I can write an appeal to Southern women, one which, thus inspired, will touch their hearts, and lead them to use their influence with their husbands and brothers. I will speak to them in such tones that they *must* hear me, and, through me, the voice of justice and humanity."

This appeal was begun that very day, but before she had written many pages, she was interrupted in her task by a letter which threw her into a state of great agitation, and added to her perplexity. This letter was from Elizur Wright, then secretary of the American

Anti-Slavery Society, the office of which was in New York. He invited her, in the name of the Executive Committee of the Society, to come to New York, and meet with Christian women in sewing circles and private parlors, and talk to them, as she so well knew how to do, on slavery.

The door of usefulness she had been looking for so long was opened at last, but it was so unexpected, so different from anything she had yet thought of, that she was cast into a sea of trouble. Naturally retiring and unobtrusive, she shrank from so public an engagement, and this proposal frightened her so much that she could not sleep the first night after receiving it. She had never spoken to the smallest assembly of Friends, and even in meeting, where all were free to speak as the spirit moved them, she had never uttered a word; and yet, how could she refuse? She delayed her answer until she could make it the subject of prayer and consult with Sarah. Desiring to leave her sister entirely free to express her opinion, she merely wrote to her that she had received the proposition.

Sarah was beginning to feel that Angelina was growing beyond her, and, may be, above her. She did not offer a word of advice, but most tenderly expressed her entire willingness to give up her "precious child," to go anywhere, and do anything she felt was right. And in a letter to a friend, alluding to this, she says: —

"My beloved sister does indeed need the prayers of all who love her. Oh! may He who laid down his life for us guide her footsteps and keep her in the hollow of His holy hand. Perhaps the Lord may be pleased to cast our lot somewhere together. If so, I feel as if I could ask no more in this world."

Sarah's willingness to surrender her to wnatever work she felt called to do was a great relief to Angelina. In writing to thank her and to speak more fully of Mr. Wright's letter, she says: —

"The bare idea that such a thing may be required of me is truly alarming, and that thy mind should be at all resigned to it increases the fear that possibly I may have to do it. It does not appear by the letter that it is expected I should extend my work *outside* of our Society. One thing, however, I do see clearly, that I am not to do it *now*, for I have begun to write an 'Appeal to the Christian Women of the South,' which I feel must be finished first."

She then proceeds to give an account of the part of this Appeal already written, and of what she intended the rest to be, and shows that she shared the feelings common among Southerners, the anticipation of a servile insurrection sooner or later. She says: —

"In conclusion I intend to take up the subject of abolitionism, and endeavor to undeceive the South as to the supposed objects of anti-slavery societies, and bear my full testimony to their pacific principles; and then to close with as feeling an appeal as possible to them as women, as Christian women, setting before them the awful responsibility resting on them at this crisis; for if the women of the South do not rise in the strength of the Lord to plead with their fathers, husbands, brothers, and sons, that country must witness the most dreadful scenes of murder and blood.

"It will be a pamphlet of a dozen pages, I suppose. My wish is to submit it to the publishing committee of the A. A. S. S., of New York, for revision, to be published by them with my name attached, for I well know my *name*

is worth more than *myself*, and will add weight to it.[1]
Now, dearest, what dost thou think of it? A pretty bold
step, I know, and one of which my friends will highly
disapprove, but this is a day in which I feel I must act
independently of consequences to myself, for of how little
consequence will my trials be, if the cause of truth is
helped forward ever so little. The South must be reached.
An address to men will not reach women, but an address
to women will reach the whole community, if it can be
reached at all.

"I mean to write to Elizur Wright by to-morrow's mail,
informing him that I am writing such a pamphlet, and
that I feel as if the proposition of the committee is one of
too much importance, either to accept or refuse, without
more reflection than I have yet been able to give to it.
The trial would indeed be great, to have to leave this
sweet, quiet retreat, but if duty calls, I must go. . . .
Many, many thanks for thy dear, long letters."

While Angelina was thus busily employed, and buoyed
up by the hope of benefiting those whose wrongs she had
all her life felt so deeply, Sarah was reaching towards her,
and in trying to be indulgent to her and just to her Society at the same time, she was awakening to her own false
position and to some of the awful mistakes of her religious
life. Through the summer, such passages as the following appear in her diary : —

"The approach of our Yearly Meeting was almost
overwhelming. I felt as if I could be thankful even for

---

[1] In a letter written some time after, she says : "I would have
liked thee to join thy name to mine in my Appeal, but thought it
would probably bring out so much opposition and violence, that I
preferred bearing it all myself."

sickness, for almost anything so I might have escaped attending it. But my dear Saviour opened no door, and after a season of unusual conflict I was favored with resignation.

"Oh! the cruel treatment I have undergone from those in authority. I could not have believed it had I not been called to endure it. But the Lord permits it. My part is not to judge how far they have been moving under divine direction, but to receive humbly and thankfully through them the lessons of meekness, lowliness, faith, patience, and love, and I trust I *may* be thankful for the opportunity thus afforded to love my enemies and to pray for them, and perhaps it is to prepare me to feel for others, that I have been thus tried and afflicted."

That she was thus prepared was evidenced through all the varied experiences of her after-life, for certainly no more sympathetic soul ever dwelt in a mortal frame, and more generously diffused its warmth and tenderness upon all who came within its radius.

After the next First Day meeting, she writes: —

"The suffering in my own meeting is so intense that I think nothing short of a settled conviction that obedience and eternal life are closely connected could enable me to open my lips there."

Two weeks later, an almost prophetic sentence is written.

"Truly discouragement does so prevail that it would be no surprise to me if Friends requested me to be silent. Hitherto, I have been spared this trial, but if it comes, O Holy Father, may my own will be so slain that I may bow in reverent adoring submission."

Notwithstanding all this distress, however, Sarah might still have lingered on some time longer, stifling in the dry dust of the Quaker Church, and refusing to partake of the living water Angelina proffered to her, but for an incident which occurred about this time, scarcely a fortnight after the last sentence quoted, — an incident which proved to be the last straw added to the heavy burden she had borne so submissively, if not patiently. It is best given in her own words, and I may add, it is the last entry in her most remarkable diary.

"8th Mo. 3d. Went this morning to Orange Street meeting after a season of conflict and prayer. I believed the Lord required this sacrifice, but I went with a heart bowed down, praying to Jesus that I might not speak my own words, that he would be pleased to make a way for me, or, if what I had to deliver brought upon me opposition, to strengthen me to endure it. The meeting had been gathered some time when I arose, and after repeating our Lord's thrice-repeated query to Peter, 'Lovest thou me?' I remarked that it was addressed to one who had been forgiven much, and who could appeal to the Searcher of hearts that he did indeed love Him. Few of us had had the temptation to endure which overcame Peter when he denied his Lord and Master. But although few of us might openly deny the Lord who bought us, yet there is, I apprehend, in many of us an evil heart of unbelief, which alienates us from God and disqualifies from answering the query as Peter did. I had proceeded so far when Jonathan Evans rose and said: 'I hope the Friend will now be satisfied.' I immediately sat down and was favored to feel perfectly calm. The language, 'Ye can have no power at all against me unless it be given you,' sustained me, and although I am branded in the public eye with the disapprobation of a poor fellow worm, and it was entirely a breach of discipline in him to publicly

silence a minister who has been allowed to exercise her
gifts in her own meeting without ever having been
requested to be silent, yet I feel no anger towards him.
Surely the feelings that could prompt to so cruel an
act cannot be the feelings of Christian love. But it
seems to be one more evidence that my dear Saviour
designs to bring me out of this place. How much has his
injunction rested on my mind of latter time. ' When
they persecute you in one city, flee ye into another.' I
pray unto Thee, O Lord Jesus, to direct the wanderer's
footsteps and to plant me where thou seest I can best promote thy glory. Expect to go to Burlington to-morrow."

To those unacquainted with the Society of Friends
fifty years ago, and its discipline at that period, so different from what it is now, this incident may seem of little
consequence; but it was, on the contrary, extremely serious. Jonathan Evans was the presiding elder of the
Yearly Meetings, a most important personage, whose authority was undisputed. He was sometimes alluded to
as "Pope Jonathan." He had disliked Sarah from the
time of her connection with the Society, and had habitually treated her and her offerings with a silent indifference most significant, and which, of course, had its effect
on many who pinned their prejudices as well as their
faith to the coats of the elders. It was owing entirely
to this secretly-exercised but well-understood opposition,
that Sarah had for nine long years used her ministerial
gift only through intense suffering. She believed, against
much rebellion in her own breast, that it had been given
her to use in God's service, and that she had no right to
withhold it; but she had been made so often to feel the
condemnation under which she labored, that she was
really not much surprised when the final blow came.

But with all her religious humility her pride was great, and her sensitiveness to any discourtesy very keen. She may not have felt anger against Elder Evans. We can imagine, on the contrary, that her heart was filled with pity for him, but a pity largely mixed with contempt; and it is certain that the Society was made, in her view, responsible for his conduct. Every slight she had ever received in it came back to her exaggerated; all her dissatisfaction with its principles of action doubled; the grief she had always felt at its indifference to the doctrine of the atonement, and its neglect to preach "Jesus Christ and him crucified," of which she had often complained, was intensified, and her first impulse was to quit the Society, as she determined to quit Philadelphia, for ever.

Angelina was greatly shocked when she learned of the treatment her sister had received, but the words, "I will break your bonds and set you free," came immediately to her mind, and so comforted her that her grief and indignation were turned to joy. She had long felt that, kind as Catherine Morris had always been, her strict orthodox principles, which she severely enforced in her household, circumscribed Sarah's liberty of thought and action, and operated powerfully in preventing her from rising out of her depressed and discouraged state. But though the question had often revolved itself in her mind, and even been discussed between her and her sister, neither had been able to see how Sarah could ever leave Catherine, bound to her as she was by such strong ties of gratitude, and feeling herself so necessary to Catherine's comfort. But now the way was made clear, and certainly no true friend of Sarah could expect her to remain longer in Philadelphia.

It is surprising that Sarah had not discovered many years earlier that the attempt must be futile to engraft a scion of the Charleston aristocracy upon the rugged stock of Quaker orthodoxy.

She went to Burlington, to the house of a dear friend who knew of all her trials, and there she remained for several weeks.

Angelina had finished her "Appeal," and, only two days before she heard of the Evans incident, wrote to Sarah to inform her of the fact. This letter is dated " Aug. 1st, 1836."

After a few affectionate inquiries, she says: " I have just finished my ' Appeal to Southern Women.' It has furnished work for two weeks. How much I wish I could have thee here, if it were only for three or four hours, that we might read it over together before I send it to Elizur Wright. I read it to Margaret, and she says it carries its own evidence with it; still, I should value thy judgment very much if I could have it, but a private opportunity offers to-morrow, and I think I had better send it. It must go just as I sent my letter to W. L. G., with fervent prayers that the Lord would do just as he pleased with it. I believe He directed and helped me to write it, and now I feel as if I had nothing to do but to send it to the Anti-Slavery Society, submitting it entirely to their judgment. . . . I cannot be too thankful for the change thou expressest in thy feelings with regard to the Anti-Slavery Society, and feel no desire at all to blame thee for former opposition, believing, as I do, that it was permitted in order to drive me closer to my Saviour, and into a deeper examination of the ground upon which I was standing. I am indeed thankful for it; how could I be otherwise, when it was so evident thou hadst my good at heart and really did for the best? And it did not hurt me at all. It did not alienate me from the blessed cause, for I think the same suffering that would drive us back from a bad cause makes us cling to and love a good one more ardently. O sister, I feel as if I could give up not only friends, but life itself, for the slave, if it is called for. I feel as if I could go anywhere to save him, even down to the South if I am called there. The conviction deepens and strengthens, as retirement affords fuller opportunity for calm reflection, that the cause of emancipation is a cause worth suffering for, yea, dying for, if need be. With regard to the proposed mission in New York, I can see nothing about it, and never did any poor creature feel more unfit to do anything than I do to undertake it. But what duty presses me into, I cannot press myself out of. . . . I sometimes feel frightened to think of how long I was standing idle in the market-place, and cannot help attributing it in a great measure to the doctrine of nothingness so constantly preached up in our Society. It is the most paralyzing, zeal-quenching doctrine that ever was preached in the Church, and I believe has produced its legitimate fruit of nothingness in reducing us to nothing, when we ought to have been a light in the Christian Church. . . . Farewell, dearest, perhaps we shall soon meet."

The Appeal was sent to New York, and this was what Mr. Wright wrote to the author in acknowledging its receipt : —

"I have just finished reading your Appeal, and not with a dry eye. I do not feel the slightest doubt that the committee will publish it. Oh that it could be rained down into every parlor in our land. I know it will carry the Christian women of the South if it can be read, and my

soul blesses that dear and glorious Saviour who has helped
you to write it."

When it was read some days after to the gentlemen of
the committee,they found in it such an intimate knowledge of the workings of the whole slave system, such
righteous denunciation of it, and such a warm interest in
the cause of emancipation, that they decided to publish it
at once and scatter it through the country, especially
through the South. It made a pamphlet of thirty-six
pages. The Quarterly Anti-Slavery Magazine for October,
1836, thus mentions it : —

"This eloquent pamphlet is from the pen of a sister of
the late Thomas S. Grimké, of Charleston, S. C. We
need hardly say more of it than that it is written with
that peculiar felicity and unction which characterized
the works of her lamented brother. Among anti-slavery
writings there are two classes — one especially adapted
to make new converts, the other to strengthen the old.
We cannot exclude Miss Grimké's Appeal from either
class. It belongs pre-eminently to the former. The converts that will be made by it, we have no doubt, will be
not only numerous, but thorough-going."

Mr. Wright spoke of it as a patch of blue sky breaking
through the storm-cloud of public indignation which had
gathered so black over the handful of anti-slavery workers.

This praise was not exaggerated. The pamphlet produced the most profound sensation wherever it was read,
but, as Angelina predicted, she was made to suffer for
having written it. Friends upbraided and denounced
her, Catherine Morris even predicting that she would be
disowned, and intimating pretty plainly that she would
not dissent from such punishment; and Angelina even
began to doubt her own judgment, and to question if she

ought not to have continued to live a useless life in Philadelphia, rather than to have so displeased her best friends.
But her convictions of duty were too strong to allow her
to remain long in this depressed, semi-repentant state. In
a letter to a friend she expresses herself as almost wondering at her own weakness; and of Catherine Morris she
says: " Her disapproval, more than anything else, shook
my resolution. Nevertheless, I told her, with many tears,
that I felt it a *religious duty* to labor in this cause, and
that I must do it even against the advice and wishes of
my friends. I think if I ever had a clear, calm view of
the path of duty in all my life, I have had it since I came
here, in reference to slavery. But I assure thee that I
expect nothing less than that my labors in this blessed
cause will result in my being disowned by Friends, but
none of these things will move me. I must confess I
value my right very little in a Society which is frowning
on all the moral reformations of the day, and almost en-
slaving its members by unchristian and unreasonable
restrictions, with regard to uniting with others in these
works of faith and labors of love. I do not believe it
would cost me one pang to be disowned for doing my
duty to the slave."

But her condemnation reached beyond the Quaker
Society — even to her native city, where her Appeal produced a sensation she had little expected. Mr. Weld's
account of its reception there is thus given : —

" When it (the Appeal) came out, a large number of
copies were sent by mail to South Carolina. Most of
them were publicly burned by postmasters. Not long
after this, the city authorities of Charleston learned that
Miss Grimké was intending to visit her mother and
sisters, and pass the winter with them. Thereupon the

mayor called upon Mrs. Grimké and desired her to inform
her daughter that the police had been instructed to prevent her landing while the steamer remained in port, and
to see to it that she should not communicate, by letter or
otherwise, with any persons in the city; and, further,
that if she should elude their vigilance and go on shore,
she would be arrested and imprisoned until the return of
the vessel. Her Charleston friends at once conveyed to
her the message of the mayor, and added that the people
of Charleston were so incensed against her, that if she
should go there despite the mayor's threat of pains and
penalties, she could not escape personal violence at the
hands of the mob. She replied to the letter that her
going would probably compromise her family; not only
distress them, but put them in peril, which she had neither
heart nor right to do; but for that fact, she would certainly exercise her constitutional right as an American
citizen, and go to Charleston to visit her relatives, and if
for that, the authorities should inflict upon her pains and
penalties, she would willingly bear them, assured that
such an outrage would help to reveal to the free States
the fact that slavery defies and tramples alike upon con-
stitutions and laws, and thus outlaws itself."

These brave words said no more than they meant, for
Angelina Grimké's moral heroism would have borne her to
the front of the fiercest battle ever fought for human
rights; and she would have counted it little to lay down
her life if that could help on the victory. She touched
as yet only the surf of the breakers into which she was
soon to be swept, but her clear eye would not have
quailed, or her cheek have blanched, if even then all their
cruelty could have been revealed to her.

CHAPTER XII.

WE have seen, a few pages back, that Angelina expressed her thankfulness at Sarah's change of views with respect to the anti-slavery cause. Again we must regret the destruction of Sarah's letters, which would have shown us by what chains of reasoning her mind at last reached entire sympathy with Angelina's. We can only infer that her progress was rapid after the public rebuke which caused her to turn her back on Philadelphia, and that her sister's brave and isolated position, appealing strongly to her affection, urged her to make a closer examination of the subject of abolitionism than she had yet done. The result we know; her entire conversion in a few weeks to Angelina's views. And from that time she travelled close by her sister's side in this as well as in other questions of reform, drawing her inspiration from Angelina's clearer intuitions and calmer judgment, and frankly and affectionately acknowledging her right of leadership.

The last of August, 1836, the sisters were once more together, Sarah having accepted Mrs Parker's invitation to come to Shrewsbury. The question of future arrangements was now discussed. Angelina felt a strong inclination to go to New England, and undertake there the same work which the committee in New York wished her to perform, and she even wrote to Mr. Wright that she expected to do so. Feeling also that Friends had the first right to her time and labors, and that, if permitted, she would prefer to work within the Society, she wrote to her old acquaintances, E. and L. Capron, the cotton manufacturers of Uxbridge, Massachusetts, to consult them on the subject. She mentions this in a letter to her friend, Jane Smith, saying : —

" My present feelings lead me to labor with Friends on the manufacture and use of the products of slave-labor. They excuse themselves from doing anything, because they say they cannot mingle in the general excitement, and so on. Now, here is a field of labor in which they need have nothing to do with other societies, and yet will be striking a heavy blow at slavery. These topics the Anti-Slavery Society has never acted upon as a body, and therefore no agent of theirs could consistently labor on them. I stated to E. and L. Capron just how I felt, and asked whether I could be of any use among them, whether they were prepared to have the morality of these things discussed on Christian principles. I have no doubt my Philadelphia friends will oppose my going there, but, Jane, I have realized very sensibly of late that I belong not to them, but to Christ Jesus, and that I must follow the Lamb whithersoever He leadeth. . . . I feel as if I was about to sacrifice every friend I thought I had, but I still believe with T. D. Weld, that this is ' a cause worth dying for.' "

This is the first mention we find of her future husband, whom she had not yet seen, but whose eloquent addresses she had read, and whose ill-treatment by Western mobs had more than once called forth the expression of her indignation.

The senior member of the firm to which she had writ-

ten answered her letter in person, and, she says, utterly
discouraged her. He said that if she should go into New
England with the avowed intention of laboring among
Friends on the subject of slavery in *any* way, her
path would be completely closed, and she would find herself entirely helpless. He even went so far as to say that
he believed there were Friends who would destroy her
character if she attempted anything of the kind. He
proposed that she should go to his house for the winter,
and employ her time in writing for the Anti-Slavery Society, and doing anything else she could incidentally.
But this plan did not suit her. She felt it right to offer
her services to Friends first, and was glad she had done
so; but if they would not accept them she must take
them elsewhere. Besides, when she communicated
her plan to Catherine Morris, Catherine objected to it
very decidedly, and said she *could not* go without a certificate and a companion, and these she knew Friends would
not grant her.

"Under all these circumstances," Angelina writes, "I
felt a little like the apostle Paul, who having first offered
the Jews the gospel, and finding they would not receive
it, believed it right for him to turn to the Gentiles.
Didst thou ever hear anything so absurd as what Catherine says about the certificate and a companion? I cannot feel bound by such unreasonable restrictions if my
Heavenly Father opens a door for me, and I do not mean
to submit to them. She knows very well that Arch
Street Meeting would grant me neither, but as the servant
of Jesus Christ I have no right to bow down thus to the
authority of man, and I do not expect ever again to suffer
myself to be trammelled as I have been. It is sinful in
any human being to resign his or her conscience and free

agency to any society or individual, if such usurpation can be resisted by moral power. The course our Society is now determined upon, of crushing everything which opposes the peculiar views of Friends, seems to me just like the powerful effort of the Jews to close the lips of Jesus. They are afraid that the Society will be completely broken up if they allow any difference of opinion to pass unrebuked, and they are resolved to put down all who question in any way the doctrines of Barclay, the soundness of Fox, or the practices which are built on them. But the time is fast approaching when we shall see who is for Christ, and who for Fox and Barclay, the Paul and Apollos of our Society."

Her plan of going to New England frustrated, Angelina hesitated no longer about accepting the invitation from New York. But first there was a long discussion of the subject with Sarah, who found it hard to resign her sister to a work she as yet did not cordially approve. She begged her not to decide suddenly, and pointed out all sorts of difficulties — the great responsibility she would assume, her retiring disposition, and almost morbid shrinking from whatever might make her conspicuous; the trial of going among strangers, made greater by her Quaker costume and speech, and lastly, of the almost universal prejudice against a woman's speaking to any audience; and she asked her if, under all these embarrassing circumstances, added to her inexperience of the world, she did not feel that she would ultimately be forced to give up what now seemed to her so practicable. To all this Angelina only answered that the responsibility seemed thrust upon her, that the call was God's call, and she could not refuse to answer it. Sarah then told her that if she should go upon this mission without the sanction of the "Meeting for Sufferings," it would be regarded as a violation of the established usages of the Society, and it would feel obliged to disown her. Angelina's answer to this ended the discussion. She declared that as her mind was made up to go, she could not ask leave of her Society — that it would grieve her to have to leave it, and it would be unpleasant to be disowned, but she had no alternative. Then Sarah, whose loving heart had, during the long talk, been moving nearer and nearer to that of her dear child, surprised her by speaking in the beautiful, tender language of Ruth: "If thou indeed feelest thus, and I cannot doubt it, then my mind too is made up. Where thou goest, I will go; thy God shall be my God, thy people my people. What thou doest, I will, to my utmost, aid thee in doing. We have wept and prayed together, we will go and work together."

And thus fully united, heart and soul and mind, they departed for New York, Angelina first writing to inform the committee of her decision, and while thanking them for the salary offered, refusing to receive any. She also told them that her sister would accompany her and co-operate with her, and they would both bear their own expense.

After this time, the sisters found themselves in frequent and intimate association with the men who, as officers of the American Anti-Slavery Society, had the direction of the movement. The marked superiority of their new friends in education, experience, culture, piety, liberality of view, statesmanship, decision of character, and energy in action, to the Philadelphia Quakers and Charleston slave-holders, must have been to them a surprise and a revelation. Working with a common purpose, these men were of varied accomplishments and qualities. William Jay and James G. Birney were cultured men of the world, trained in legal practice and public life; Arthur Tappan, Lewis Tappan, John Rankin, and Duncan Dunbar, were successful merchants; Abraham L. Cox, a physician in large practice; Theodore D. Weld, Henry B. Stanton, Alvan Stewart, and Gerrit Smith were popular orators; Joshua Leavitt, Elizur Wright, and William Goodell were ready writers and able editors; Beriah Green and Amos A. Phelps were pulpit speakers and authors, and John G. Whittier was a poet. Some of them had national reputations. Those who in December, 1835, protested against the false charges of publishing incendiary documents calculated to excite servile war, made against the Society by President Jackson, had signed names almost as well known as his, and had written better English than his message. Several of them had been officers of the American Anti-Slavery Society from its formation. Their energy had been phenomenal: they had raised funds, sent lecturers into nearly every county in the free States, and circulated in a single year more than a million copies of newspapers, pamphlets, magazines, and books. Their moderation, good judgment, and piety had been seen and known of all men. Faithful in the exposure of unfaithfulness to freedom on the part of politicians and clergymen, they denounced neither the Constitution nor the Bible. Their devotion to the cause of abolition was pure; for its sake they suppressed the vanity of personal notoriety and of oratorical display. Among them, not one can be found who sought to make a name as a leader, speaker, or writer; not one who was jealous of the reputation of co-adjutors; not one who rewarded adherents with flattery and hurled invectives at dissentients; not one to whom personal flattery was acceptable or personal prominence desirable; not one whose writings betrayed egotism, self-inflation or bombast. Such was their honest aversion to personal publicity, it is now almost impossible to trace the work each did. Some of their noblest arguments for Freedom were published anonymously. They made no vainglorious claims to the original authorship of ideas. But never in the history of reform was work better done than the old American Anti-Slavery Society did from its formation in 1833 to its disruption in 1840. In less than seven years it regained for Freedom most of the vantage-ground lost under the open assaults and secret plottings, beginning in 1829, of the Jackson administration, and in the panic caused by the Southampton insurrection; blew into flame the embers of the national anti-slavery senti-ment; painted slavery as it was; vindicated the anti-slavery character of the Constitution and the Bible; defended the right of petition; laid bare the causes of the Seminole war: exposed the Texas conspiracy and the designs of the slave power for supremacy; and freed the legitimate abolition cause from " no human government," secession, and anti-constitution heresies. In short, it planted the seed which flowered and fruited in a political party, around which the nation was to gather for defence against the aggressions of the slave power.

At the anti-slavery office in New York, Angelina and Sarah learned, much to their satisfaction, that the work that would probably be required of Angelina could be done in a private capacity; that it was proposed to orga-nize, the next month (November), a National Female Anti-Slavery Society, for which women agents would be needed, and they could make themselves exceedingly useful travelling about, distributing tracts, and talking to women in their own homes.

There the matter rested for a time.

Writing to her friend Jane Smith in Philadelphia after their return to Shrewsbury, Angelina says: —

"I am certain of the disapproval of nearly all my friends. As to dear Catherine, I am afraid she will hardly want to see me again. I wrote to her all about it, for I wanted her to know what my prospects were. I expect nothing less than the loss of her friendship and of my membership in the Society. The latter will be a far less trial than the former. . . . I cannot describe to thee how my dear sister has comforted and strengthened me. I cannot regard the change in her feelings as any other than as a strong evidence that my Heavenly Father has called me into the anti-slavery field, and after having tried my faith by her opposition, is now pleased to strengthen and confirm it by her approbation."

In a postscript to this letter, Sarah says: —

"God does not willingly grieve or afflict the children of men, and if my suffering or even my beloved sister's, which is harder to bear than my own, can help forward the cause of Truth and Righteousness, I may rejoice in that we are found worthy not only to believe on, but also to suffer for, the name of Jesus."

Angelina adds that she shall be obliged to go to Philadelphia for a week or so, to dispose of her personal effects, and asks Jane to receive her as a boarder, as she did not think it would be right to impose herself upon either her sister, Mrs. Frost, or Catherine, on account of their disapproval of anti-slavery measures.

"I never felt before," she says, "as if I had *no* home. It seems as if the Lord had completely broken up my rest and driven me out to labor for the poor slave. It is *His* work — I blame no one."

A few weeks later, the sisters were again in New York,

the guests of that staunch abolitionist, Dr. Cox, and his
good wife, Abby, as earnest a worker in the cause as her
husband. An anti-slavery convention had been called for
the first week in the month of November, and met soon
after their arrival. It was at this convention that Angelina first saw and listened to Theodore D. Weld.
Writing to her friend Jane, she says: —

"The meetings are increasingly interesting, and to-day
(11th) we enjoyed a moral and intellectual feast in a
most noble speech from T. D. Weld, of more than two
hours, on the question, 'What is slavery?' I never
heard so grand and beautiful an exposition of the dignity
and nobility of man in my life."

She goes on to give a synopsis of the entire speech,
and by her frequent enthusiastic comments reveals how
much it and the speaker impressed her. She continues: —

"After the meeting was over, W. L. Garrison introduced Weld to us. He greeted me with the appellation
of 'my dear sister,' and I felt as though he was a brother
indeed in the holy cause of suffering humanity; a man
raised up by God and wonderfully qualified to plead the
cause of the oppressed. Perhaps now thou wilt want to
know how this lion of the tribe of abolition *looks*. Well,
at first sight, there was nothing remarkable to me in his
appearance, and I wondered whether he was really as
great as I had heard. But as soon as his countenance
became animated by speaking, I found it was one which
portrayed the noblest qualities of the heart and head
beaming with intelligence, benevolence, and frankness."

On the last page of her letter she says: "It is truly
comforting to me to find that sister is so much pleased
with the Convention, that she acknowledges the spirit of
brotherly love and condescension manifest there, and that

earnest desire after truth which characterizes the addresses. We have been introduced to a number of abolitionists, Thurston, Phelps, Green, the Burleighs, Wright, Pritchard, Thome, etc., and Amos Dresser, as lovely a specimen of the meekness and lowliness of the great Master as I ever saw. His countenance betrayeth that he has been with Jesus, and it was truly affecting to hear him on Sixth Day give an account of the Nashville outrage to a very large colored school.[1]

"The F. A. S. Society is to have its first public meeting this week, at which we hope to hear Weld, but fear he will not have time, as he is not even able to go home to meals, and told me he had sat up until two o'clock every night since he came to New York. As to myself, I feel I have nothing to do but to attend the Convention at present. I am very comfortable, feeling in my right place, and sister seems to feel so too, though neither of us sees much ahead."

In her next letter she describes the deepening interest of the Convention, and Sarah's increasing unity with its members.

---

[1] Amos Dresser was one of the Lane Seminary students. After leaving that institution, in order to raise funds to continue his studies, he accepted an agency for the sale of the " Cottage Bible." While peacefully prosecuting his business in Nashville, in 1834, it became known that he was an abolitionist. This was enough. He was arrested, his trunk broken open, and its contents searched and scattered. He was then taken before a vigilance committee, and without a single charge, except that of his anti-slavery principles, being brought against him, was condemned to receive twenty lashes, " well laid on," on the bare back, and then to be driven from the town. The sentence was carried out by the votes and in the presence of thousands of people, and was presided over by the mayor and the elders of the Presbyterian Church from whose hands Mr. Dresser had, the Sunday before, received the Holy Communion.

" We sit," she says, " from 9 to 1, 3 to 5, and 7 to 9, and never feel weary at all. It is better, *far* better than any Yearly Meeting I ever attended. It is still uncertain when we shall adjourn, and it is so good to be here that I don't know how to look forward to the end of such a feast. . . . T. D. Weld is to begin his Bible argument to-morrow. It will occupy, he says, four days."

The Convention adjourned the latter part of November, 1836, and we may judge how profitable its meetings had proved to Sarah Grimké, from the fact that she at once began the preparation of an " Epistle to the Clergy of the Southern States," which, printed in pamphlet form, was issued some time in December, and was as strong an argument against the stand on the subject of slavery taken by the majority of the clergy as had yet appeared. Reading it, one would little suspect how recent had been the author's opposition to just such protests as this, calculated to stir up bitter feelings and create discussion and excitement in the churches. It is written in a spirit of gentleness and persuasion, but also of firm admonition, and evidently under a deep sense of individual responsibility. It shows, too, that Sarah had reached full accord with Angelina in her views of immediate emancipation.

By the time the Convention was over, the sisters, and portions of their history, had become so well known to abolitionists, that the leaders felt they had secured invaluable champions in these two Quaker women, one so logical, brilliant, and persuasive ; the other so intelligent, earnest, and conscientious ; and both distinguished by their ability to testify as eye-witnesses against the monstrous evils of slavery.

It was proposed that they should begin to hold a series of parlor meetings, for women only, of course. But it was soon found that they had, in private conversations, made such an impression, that no parlors would be large enough to accommodate all who desired to hear them speak more at length. Upon learning this, the Rev. Mr. Dunbar, a Baptist clergyman, offered them the use of his Session room, and the Female Anti-Slavery Society embraced the opportunity to make this the beginning of regular quarterly meetings. On the Sunday previous to the meeting, notice of it was given out in four churches, without however, naming the proposed speakers. But it became known in some way that the Misses Grimké were to address the meeting, and a shock went through the whole community. Not a word would have been said if they had restricted themselves to a private parlor meeting, but that it should be transferred to such a public place as the parlor of a church made quite a different affair of it. Friends were of course as loud as Friends could properly be in their expressions of disapproval, while other denominations, not so restrained, gave Mr. Dunbar, the abolitionists, and the "two bold Southern women" an unmistakable piece of their mind. Even Gerrit Smith, always the grandest champion of woman, advised against the meeting, fearing it would be pronounced a Fanny Wright affair, and do more harm than good. Sarah and Angelina were appalled, the latter especially, feeling almost as if she was the bold creature she was represented to be. She declared her utter inability, in the face of such antagonism, to go on with the work she had undertaken, and the more she looked at it, the more unnatural and unwise it seemed to her; and when printed hand-bills were scattered about, calling attention in a slighting manner to their names, both felt as if it were humanly impossible for them to proceed any further. But the meeting had been called, and as there was no business to come before it, they did not know what to do.

"In this emergency," Angelina writes, "I called upon Him who has ever hearkened unto my cry. My strength and confidence were renewed, my burden slipped off, and from that time I felt sure of God's help in the hour of need, and that He would be mouth and wisdom, tongue and utterance to us both."

"Yesterday," she continues, "T. D. Weld came up, like a brother, to sympathize with us and encourage our hearts. He is a precious Christian, and bade us not to fear, but to trust in God. In a previous conversation on our holding meetings, he had expressed his full unity with our doing so, and grieved over that factitious state of society which bound up the energies of woman, instead of allowing her to exercise them to the glory of God and the good of her fellow creatures. His visit was really a strength to us, and I felt no more fear. We went to the meeting at three o'clock, and found about three hundred women there. It was opened with prayer by Henry Ludlow; we were warmly welcomed by brother Dunbar, and then these two left us. After a moment, I arose and spoke about forty minutes, feeling, I think, entirely unembarrassed. Then dear sister did her part better than I did. We then read some extracts from papers and letters, and answered a few questions, when at five the meeting closed; after the question had been put whether our sisters wished another meeting to be held. A good many rose, and Henry Ludlow says he is sure he can get his session room for us."

This account of the first assembly of women, not Quakers, in a public place in America, addressed by

American women, is deeply interesting, and touching from its very simplicity.

We who are so accustomed to hear women speak to promiscuous audiences on any and every subject, and to hear them applauded too, can scarcely realize the prejudice which, half a century back, sought to close the lips of two refined Christian ladies, desirous only of adding their testimony against the greatest evil of any age or country. But those who denounced and ridiculed them builded better than they knew, for then and there was laid the corner-stone of that temple of equal rights for women, which has been built upon by so many brave hearts and willing hands since, and has brought to the front such staunch supporters and brilliant advocates as now adorn every convention of the Woman's Rights Associations.

After mentioning some who came up and spoke to them after the meeting was over, Angelina adds: —

" We went home to tea with Julia Tappan, and Brother Weld was all anxiety to hear about the meeting. Julia undertook to give some account, and among other things mentioned that a warm-hearted abolitionist had found his way into the back part of the meeting, and was escorted out by Henry Ludlow. Weld's noble countenance instantly lighted up, and he exclaimed: 'How supremely ridiculous to think of a man's being shouldered out of a meeting, for fear he should hear a woman speak!' . . .

" In the evening a colonizationist of this city came to introduce an abolitionist to Lewis Tappan. We women soon hedged in our expatriation brother, and held a long and interesting argument with him until near ten o'clock. He gave up so much that I could not see what he had to stand on when we left him."

Another meeting, similar to the first, was held the next week, when so much interest was manifested that it was decided to continue the meetings every week until further notice. By the middle of January they had become so crowded, and were attended by such an influential class of women, that Mr. Ludlow concluded to offer his church to them. He always opened the meetings with prayer, and then retired. The addresses made by the sisters were called " lectures," but they were rather familiar talks, occasionally a discussion, while many questions were asked and answered. Angelina's confidence in herself increased rapidly, until she no longer felt the least embarrassment in speaking; though she alludes to the exhausting effect of the meetings on her physical system. Of Sarah, she says, writing to Jane Smith : —

" It is really delightful to see dear sister so happy in this work. . . . Some Friends come to hear us, but I do not know what they think of the meetings — or of us. How little, how very little I supposed, when I used so often to say ' I wish I were a man,' that I could go forth and lecture, that *I* ever would do such a thing. The idea never crossed my mind that as a *woman* such work could possibly be assigned to me."

To this letter there is a postscript from Sarah, in which she says : —

" I would not give up my abolition feelings for anything I know. They are intertwined with my Christianity. They have given a new spring to my existence, and shed over my whole being sweet and hallowed enjoyments."

Angelina's next letter to her friend is dated, " 2d Mo. 4th, 1837," and continues the account of the meetings. She mentions that, at the last one, they had one *male* auditor, who refused to go out when told he must, so he was allowed to stay, and she says: "Somehow, I did not feel his presence embarrassing at all, and went on just as though he had not been there. Some one said he took notes, and I think he was a Southern spy, and shall not be at all surprised if he publishes us in some Southern paper."

Truly it was a risky thing for a lord of creation to intrude himself into a woman's meeting in those days!

Angelina goes on to remark that more Friends are attending their meetings, and that if they were not opened with prayer, still more would come. Also, that Friends had been very kind and attentive to them in every way, and never said a discouraging word to them. She then discourses a little on phrenology, at that time quite a new thing in this country, and relates an anecdote of "Brother Weld," as follows : —

"When he went to Fowler in this city, he disguised himself as an omnibus driver. The phrenologist was so struck with the supposed fact that an omnibus driver should have such an extraordinary head, that he preserved an account of it, and did not know until some time after that it was Weld's. He says that when he first had his head examined at Utica, he was told he was deficient in the organ of color, his eyebrow showing it. He immediately remembered that his mother often told him: 'Theodore, it is of no use to send you to match a skein of silk, for you never bring the right color.' When relating this, he observed a general titter in the room, and on inquiring the reason a candle was put near him, and, to his amazement, all agreed that the legs of his pantaloons were of different shades of green. Instead of a ridge all around his eyebrow, he has a little hollow in one spot."

A society for the encouragement of abstinence from the use of slave products had just been formed in Philadelphia, and Angelina desired her friend to put *her* name to the pledge, but not Sarah's. In a postscript Sarah explains this, saying : —

" I do abstain from slave produce as much as I can, just because I feel most easy to do so, but I cannot say my judgment is convinced; therefore, I would rather not put my name to the pledge."

Her judgment *was* convinced, however, very shortly afterwards, by a discussion of the subject with Weld and some others, and she then wrote to Jane Smith to set her name down, as she found her testimony in the great cause was greatly strengthened by keeping clean hands.

There is much told of their meetings, and their other experiences in New York, which is very interesting, and for which I regret I have not room. Angelina describes in particular one visit they made to a poor family, that of one of her Sunday-school pupils, where they stayed to tea, being afterwards joined by Mr. Weld, who came to escort them home. She says of him : —

" I have seen him shine in the Convention and in refined circles, but never did I admire him so much. His perfect ease at this fireside of poverty showed that he was accustomed to be the friend and companion of the poor of this world."

The family here mentioned was doubtless a colored one, as it was in the colored Sunday school that both sisters taught. They had already proved, by their friendship for Sarah Douglass, the Fortens, and other colored families of Philadelphia, how slight was their prejudice against color, but the above incident proves the entire sincerity of their convictions and their desire to avail themselves of every opportunity to testify to it. Still, there is no doubt that to the influence of Theodore Weld's conversations they owed much of their enlightenment on this as well as on some other points of radical abolitionism. It was after a talk with him that Angelina describes the Female Anti-Slavery Society of New York as utterly inefficient, "doing literally nothing," and ascribes its inefficiency to the sinful prejudice existing there, which shut out colored women from any share in its management, and gave little encouragement to them even to become members.

She adds: " I believe it is our duty to visit the poor, white and colored, just in this way, and to receive them at our houses. I think that the artificial distinctions in society, the separation between the higher and the lower orders, the aristocracy of wealth and education, are the very rock of pauperism, and that the only way to eradicate this plague from our land will be to associate with the poor, and the wicked too, just as our Redeemer did. To visit them as our inferiors, the recipients of our bounty, is quite a different thing from going among them as our equals."

In her next letter to Jane Smith, Angelina gives an interesting account of H. B. Stanton's great speech before the Committee of the Massachusetts legislature on the abolition of slavery in the District of Columbia; a speech which still ranks as one of the ablest and most brilliant ever delivered in this country. There is no date to this letter, but it must have been written the last of February or first of March, 1837. She begins thus: —

"I was wondering, my dear Jane, what could be the reason I had not heard from thee, when brother Weld came in with thine and Mira's letters *hanging* from the paper on which they had been tied. 'I bring you,' he said, ' a good emblem of the fate of abolitionists, — so take warning ;' and held them up to our view. . . .

" Brother Garrison was here last Sixth Day and spent two hours with us. He gave us a most delightful account of recent things in Boston, which I will try to tell thee of. When the abolitionists found how their petitions were treated in Congress, they sent in, from all parts of Massachusetts, petitions to the legislature, requesting it to issue a protest against such contempt of the people's wishes and rights. The legislature was amazed at the number and respectability of these petitions, and appointed a committee to take them under consideration. Abolitionists then asked for a hearing before that committee, *not* in the lobby, but in the Hall of Representatives. The request was granted, and though the day was exceedingly stormy, a good number were out. A young lawyer of Boston first spoke an hour and a half; H. B. Stanton followed, and completely astonished the audience, but could not get through by dark, and asked for another meeting. The next afternoon an overflowing audience greeted him; he spoke three hours, and did not yet finish. Another meeting was appointed for the next evening, and he says he thinks hundreds went away because they could not get in. Stanton spoke one hour and a quarter, and then broke down from the greatness of the effort, added to the unceasing labors of the winter. A profound silence reigned through the crowded hall. Not one moved to depart. At last a member of the committee arose, and asked if there was any other abolitionist present who wished to speak. Stanton said he believed not, as they now had the views of the Anti-Slavery Society. The committee were not satisfied ; and one of them said if there was any abolitionist who wished to follow Mr. Stanton, they would gladly hear all he had to say, but all declined. Brother Garrison said such was the desire to hear more on this subject, that he came directly to New York to get Weld to go and speak before them, but his throat is still so much affected that it will be impossible for him to do so. Isn't this cheering news? Here are seven hundred men in the Massachusetts legislature, who, if they can be moved to protest against the unconstitutional proceedings of Congress, will shake this nation to its cent; e, and rock it in a revolutionary storm that must either sink it or save it."

After closing their meetings in New York, the sisters held similar ones in Newark, Bloomfield, and other places in New Jersey, in all of which Sarah was as active and enthusiastic as Angelina, and from this time we hear no more of the gloom and despondency which had saddened so many of the best years of her life. But, identified completely with her sister's work, she was busy, contented and satisfied of the Lord's goodness and mercy.

These meetings had all been quiet and undisturbed in every way, owing of course, to the fact that only women attended, but the newspapers had not spared them. Ridicule, sarcasm, and pity were liberally bestowed upon the " deluded ladies " by the press generally, and the *Richmond Whig* published several editorials about "those fanatical women, the Misses Grimké." But writing against them was the extent of the opposition at that time, and this affected them very little.

From New Jersey they went up the North River with Gerrit Smith, holding interesting meetings at Hudson and Poughkeepsie. At the latter place they spoke to an assembly of colored people of both sexes, and this was the first time Angelina ever addressed a mixed audience, and it was perhaps in accordance with the fitness of things that it should have been a colored one. She often spoke of this in after years, looking back to it with pleasure. Here, also, they attended a meeting of the Anti-slavery Society of the Protestant Episcopal Methodist Church, and spoke against the sin of prejudice. In a letter to Sarah Douglass, Sarah says : —

" My feelings were so overcome at this meeting that I sat down and wept. I feel as if I had taken my stand by the side of the colored American, willing to share with him the odium of a darker skin, and I trust if I am permitted again to take my seat in Arch Street Meeting House, it will be beside thee and thy dear mother."

These Hudson River meetings ended the labors of the sisters in New York for the time. They returned to the city to take a little needed rest, and to prepare for the Female Anti-Slavery Convention, which was to meet there early in May. The Society which had sent them forth had reason to be well satisfied with its experiment. Not only had they awakened enthusiasm and sincere interest in abolition, but had demonstrated the ability of women to publicly advocate a great cause, and the entire propriety of their doing so. One of the members of the committee asserted that it would be as impossible to calculate the number of converts they had made, as to estimate the encouragement and strength their zeal and eloquence had given to abolitionists all over the country. Men were slow to believe the reports of their wives and sisters respecting Angelina's wonderful oratory, and this incredulity produced the itching ears which soon drew to the meetings where the Grimké sisters were to speak more men than women, and gave them the applause and hearty support of some of the ablest minds of New England. The Female Anti-slavery Convention opened with seventy-one delegates; the Misses Grimké, at their own request, representing South Carolina. During this convention they met many congenial souls, among whom they particularize Lydia M. Child, Mary T. Parker, and Anna Weston, as sympathizing so entirely with their own views respecting prejudice and the province of woman.

The latter question had long been Sarah's pet problem, to the solution of which she had given much thought and study, ever since the time when she was denied participation in her brother's education because of her sex. It is scarcely too much to say that to her mind this question was second in importance to none, and though the word *enfranchisement*, as applied to woman, had not yet been uttered, the whole theory of it was in Sarah's heart, and she eagerly awaited the proper time and place to develop it. Angelina, while holding the same views, would probably have kept them in the background longer, but for Sarah's arguments, supported by the objection so frequently urged against the encouragement of their meetings, — that slavery was a political subject with which women had nothing to do. This objection she answered in a masterly paper, an " Appeal to the Women of the Nominally Free States," which was printed in pamphlet form and sent out by the Female Anti-Slavery Convention, and attracted wide attention. The chief point she took was this: " The denial of our duty to act in this cause is a denial of our right to act; and if we have no right to act, then may *we* well be termed ' the white slaves of the North,' for, like our brethren in bonds, we must seal our lips in silence and despair."

The whole argument, covering nearly seventy pages, is

remarkable in its calm reasoning, sound logic, and fervid eloquence, and will well repay perusal, even at this day. About the same time a beautiful and most feeling "Address to Free Colored Americans" was written by Sarah, and likewise circulated by the Convention. These two pamphlets made the sisters so widely known, and so increased the desire in other places to hear them speak, that invitations poured in upon them from different parts of the North and West, as well as from the New England States. It was finally decided that they should go to Boston first, to aid the brave, good women there, who, while willing to do all that women could do for the cause in a private capacity, had not yet been persuaded to open their lips for it in any kind of a public meeting. It was not contemplated, however, that the sisters should address any but assemblies of women. Even Boston was not yet prepared for a greater infringement of the social proprieties.

CHAPTER XIII.

The Woman's Rights agitation, while entirely separate from Abolitionism, owes its origin to the interest this subject excited in the hearts and minds of American women; and to Sarah and Angelina Grimké must be accorded the credit of first making the woman question one of reform. Their broad views, freely expressed in their New York meetings, opened up the subject of woman's duties under the existing state of public sentiment, and, in connection with the revelations made concerning the condition of her white and colored sisters at the South, and the frantic efforts used to prevent her from receiving these revelations, she soon began to see that she had some moral obligations outside of her home sphere and her private circle. At first her only idea of aid in the great cause was that of prayer, which men universally granted was her especial privilege, even encouraging her to pray for *them;* but it must be private prayer — prayer in her own closet — with no auditor but the God to whom she appealed. As soon as it became public, and took the form of petitions to legislatures and to Congress, the reprobation began. The enemies of freedom, fully realizing woman's influence, opposed her interference at every point; and when a Southern representative declared from his seat that women had no right to send up petitions to Congress, he was sustained by the sycophantic response which came from the North, that slavery was a political question, with which women had nothing to do. Angelina Grimké answered this so fully and so eloquently in her " Appeal to Northern Women," that no doubt could have been left in the minds of those who read it, not only of woman's right, but of her duty to interfere in this matter. The appeal is made chiefly to woman's tenderest and holiest feelings, but enough is said of her rights to show whither Angelina's own reflections were leading her, and it must have turned the thoughts of many other women in the same direction. A passage or two may be quoted as examples.

" Every citizen should feel an intense interest in the political concerns of the country, because the honor, happiness and well-being of every class are bound up in its politics, government, and laws. Are we aliens because we are women? Are we bereft of citizenship because we are the *mothers, wives, and daughters* of a mighty people? Have *women* no country — no interests staked on the public weal — no partnership in a nation's guilt and shame? Has *woman* no home nor household altars, nor endearing ties of kindred, nor sway with man, nor power at the mercy-seat, nor voice to cheer, nor hand to raise the drooping, or to bind the broken? . . . The Lord has raised up men whom he has endowed with 'wisdom and understanding, and knowledge,' to lay deep and broad the foundations of the temple of liberty. This is a great moral work in which they are engaged. No war-trumpet summons to the field of battle; but Wisdom crieth without, 'Whosoever is of a willing heart, let him bring an offering.' Shall *woman* refuse her response to the call? Was she created to be a helpmeet for man —

his sorrows to divide, his joys to share, and all his toils to lighten by her willing aid, and shall she refuse to aid him with her prayers, her labors, and her counsels too, *at such a time, in such a cause as this*?"

There had been, from the beginning of the anti-slavery agitation, no lack of women sympathizers with it. Some of the best and brightest of the land had poured forth their words of grief, of courage, and of hope through magazines and newspapers, in prose and in verse, and had proved their willingness to suffer for the slave, by enduring unshrinkingly ridicule and wrath, pecuniary loss and social ostracism. All over the country, in almost every town and village, women labored untiringly to raise funds for the printing of pamphlets, sending forth lecturers and for the pay of special agents. They were regular attendants also on the anti-slavery meetings and conventions, often outnumbering the men, and privately made some of the best suggestions that were offered. But so strong and general was the feeling against women speaking in any public place, that, up to the time when Sarah and Angelina Grimké began their crusade, it was an almost unheard of thing for a woman to raise her voice in any but a church prayer-meeting. During the sittings of the Anti-Slavery Convention in Philadelphia, in 1833, which was attended by a number of women, chiefly Friends, Lucretia Mott, though she had had experience in speaking in Quaker meetings, *timidly* arose one day, and, in fear lest she might offend, ventured to propose an amendment to a certain resolution. With rare indulgence and good sense, Beriah Green, the president of the convention, encouraged her to proceed; and May, in his "Recollections," says: "She made a more impressive and effective speech than any other that was made in the convention, excepting only the closing address of our president."

Two other ladies, Esther Moore and Lydia White, emboldened by Mrs. Mott's example, afterwards said a few words on one or two occasions, but these were the only infringements, during all those early years of agitation, of St. Paul's oft-quoted injunction.

When Sarah and Angelina Grimké accepted the invitation of the Female Anti-Slavery Society of Boston, to come and labor there, they found friends on every hand — women of the highest culture and purest religion, eager to hear them, not only concerning what their eyes had witnessed in that land of worse than Egyptian bondage, but ready to be enlightened upon their own duties and rights in the matter of moral reform, and as willing as resolute to perform them. Without experience, as the sisters were, we can hardly be surprised that they should have been carried beyond their original moorings, and have made what many of their best friends felt was a serious mistake, in uniting the two causes, thus laying upon abolitionists a double burden, and a responsibility to which the great majority of them were as much opposed as were their bitterest enemies. But no movement in this direction was made for some time. Indeed, it seems to have grown quite naturally out of, or been forced forward by, the alarm among men, and the means they took to frighten and warn women away from the dangerous topic.

The Massachusetts Anti-Slavery Convention met early in June, 1837. In writing about it to Jane Smith, Angelina first touches upon the dawning feeling on this woman question. She says : —

" We had Stanton and Burleigh, Colver and Birney,

Garrison and Goodell, etc. Their eloquence was no less delightful to the ear than the soundness of their doctrine was comforting to the heart. . . . A peace resolution was brought up, but this occasioned some difficulty on account of non-resistance here meaning a repudiation of civil government, and of course we cannot expect many to be willing to do this. . . . At Friend Chapman's, where we spent a social evening, I had a long talk with the brethren on the rights of women, and found a very general sentiment prevailing that it is time our fetters were broken. L. M. Child and Maria Chapman strongly supported this view; indeed, very many seem to think a new order of things is very desirable in this respect. . . . And now, my dear friend, in view of these things, I feel that it is not the cause of the slave only that we plead, but the cause of woman as a moral, responsible being, and I am ready to exclaim, 'Who is sufficient for these things?' These holy causes must be injured if they are not helped by us. I see not to what point all these things are leading us. But one thing comforts me : I do feel as though the Lord had sent us, and as if I was leaning on his arm."

And in this reliance, in a meek and lowly spirit, impelled not by inclination, but by an overpowering sense of duty, these gentle women, fully realizing the singularity of their position, prepared to enter upon entirely new scenes of labor, encompassed by difficulties peculiarly trying to their delicate natures.

A series of public meetings was arranged for them as soon as the Convention adjourned, and the first was held in Dorchester, in the town hall, to which they repaired upon finding the number of those who wished to hear them too great to be accommodated in a private house.

Their next was in Boston on the following afternoon. Angelina's heart here almost failed her as she glanced over the assemblage of women of all classes, and thought of the responsibility resting upon her. It was at this meeting that a reverend gentleman set the example, which was followed by two or three other men, of slyly sliding into a back seat to hear for himself what manner of thing this woman's speaking was. Satisfied of its superior quality, and alarmed at its effects upon the audience, he shortly afterwards took great pains to prove that it was unscriptural for a woman to speak in public.

As the meetings were held at first only in the daylight, there was little show of opposition for some time. The sisters went from one town to another, arousing enthusiasm everywhere, and vindicating, by their power and success, their right to speak. Angelina's letters to Jane Smith contain memoranda of all the meetings she and Sarah held during that summer and fall. It is surprising that they were able to endure such an amount of mental and physical labor, and maintain the constantly increasing eagerness to hear them. Before the end of the first week, she records:— " Nearly thirty men present, pretty easy to speak." A few days later the number of men had increased to fifty, with "great openness on their part to hear."

After having held meetings every day, their audience numbering from one hundred and fifty to one thousand, Angelina records on the 21st July, at Lynn : —

" In the evening of the same day addressed our first *mixed* audience. Over one thousand present, great openness to hear, and ease in speaking."

This, so briefly mentioned, was the beginning of the revolution in sentiment respecting woman's sphere, which,

though it was met at the outset with much the same
spirit which opposed abolitionism, soon spread and became a principle of reform as conscientiously and as ably
advocated as any other, moral or political. Neither Sarah
nor Angelina had any idea of starting such a revolution,
but when they found it fairly inaugurated, and that many
women had long privately held the same views as they
did and were ready to follow in their lead, they bravely
accepted, and to the end of their lives as bravely sustained
all the responsibilities their opinions involved. They
were the pioneers in the great cause of political freedom
for women, and opened the way in the true pioneer spirit.
The clear sense of justice and the broad humanity which
inspired their trenchant rebukes and fervid appeals not
only enlightened and encouraged other women, but led to
inquiry into various wrongs practised towards the sex
which had up to that time been suffered in silence and in
ignorance, or in despair of any possibility of relief. The
peculiar tenderness of Sarah Grimké's nature, and her
overflowing sympathy with any form of suffering, led her,
earlier than Angelina, to the consideration of the necessity of some organized system of protection of helpless
women and children; and, from the investigation of the
impositions and abuses to which they were subjected, was
evolved, without much difficulty, the doctrine of woman's
equality before the law, and her right to a voice on every
subject of public interest, social or political. Sarah's
published letters during the summer of 1837 show her to
have been as deeply interested in this reform as in abolitionism, and to her influence was certainly due the intro-
duction of the " Woman Question " into the anti-slavery
discussions. That this question was as yet a secondary
one in Angelina's mind is evident from what she writes

to Jane Smith about this time. She says: "With regard to speaking on the rights of woman, it has really
been wonderful to me that though, everywhere I go, I
meet prejudice against our speaking, yet, in addressing an
audience, I never think of referring to it. I was particularly struck with this two days ago. Riding with Dr.
Miller to a meeting at Franklin, I found, from conversation with him, that I had a great amount of prejudice to
meet at that town, and very much in his own mind. I
gave him my views on women's preaching, and verily believe I converted him, for he said he had no idea so much
could be adduced from the Bible to sustain the ground I
had taken, and remarked: 'This will be quite new to
the people, and I believe they will gladly hear these
things,' and pressed me so much to speak on the subject
at the close of my lecture that I was obliged to promise I
would if I could remember to do so. After speaking two
hours, we returned to his house to tea, and he asked:
'Why did you not tell the people why you believed you
had a right to speak?' I had entirely forgotten all
about it until his question revived the conversation
we had on the road. Now I believe the Lord orders
these things so, driving out of my mind what I ought not
to speak on. If the time ever comes when this shall be
a part of my public work, then I shall not be able to
forget it."

But to return to the meeting at Lynn. We are told
that the men present listened in amazement. They were
spell-bound, and impatient of the slightest noise which
might cause the loss of a word from the speakers. Another meeting was called for, and held the next evening.
This was crowded to excess, many going away unable to
get even standing-room.

"At least one hundred," Angelina writes, "stood around the doors, and, on the outside of each window, men stood with their heads above the lowered sash. Very easy speaking indeed."

But now the opposers of abolitionism, and especially the clergy, began to be alarmed. It amounted to very little that (to borrow the language of one of the newspapers of the day) "two fanatical women, forgetful of the obligations of a respected name, and indifferent to the feelings of their most worthy kinsmen, the Barnwells and the Rhetts, should, by the novelty of their course, draw to their meetings idle and curious women." But it became a different matter when men, the intelligent, respectable and cultivated citizens of every town, began to crowd to hear them, even following them from one place to another, and giving them loud and honest applause. Then they were adjudged immodest, and their conduct denounced as unwomanly and demoralizing. Their devotion to principle, the purity of their lives, the justice of the cause they pleaded, the religious stand-point from which they spoke, all were overlooked, and the pitiless scorn of Christian men and women of every sect was poured down upon them. Nor should we wonder when we remember that, at that time, the Puritan bounds of propriety still hedged in the education and the training of New England women, and limited the views of New England men. Even many of the abolitionists had first to hear Sarah and Angelina Grimké to be convinced that there was nothing unwomanly in a woman's raising her voice to plead for those helpless to plead for themselves. So good a man and so faithful an anti-slavery worker as Samuel J. May confesses that his sense of propriety was a little disturbed at first. Letters of reproval, admonition, and persuasion, some anonymous, some signed by good conscientious people, came to the sisters frequently. Clergymen denounced them from their pulpits, especially warning their women members against them. Municipal corporations refused the use of halls for their meetings, and threats of personal violence came from various quarters. *Friends* especially felt outraged. The New England Yearly Meeting went so far as to advise the closing of meeting-house doors to all anti-slavery lecturers and the disownment the sisters had long expected now became imminent.

We can well imagine how terrible all this must have been to their shrinking, sensitive, and proud spirits. But their courage never failed, nor was their mighty work for humanity stayed one instant by this storm of indignation and wrath. Angelina, writing to her dear Jane an account of some of the opposition to them, says:

" And now, thou wilt want to know how we feel about all these things. Well, dear, poor enough in ourselves, and defenceless; but rich and strong in the help which our Master is pleased to give from time to time, making perfect his strength in our weakness. This is a truly humbling dispensation, but when I am speaking I am favored to forget little *I* entirely, and to feel altogether hidden behind the great cause I am pleading. Were it not for this, I do not know how I could face such audiences and such opposition. O Jane, how good it is that we can cast all our burdens upon the Lord."

And Sarah, writing to Sarah Douglass, says: " They think to frighten us from the field of duty ; but they do not move us. God is our shield, and we do not fear what man can do unto us." A little further on she says: " It is really amusing to see how the clergy are arrayed against two women who are telling the story of the slave's wrongs."

This was before the celebrated "Pastoral Letter" appeared. Sarah's answer to that in her letters to the *N. E. Spectator* shows how far the clergy had gone beyond amusing her.

There were, of course, many church members of every denomination, and many ministers, in the abolition ranks. Indeed, at some of the Anti-Slavery Conventions, it was a most edifying sight to see clergymen of different churches sitting together and working together in harmony, putting behind them, for the time being, all creeds and dogmas, or, rather, sinking them all in the one creed taught by the blessed command to do unto others as they would be done by.

Some of the more conservative of the clergy objected, it is true, to the great freedom of thought and speech allowed generally in the Conventions, but this was slight compared to the feeling excited by the encouragement given to women to take prominent and public part in the work, even to speaking from the platform and the pulpit.

The general prejudice against this was naturally increased by the earnest eloquence with which Angelina Grimké pointed out the inconsistent attitude of ministers and church members towards slavery; by Sarah's strongly expressed views concerning a paid clergy; and the indignant protests of both sisters against the sin of prejudice, then as general in the church as out of it.

The feeling grew very strong against them. They were setting public sentiment at defiance, it was said; they were seeking to destroy veneration for the ministers of the Gospel; they were casting contempt upon the consecrated forms of the Church; and much more of the same kind. Nowhere, however, did the feeling find decided public expression until the General Association of Congregational Ministers of Massachusetts saw proper to pass a resolution of censure against Sarah and Angelina Grimké, and issued a pastoral letter, which, in the light and freedom of the present day, must be regarded as a most extraordinary document, to say the least of it. The opening sentences show the degree of authority felt and exercised by the clergy at that time. It maintained that, as ministers were ordained by God, it was their place and duty to judge what food was best to feed to the flock over which they had been made overseers by the Holy Ghost; and that, if they did not preach on certain topics, as the flock desired, the flock had no right to put strangers in their place to do it; that deference and subordination were necessary to the happiness of every society, and peculiarly so to the relation of a people to their pastor; and that the sacred rights of ministers had been violated by having their pulpits opened *without their consent* to lecturers on various subjects of reform.

All this might pass without much criticism: but it was followed by a tirade against woman-preachers, aimed at the Grimké sisters especially, which was as narrow as it was shallow. The dangers which threatened the female character and the permanent injury likely to result to society, if the example of these women should be followed, were vigorously portrayed. Women were reminded that their power was in their dependence; that God had given them their weakness for their protection; and that when they assumed the tone and place of man, as public reformers, they made the care and protection of man seem unnecessary. "If the vine," this letter fancifully said, " whose strength and beauty is to lean upon the trellis-work, and half conceal its clusters, thinks to assume the independence and the overshadowing nature of the elm, it will not only cease to bear fruit, but will fall in shame and dishonor into the dust."

Sarah Grimké had just begun a series of letters on the " Province of Woman" for the *N. E. Spectator*, when this pastoral effusion came out. Her third letter was devoted to it. She showed in the clearest manner the unsoundness of its assertions, and the unscriptural and unchristian spirit in which they were made. The delicate irony with which she also exposed the ignorance and the shallowness of its author must have caused him to blush for very shame.

Whittier's muse, too, found the Pastoral Letter a fitting theme for its vigorous, sympathetic utterances. The poem thus inspired is perhaps one of the very best among his many songs of freedom. It will be remembered as beginning thus : —

> " So this is all! the utmost reach
> Of priestly power the mind to fetter,
> When laymen *think*, when women *preach*,
> A war of words, a ' Pastoral Letter!' "

Up to this time nothing had been said by either of the sisters in their lectures concerning their views about women. They had carefully confined themselves to the subject of slavery, and the attendant topics of immediate emancipation, abstinence from the use of slave products, the errors of the Colonization Society, and the sin of prejudice on account of color. But now that they found their own rights invaded, they began to feel it was time to look out for the rights of their whole sex.

The Rev. Amos Phelps, a staunch abolitionist, wrote a private letter to the sisters, remonstrating earnestly but kindly against their lecturing to men and women, and requesting permission to publish the fact of his having done so, with a declaration on their part that they preferred having female audiences only. Angelina says to Jane Smith : —

"I wish you could see sister's admirable reply to this. We told him we were entirely willing he should publish anything he felt it right to, but that we could not consent to his saying in our name that we preferred female audiences only, because in so saying we should surrender a fundamental principle, believing, as we did, that as *moral* beings it was our duty to appeal to all moral beings on this subject, without any distinction of sex. He thinks we are throwing a responsibility on the Anti-Slavery Society which will greatly injure it. To this we replied that we would write to Elizur Wright, and give the Executive Committee an opportunity to throw off all such responsibility by publishing the facts that we had no commission from them, and were not either responsible to or dependent on them. I wrote this letter. H. B. Stanton happened to be here at the time; after reading all the letters, he wrote to Elizur Wright, warning him by *no* means to publish anything which would in the least appear to disapprove of what we were doing. I do not know what the result will be. My only fear is that some of our anti-slavery brethren will commit themselves, in this excitement, against *women's rights and duties* before they examine the subject, and will, in a few years, regret the steps they may now take. This will soon be an absorbing topic. It must be discussed whether women are moral and responsible beings, and whether there is such a thing as male and female virtues, male and female duties, etc. My opinion is that there is no difference, and that this false idea has run the ploughshare of ruin over the whole field of morality. My idea is that whatever is morally right for a man to do is morally right for a woman to do. I recognize no rights but human rights. I know nothing of men's rights and women's rights; for in Christ Jesus there is neither male nor female. . . . I am persuaded that woman is not to be as she has been, a mere second-hand agent in the regeneration of a fallen world, but the acknowledged equal and co-worker with man in this glorious work. . . . Hubbard Winslow of Boston has just preached a sermon to set forth the proper sphere of our sex. I am truly glad that men are not ashamed to come out boldly and tell us just what is in their hearts."

In another letter she mentions that a clergyman gave out a notice of one of their meetings, at the request, he said, of his deacons, but under protest; and he earnestly advised his members, particularly the women, not to go and hear them. At a meeting, also, at Pepperell, where they had to speak in a barn, on account of the feeling against them, she mentions that an Orthodox clergyman opened the meeting with prayer, but went out immediately after finishing, declaring that he would as soon rob a hen-roost as remain there and hear a woman speak in public.

This, however, did not prevent the crowding of the barn "almost to suffocation," and deep attention on the part of those assembled.

In the face of all this censure and ridicule, the two sisters continued in the discharge of a duty to which they increasingly felt they were called from on high. The difficulties, inconveniences, and discomforts to which they were constantly subjected, and of which the women reformers of the present day know so little, were borne cheerfully, and accepted as means of greater refinement and purification for the Lord's work. They were often obliged to ride six or eight or ten miles through the sun or rain, in stages or wagons over rough roads to a meeting, speak two hours, and return the same distance to their temporary abiding-place. For many weeks they held five and six meetings a week, in a different place every time, were often poorly lodged and poorly fed, especially the latter, as they ate nothing which they did not know to be the product of free labor; taking cold frequently, and speaking when ill enough to be in bed, but sustained through all by faith in the justice of their cause, and by their simple reliance upon the love and guidance of an Almighty Father. The record of their journeyings, as copied by Angelina from her day-book for the benefit of Jane Smith, is very interesting, as showing how, in spite of continued opposition to them, anti-slavery sentiment grew under their eloquent preaching. Wendell Phillips says: "I can never forget the impulse our cause received when those two sisters doubled our hold on New England in 1837 and 1838, and made a name, already illustrious in South Carolina by great services, equally historical in Massachusetts, in the two grandest movements of our day."

Angelina's eloquence must have been something marvellous. The sweet, persuasive voice, the fluent speech, and occasionally a flash of the old energy, were all we who knew her in later years were granted, to show us what had been; but it was enough to confirm the accounts given by those who had felt the power of her oratory in those early times. Says Wendell Phillips: "I well remember evening after evening listening to eloquence such as never then had been heard from a woman. She swept the chords of the human heart with a power that has never been surpassed and rarely equalled."

Mr. Lincoln, in whose pulpit she lectured in Gardiner, says : " Never before or since have I seen an audience so held and so moved by any public speaker, man or woman ; and never before or since have I seen a Christian pulpit so well filled, nor in the pews seen such absorbed hearers."

Robert F. Walcutt testifies in the same manner. " Angelina," he says, " possessed a rare gift of eloquence, a calm power of persuasion, a magnetic influence over those who listened to her, which carried conviction to hearts that nothing before had reached. I shall never forget the wonderful manifestation of this power during six successive evenings, in what was then called the Odeon. It was the old Boston Theatre, which had been converted into a music hall ; the four galleries rising above the auditorium all crowded with a silent audience carried away with the calm, simple eloquence which narrated what she and her sister had seen from their earliest days. And yet this Odeon scene, the audience so quiet and intensely absorbed, occurred at the most enflamed period of the anti-slavery contest. The effective agent in this phenomenon was Angelina's serene, commanding eloquence, a wonderful gift, which enchained attention, disarmed prejudice, and carried her hearers with her."

Another, who often heard her, speaks of the gentle, firm, and impressive voice which could ring out in clarion tones when speaking in the name of the Lord to let the oppressed go free.

Many travelled long distances to hear her. Mechanics left their shops, and laborers came in out of the field, and sat almost motionless throughout her meetings, showing impatience only when the lecture was over and they could hear no more. Sarah's speaking, though fully as earnest, was not nearly so effective as Angelina's. She was never very fluent, and cared little for the flowers of rhetoric. She could state a truth in clear and forcible terms, but the language was unvarnished, sometimes harsh, while the manner of speaking was often embarrassed. She understood and felt her deficiencies, and preferred to serve the cause through her pen rather than through her voice. Writing to Sarah Douglass, in September, 1837, she says: —

"That the work in which we are engaged is in a peculiar manner dear Angelina's, I have no doubt. God called and qualified her for it by deep travail of spirit. I do not think my mind ever passed through the preparation hers did, and I regard my being with her more as an evidence of our dear Saviour's care for us, than a design that I should perform a conspicuous part in this labor of love. Hence, although at first I was permitted to assist her, as her strength increased and her ability to do the work assigned her was perfected, I was more and more withdrawn from the service. Nor do I think anyone ought to regret it. My precious sister has a gift in lecturing, in reasoning and elucidating, so far superior to mine, that I know the cause is better pleaded if left entirely in her hands. My spirit has not bowed to this dispensation without prayer for resignation to being thus laid aside, but since I have been enabled to take the above view, I have been contented to be silent, believing that so is the will of God."

Sarah's religious anxieties seem all to have vanished before the absorbing interest of her new work. She had no longer time to think of herself, or to stand and question the Lord on every going-out and coming-in. She relied upon Him as much as ever, but she understood Him better, and had more faith in His loving-kindness. In a letter to T. D. Weld, she says: —

" For many years I have been inquiring the way to Zion, and now I know not but I shall have to surrender all or many long-cherished points of religion, and come back to the one simple direction: 'Follow after holiness, without which no man shall see the Lord.' "

All her letters show how much happier she was under her new experiences. Angelina thus writes of her: —

" Sister Sarah enjoys more real comfort of mind than I ever saw her enjoy before, and it is delightful to be thus yoked with her in this work."

But with Sarah's wider, fuller sympathies came bitter regrets over the spiritual bondage which had kept her idle and useless so long. And yet, in spite of all, her heart still clung to the Society of Friends, and the struggle to give them up, to resign the long-cherished hope of being permitted to preach among them the unsearchable riches of Christ, was very great. But conscientious and true to her convictions even here, as her own eyes had been mercifully opened to the faults of this system of religion, she must do what she could to help others. Under a solemn sense of responsibility, she wrote and printed a pamphlet exposing the errors of the Quaker Church, and showing the withering influence it exerted over all moral and religious progress. For this, she doubted not, she would be at once disowned; but Friends seem to have been very loth to part with the two rebellious subjects, who had certainly given them much trouble, but in whom they could not help feeling a certain pride of ownership. They showed their willingness to be patient yet a little while longer.

All through the summer and early fall, the meetings were continued with slightly decreasing opposition, and continued abuse from press and pulpit and "good society." Sarah still bore her share of the labors, frequently speaking an hour at a time, and taking charge chiefly of the legal side of the question of slavery, while the moral and religious sides were left for Angelina. At Amesbury, Angelina writes: —

"We met the mother, aunt, and sister of brother Whittier. They received us at their sweet little cottage with sincere pleasure, I believe, they being as thoroughgoing as their dear J. G. W., whom they seem to know how to value. He was absent, serving the good cause in New York."

At an evening meeting they held at Amesbury, a letter was handed Angelina, which stated that some gentlemen were present, who had just returned from the South, and had formed very different opinions from those of the lecturers, and would like to state them to the meeting. Sarah read the letter aloud, and requested the gentlemen to proceed with their remarks. Two arose, and soon showed how little they really knew, and how close an affinity they felt with slave-holders. A discussion ensued, which lasted an hour, when Angelina went on with her lecture on the "Dangers of Slavery." When it was over, the two gentlemen of Southern sympathies requested that another opportunity be granted for a free discussion of the subject. This was agreed to, and the 19th of the month, August, settled upon.

This was another and a great step forward, and when known gave rise to renewed denunciations, the press being particularly severe against such an unheard-of thing, which, it was declared, would not be tolerated if the

Misses Grimké were not members of the Society of
Friends. The abolitionists, however, rallied to their support, H. B. Stanton even proposing to arrange some
meeting where he and they could speak together. But
even Angelina shrank from such an irretrievable committal
on his part as this would be, and did not think the time
had yet come for such an anomaly. On the 19th they
returned to Amesbury, and Angelina writes that great
excitement prevailed, and that many had come from
neighboring towns to hear two *Massachusetts men defend*
slavery against the accusations of two *Southern women.*
" May the blessed Master," she adds, " stand at our right
hand in this trying and uncommon predicament."

Two evenings were given to the discussion, the hall
being packed both evenings, many, even ladies, standing
the whole time. Angelina gives no details about it, as,
she says, she sends a paper with a full account to Jane
Smith; but we may judge of the interest it excited from
the fact that the people urged a continuance of the discussion for two more evenings, which, however, the sisters
were obliged to decline. Angelina adds : —

" Everyone is talking about it; but we have given
great offence on account of our womanhood, which seems
to be as objectionable as our abolitionism. The whole
land seems aroused to discussion on the province of
woman, and I am glad of it. We are willing to bear the
brunt of the storm, if we can only be the means of
making a breach in the wall of public opinion, which lies
right in the way of woman's true dignity, honor, and
usefulness. Sister Sarah does preach up woman's rights
most nobly and fearlessly, and we find that many of our
New England sisters are prepared to receive these strange
doctrines, feeling, as they do, that our whole sex needs

emancipation from the thraldom of public opinion. What dost thou think of some of *them walking* two, four, six, and eight miles to attend our meetings?"

This preaching of the much-vexed doctrine was, however, done chiefly in private, indeed altogether so by Angelina. Sarah's nature was so impulsive that she could not always refrain from putting in a stroke for her cherished views when it seemed to fit well into the argument of a lecture. What prominent abolitionists thought of the subject in its relation to the anti-slavery cause, and especially what T. D. Weld and John G. Whittier thought, must be told in another chapter.

CHAPTER XIV.

AMONG the most prominent opposers of immediate emancipation were Dr. Lyman Beecher and the members of his remarkable family; and though they ultimately became converts to it, even so far as to allow a branch of the " underground railway" to run through their barn, their conversion was gradual, and only arrived at after various controversies and discussions, and much bitter feeling between them and the advocates of the unpopular cause. Opposed to slavery in the abstract, that is, believing it to be a sin to hold a fellow creature in bondage for the "*mere purposes of gain*," they utterly condemned all agitation of the question. The Church and the Gospel were, with them, as with so many evangelical Christians, the true means through which evils should be reached and reforms effected. All efforts outside were unwise and useless, not to say sinful. And further, as Catherine Beecher expressed it, they considered the matter of Southern slavery as one with which the North was no more called to interfere than in the abolition of the press-gang system in England, or the tithe system in Ireland. Some chapters back, the short but pleasant friendship of Catherine Beecher and Angelina Grimké was mentioned. Very soon after that little episode, the Beechers removed to

Cincinnati, where the doctor was called to the Presidency
of the Lane Theological Seminary. We can well understand that the withdrawal of nearly all its students after
the great discussion was a sore trial to the Beechers, and
intensified their already adverse feelings towards abolitionists. The only result of this with which we have to
do is the volume published by Catherine Beecher during
the summer of 1837, entitled " Miss Beecher on the Slave
Question," and addressed to Angelina Grimké.

Catherine was the true counterpart of her father, and
the most intellectual of his children, but she lacked the
gentle, feminine graces, and was so wanting in tenderness
and sympathy that Angelina charitably implies that her
heart was sunk forever with her lover, Professor Fisher of
Yale, who perished in a storm at sea. With independence, striking individuality, and entire freedom from
timidity of any sort, it would appear perfectly natural
that Catherine should espouse the Woman's Rights reform, even though opposing that of abolitionism. But
she presented the singular anomaly of a strong-minded
woman, already successful in taking care of herself, advo-
cating woman's subordination to man, and prescribing for
her efforts at self-help limits so narrow that only the few
favored as she was could venture within them.

Her book was received with much favor by slave-holders and their apologists, though it was harshly criticised
by a few of the more sensible of the former. These declared that they had more respect for abolitionists who
openly denounced the system of slavery, than for those
people who, in order to please the South, cloaked their
real sentiments under a garb like that of Miss Beecher's
book. It was also severely handled by abolitionists, and
Lucretia Mott wrote a very able review of it, which

Angelina, however, pronounced entirely too mild. She writes to Jane Smith:

"Catherine's arguments are the most insidious things I ever read, and I feel it my duty to answer them; only, I know not how to find language strong enough to express my indignation at the view she takes of woman's character and duty."

The answer was given in a number of sharp, terse, letters, sent to the *Liberator* from various places where the sisters stopped while lecturing. A few passages will convey some idea of the spirit and style of these letters, thirteen in number. In the latter part of the second letter she says: —

"Dost thou ask what I mean by emancipation? I will explain myself in a few words.

"1st. It is to reject with indignation the wild and guilty phantasy that man can hold *property* in man.

"2d. To pay the laborer his hire, for he is worthy of it.

"3d. No longer to deny him the right of marriage, but to let every man have his own wife, and let every woman have her own husband, as saith the apostle.

"4th. To let parents have their own children, for they are the gift of the Lord to them, and no one else has any right to them.

"5th. No longer to withhold the advantages of education, and the privilege of reading the Bible.

"6th. To put the slave under the protection of equitable laws.

"Now why should not *all* this be done immediately? Which of these things is to be done next year, and which the year after? and so on. *Our* immediate emancipation means doing justice and loving mercy *to-day*, and this is what we call upon every slave-holder to do. . . .

"I have seen too much of slavery to be a gradualist. I dare not, in view of such a system, tell the slave-holder that he is 'physically unable to emancipate his slaves.'[1] I say *he is able* to let the oppressed go free, and that such heaven-daring atrocities ought to cease *now*, henceforth, and forever. Oh, my very soul is grieved to find a Northern woman 'thus sewing pillows under all arm-holes,' framing and fitting soft excuses for the slave-holder's conscience, whilst with the same pen she is *professing* to regard slavery as a sin. 'An open enemy is better than such a secret friend.'

"Hoping that thou mayst soon be emancipated from such inconsistency, I remain until then,

"Thine *out* of the bonds of Christian abolitionism.

"A. E. GRIMKÉ."

The last letter, which Angelina says she wrote in sadness and read to her sister in tears, ends thus : —

"After endeavoring to show that woman has no moral right to exercise the right of petition for the dumb and stricken slave; no business to join, in any way, in the excitement which anti-slavery principles are producing in our country; no business to join abolition societies, etc., thou professest to tell our sisters what they are to do in order to bring the system of slavery to an end. And now, my dear friend, what does all thou hast said in many pages amount to? Why, that women are to exert their influence in private life to allay the excitement which exists on this subject, and to quench the flame of sympathy

---

[1] The plea made by many of the apologists was that, as the laws of some of the States forbade emancipation, the masters were physically unable to free their slaves.

in the hearts of their fathers, husbands, brothers, and sons. Fatal delusion! Will Christian women heed such advice?

"Hast thou ever asked thyself what the slave would think of thy book if he could read it? Dost thou know that, from the beginning to the end, not a word of compassion for *him* has fallen from thy pen? Recall, I pray, the memory of hours which thou spent in writing it. Was the paper once moistened by the tear of pity? Did thy heart once swell with sympathy for thy sister in *bonds?* Did it once ascend to God in broken accents for the deliverance of the captive? Didst thou even ask thyself what the free man of color would think of it? Is it such an exhibition of slavery and prejudice as will call down *his* blessing on thy head? Hast thou thought of *these* things? or carest thou not for the blessings and prayers of these our suffering brethren? Consider, I entreat, the reception given to thy book by the apologists of slavery. What meaneth that loud acclaim with which they hail it? Oh, listen and weep, and let thy repentings be kindled together, and speedily bring forth, I beseech thee, fruits meet for repentance, and henceforth show thyself faithful to Christ and His bleeding representative, the slave.

"I greatly fear that thy book might have been written just as well, hadst thou not had the heart of a woman. It bespeaks a superior intellect, but paralyzed and spell-bound by the sorcery of a worldly-minded expediency. Where, oh, where in its pages are the outpourings of a soul overwhelmed with a sense of the heinous crimes of our nation, and the necessity of immediate repentance? . . . Farewell! Perhaps on a dying bed thou mayst vainly wish that '*Miss Beecher on the Slave Question*' might perish with the mouldering hand which penned its cold and heartless pages. But I forbear, and in deep sadness of heart, but in tender love though I thus speak, I bid thee again, farewell. Forgive me if I have wronged thee, and pray for her who still feels like

"Thy sister in the bonds of a common sisterhood.

"A. E. GRIMKE."

While Angelina was writing these letters, Sarah was publishing her letters on the "Province of Woman" in the *Spectator*. This was a heavier dose than Boston could stand at one time; harsh and bitter things were said about the sisters, notices of their meetings were torn down or effaced, and abolitionism came to be so mixed up in the public mind with Woman's Rights, that anti-slavery leaders generally began to feel anxious lest their cause should suffer by being identified with one to which the large majority of abolitionists was decidedly opposed. Even among them, however, there was a difference of opinion, Garrison, H. C. Wright and others, non-resistants, encouraging the agitation of Woman's Rights. A few lines from one of Angelina's letters will best define the position taken by herself and Sarah.

"Sister and I," she writes, "feel quite ready for the discussion about women, but brothers Whittier and Weld entreat us to let it alone for the present, because it will involve topics of such vast importance, — a paid ministry, clerical domination, etc., — and will, they fear, divert our attention and that of the community from the anti-slavery cause; and that the wrongs of the slave are so much greater than the wrongs of woman, they ought not to be confounded. In their letters, received last week, they regret exceedingly that the letters in the *Spectator* had been written. They think just as we do, but believe that, for the time being, a persevering, practical assertion of woman's right to speak to mixed audiences is the best one we can make, and that we had better keep out of controversies, as our hands are full. On the other hand, we fear that the leaven of the Pharisees will be so assiduously worked into the minds of the people, that if they come to hear us, they will be constantly thinking it is a *shame* for us to speak in the churches, and that we shall lose that influence which we should otherwise have. We know that *our* views on this subject are quite new to the mass of the people of this State, and I think it best to throw them open for their consideration, just letting them have both sides of the argument to look at, at the same time. Indeed some wanted to have a meeting in Boston for us to speak on this subject now, and we went into town on purpose to hold a conference about it at Maria Chapman's. She, Mary Parker, and sister were against it for the present, fearing lest it would bring down such a storm upon our heads, that we could not work in the country, and so Henrietta Sargent and I yielded, and I suppose this is the wisest plan, though, as brother Stanton says, I am ready for the battle *now.* I am still glad of sister's letters, and believe they are doing great good. Some noble-minded women cheer her on, and she feels encouraged to persevere, the brethren notwithstanding. I tell them that this is *a part* of the great doctrine of Human Rights, and can no more be separated from emancipation than the light from the heat of the sun ; the rights of the slave and of woman blend like the colors of the rainbow. However, I rarely introduce this topic into my addresses, except to urge my sisters up to duty. Our *brethren* are dreadfully afraid of this kind of amalgamation. I am very glad to hear that Lucretia Mott addressed the Moral Reform Society, and am earnest in the hope that *we* are only pioneers, going before a host of worthy women who will come up to the help of the Lord against the mighty."

The letters of Whittier and Weld, alluded to by Angelina, are so good and so important that I feel no reluctance in giving them here almost entire. The first is Whittier's, and is dated : " Office of Am. A. S. Soc., 14th of 8th Mo., 1837," — and is as follows :

" MY DEAR SISTERS, — I have been waiting for an opportunity to answer the letter which has been so kindly sent me. I am anxious, too, to hold a long conversation with you on the subject of *war*, human government, and church and family government. The more I reflect on this subject, the more difficulty I find, and the more decidedly am I of opinion that we ought to hold all these matters far aloof from the cause of abolition. Our good friend, H. C. Wright, with the best intentions in the world, is doing great injury by a different course. He is making the anti-slavery party responsible in a great degree, for his, to say the least, startling opinions. I do not censure him for them, although I cannot subscribe to them in all their length and breadth. But let him keep them distinct from the cause of emancipation. This is his duty. Those who subscribe money to the Anti-Slavery Society do it in the belief that it will be spent in the propagation, not of Quakerism or Presbyterianism, but of the doctrines of Immediate Emancipation. To employ an agent who devotes half his time and talents to the propagation of 'no human or no family government' doctrines in connection — *intimate connection* — with the doctrines

of abolition, is a fraud upon the patrons of the cause. Just
so with papers. Brother Garrison errs, I think, in this
respect. He takes the 'no church, and no human government' ground, as, for instance, in his Providence
speech. Now, in his prospectus, he engaged to give his
subscribers an anti-slavery paper, and his subscribers made
their contract with him on that ground. If he fills his
paper with Grahamism and no governmentism, he de-
frauds his subscribers. However, I know that brother
Garrison does not look at it in this light.

"In regard to another subject, '*the rights of woman*,'
you are now doing much and nobly to vindicate and
assert the rights of woman. Your lectures to crowded
and promiscuous audiences on a subject manifestly, in
many of its aspects, *political*, interwoven with the frame-
work of the government, are practical and powerful
assertions of the right and the duty of woman to labor
side by side with her brother for the welfare and redemption of the world. Why, then, let me ask, is it necessary
for you to enter the lists as controversial writers on this
question? Does it not *look*, dear sisters, like abandoning
in some degree the cause of the poor and miserable slave,
sighing from the cotton plantations of the Mississippi,
and whose cries and groans are forever sounding in our
ears, for the purpose of arguing and disputing about
some trifling oppression, political or social, which we may
ourselves suffer? Is it not forgetting the great and
dreadful wrongs of the slave in a selfish crusade against
some paltry grievance of our own? Forgive me if I have
stated the case too strongly. I would not for the world
interfere with you in matters of conscientious duty, but I
wish you would weigh candidly the whole subject, and
see if it does not *seem* an abandonment of your first love.

Oh, let us try to forget everything but our duty to God and our fellow beings; to dethrone the selfish principle, and to strive to win over the hard heart of the oppressor by truth kindly spoken. The Massachusetts Congregational Association can do you no harm if you do not allow its splenetic and idle manifesto to divert your attention from the great and holy purpose of your souls.

"Finally, dear sisters, rest assured that you have my deepest and warmest sympathy; that my heart rejoices to know that you are mighty instruments in the hands of Him who hath come down to deliver. May the canopy of His love be over you, and His peace be with you!

"Your friend and brother,

"Jno. G. Whittier."

Weld's first letter, written the day after Whittier's, begins by defining his own position on the disturbing question. He says: "As to the rights and wrongs of woman, it is an old theme with me. It was the *first* subject I ever discussed. In a little debating society, when a boy, I took the ground that sex neither qualified nor disqualified for the discharge of any functions, mental, moral, or spiritual: that there is no reason why woman should not make laws, administer justice, sit in the chair of State, plead at the Bar, or in the pulpit, if she has the qualifications, just as much as man. What I advocated in boyhood, I advocate now — that woman, in *every particular*, shares, equally with man, rights and responsibilities. Now that I have made this statement of my creed on this point, to show you that we fully agree, except that I probably go much further than you do, I must say I do most deeply regret that you have begun a series of articles in the papers on the rights of woman. Why, my dear sisters, the best possible advocacy which you can make is just what you are making day by day. Thousands hear you every week who have all their lives held that women must not speak in public. Such a practical refutation of the dogma which your speaking furnishes has already converted multitudes."

He then goes on to urge two strong points: —

1st. That as Southerners, and having been brought up among slaveholders, they could do more to convince the North than twenty Northern women, though they could speak as well, and that they would lose this peculiar advantage the moment they took up another subject.

2d. That almost any other women of their capacity and station could produce a greater effect on the public mind on that subject than they, because they were Quakers, and woman's right to speak and minister was a Quaker doctrine. Therefore, for these and other reasons, he urged them to leave the lesser work to others who could do it better than they, and devote, consecrate their whole souls, bodies, and spirits to the greater work which they could do far better than anybody else. He continues: "Let us all first wake up the nation to lift millions of slaves from the dust and turn them into men, and then, when we all have our hand in, it will be an easy matter to take millions of women from their knees and set them on their feet; or, in other words, transform them from *babies* into *women*."

A spirited, almost dogmatic, controversy was the result of these letters. In a letter to Jane Smith, Angelina says: "I cannot understand why they (the abolitionists) so exceedingly regret sister's having begun those letters. Brother Weld was not satisfied with writing us *one* letter about them, but we have received two more setting forth various reasons why we should not moot the subject of woman's rights *at all*, but our judgment is not convinced, and we hardly know what to do about it, for we have just as high an opinion of Brother Garrison's views, and *he* says, '*go on.*' . . . The great effort of abolitionists now seems to be to keep every topic but slavery out of view, and hence their opposition to Henry C. Wright and his preaching anti-government doctrines, and our even *writing* on woman's rights. Oh, if I *only* saw they were *right* and *we* were *wrong*, I would yield immediately."

One of the two other letters from T. D. Weld, referred to by Angelina, is a very long one, covering over ten pages of the old-fashioned foolscap paper, and is in reply to letters received from the sisters, and which were afterwards returned to them and probably destroyed. I have concluded to make some extracts from this long letter from Mr. Weld, not only on account of the arguments used, but to show the frank, fearless spirit with which he met the reasoning of his two " sisters." When we consider that he was even then courting Angelina, his hardihood is a little surprising.

After observing that he had carefully read their letters, and made an abstract on half a sheet of paper of the " positions and conclusions found therein," he continues: —

" This abstract I have been steadily looking at with great marvelling,

" 1st. That you should argue at length the doctrine of Woman's Rights, as though I was a *dissentient ;*

" 2d. That you should so magnify the power of the New England clergy ;

" 3d. That you should so misconceive the actual convictions of ministers and Christians, and almost all, as to the public speaking of women ;

"4th. That you should take the ground that the clergy, and the whole church government, must come down *before* slavery can be abolished (a proposition which to my mind is absurd).

"5th. That you should so utterly overlook the very *threshold* principle upon which alone any moral reformation can be effectually promoted. Oh, dear! There are a dozen other things — marvellables — in your letters; but I must stop short, or I can say nothing on other points.

". . . Now, before we commence action, let us clear the decks; for if they are clogged we shall have foul play. *Overboard* with everything that don't *belong on board.* Now, first, *what is the precise point at issue between us?* I answer first *negatively*, that we may understand each other on all points kindred to the main one. 1st. It is *not* whether *woman's* rights are inferior to *man's* rights."

He then proceeded to state the doctrine of Woman's Rights very forcibly. Of *sex*, he says: —

" Its *only* design is not to give nor to take away, nor in any respect to modify, or even touch, rights or responsibilities in any sense, except so far as the peculiar offices of each sex may afford less or more *opportunity* and ability for the exercise of rights, and the discharge of responsibilities, but merely to continue and enlarge the human department of God's government."

For an entire page he continues in this manner of " *negatives* " to " *clear the decks*," until he has shown through seven negative specifications what do *not* constitute the point at issue, and then goes on: —

" Well, waving further negatives, the question at issue between us *is*, whether *you*, S. M. G. and A. E. G., should engage in the public discussion of the rights of

women as a distinct topic. Here you affirm, and I deny.
Your reasons for doing it, as contained in your *two* letters,
are the following : —

"1st. The *New England Spectator* was *opened;* you
were invited to write on the subject, and some of the
Boston abolitionists *urged* you to do so, and you say,
' We viewed this unexpected opportunity of throwing
our views before the public, as *providential.*'

"*Answer.* When the devil is hard pushed, and likely to
be run down in the chase, it is an old trick of his to start
some smaller game, and thus cause his pursuers to strike
off from his own track on to that of one of his imps. It
was certainly a very *providential* opportunity for Ne-
hemiah to 'throw his views before the public,' when Ge-
shem, Sanballat, and Tobiah *invited* and urged him to stop
building the wall and hold a public discussion as to the
right to build. And doubtless a great many Jews said to
him, 'Unless we *establish* the right in the first place, it
will surely be taken from us utterly. This is a providential opportunity to preach truth in the very camp of the
enemy.' But who got it up, God or the devil? . . . Look
over the history of the world, and in nine cases out of
ten we shall find that Satan, after being foiled in his arts
to stop a great moral enterprise, has finally succeeded by
diverting the reformers from the *main* point to a *colla-
teral,* and that too just at the *moment* when such diver-
sion brought ruin. Now, even if this opportunity made
it the duty of *somebody* to take up the subject (which is
not proved by the *fact* of the opportunity), why should
you give *your* views, and with *your name ?* Others as
able might be found, and as familiar with the subject.
But you say, others 'are driven off the field, and cannot
answer the objections.' I answer, your *names* do not an-

swer the objections. . . . How very easy to have helped
a third person to the argument. By publicly making an
onset in your own names, in a widely-circulated periodical, upon a doctrine cherished as the apple of their eye
(I don't say really *believed*) by nine tenths of the church
and the world; what was it but a formal challenge to
the whole community for a regular set-to ?"

He proceeds to speak of such a " set to " and debate as
" producing alienation wide-spread in our own ranks, and
introducing confusion and every evil work." He urges
the necessity of vindicating a right "by exercising it,"
instead of simply arguing for it.

Of ministers he says: "True, there is a pretty large
class of ministers who are fierce about it, and will fight,
but a still larger class that will come over *if* they first
witness the successful practice rather than meet it in the
shape of a doctrine to be swallowed. Now, if instead of
blowing a blast through the newspapers, sounding the onset, and summoning the ministers and churches to surrender, you had without any introductory flourish just gone
right among them and lectured, *when* and *where* and *as*
you could find opportunity, and paid no attention to criticism, but pushed right on, without making any ado about
' attacks,' and ' invasions,' and ' opposition,' and have let
the barkers bark their bark out, — within one year you
might have practically brought over five hundred thousand persons, of the very moral *élite* of New England.
You may rely upon it. . . . No moral enterprise, when
prosecuted with ability and any sort of energy, *ever* failed
under heaven so long as its conductors pushed the *main*
principle, and did not strike off until they reached the
summit level. On the other hand, every reform that ever
foundered in mid-sea, was capsized by one of these gusty

side-winds. Nothing more utterly amazes me than the fact that the *conduct* of a great, a *pre-eminently* great moral enterprise, should exhibit so little of a wise, far-sighted, comprehensive *plan.* Surely it is about plain enough to be called *self-evident*, that the only common-sense method of conducting a great moral enterprise is to *start* with a *fundamental, plain principle, so* fundamental as not to involve side-relations, and *so* plain, that it cannot be denied."

The main obvious principle he urges is to be pushed until the community surrenders to it. He adds : —

"Then, when you have drawn them up to the top of the general principle, you can slide them down upon all the derivative principles *all at once.* But if you attempt to start off on a derivative principle, from any other point than the summit level of the main principle, you must beat up stream — yes, up a cataract. It reverses the order of nature, and the laws of mind. . . .

"You put the cart before the horse; you drag the tree by the top, in attempting to push your woman's rights until human rights have gone ahead and broken *the path.*

.   .   .   .   .

"You are both liable, it seems to me, from your structure of mind, to form your opinions upon *too slight* data, and too narrow a range of induction, and to lay your plans and adopt your measures, rather *dazzled* by the glare of false *analogies* than *led on* by the relations of cause and effect. Both of you, but especially Angelina, unless I greatly mistake, are constitutionally tempted to push for *present* effect, and upon the suddenness and impulsiveness of the onset rely mainly for victory. Besides from *her* strong *resistiveness* and constitutional obstinacy, she is liable every moment to turn short from the main point

and spend her whole force upon some little one-side annoy-
ance that might temporarily nettle her. In doing this she
might win a *single battle*, but *lose a whole campaign*. Add
to this, great pride of character, so closely curtained as
to be almost searchless to herself, with a passion for ad-
venture and novel achievements, and she has in all an
amount of temptation to poor human nature that can be
overmastered only by strong conflicts and strong faith.
Under this, a sense of justice so keen that violation of
justice would be likely to lash up such a tide of indignation as would drive her from all anchorage. I say this to
her *not* in raillery. I *believe* it, and therefore utter it. It
is either fiction or fact. If *fiction* it can do no hurt ; if
fact, it may not be in vain in the Lord, and then my
heart's desire and prayer will be fulfilled. May the Lord
have you in his keeping, my own dear sisters.

"Most affectionately, your brother ever,

"T. D. Weld."

"One point I designed to make *more* prominent. It is
this: What is done for the *slave* and *human rights* in
this country *must be done now, now, now.* Delay is
madness, ruin, whereas woman's rights are not a life
and death business, *now or never.* Why can't you have
eyes to see this? The wayfaring man, though a *fool*,
need not err *here*, it is so plain. What will you run a tilt
at next?"

And he names several things, — the tariff, the banks,
English tithe system, burning widows, etc., and adds : —

"If you adopt the views of H. C. Wright, as you are
reported to have done, in his official bulletin of a ' domestic scene' (where you are made to figure conspicuously
among the conquests of the victor as rare spoils gracing

the triumphal car), why then we are in one point of doctrine just as wide asunder as extremes can be."

This letter was answered by Sarah, and with the most admirable patience and moderation. She begins by saying : —

"Angelina is so wrathy that I think it will be unsafe to trust the pen in her hands to reply to thy two last *good* long letters. As I feel nothing but gratitude for the kindness which I am sure dictated them, I shall endeavor to answer them, and, as far as possible, allay thy uneasiness as to the course we are pursuing."

She then proceeds to calmly discuss his objections, and to defend their views on the woman question, which, she says, she regards as second in importance to none, but that she does not feel bound to take up every *caviller* who presents himself, and therefore will not notice some others who had criticised her letters in the *Spectator*.

About H. C. Wright, she says: "I must say a few words concerning Brother Wright, towards whom I do not feel certain that the law of love predominated when thou wrote that part of thy letter relative to him. . . . We feel prepared to avow the principles set forth in the 'domestic scene.' I wonder thou canst not perceive the simplicity and beauty and consistency of the doctrine that all government, whether civil or ecclesiastical, conflicts with the government of Jehovah, and that by the Christian no other can be acknowledged, without leaning more or less on an arm of flesh. Would to God that all abolitionists put their trust where I believe H. C. Wright has placed his, in God alone. . . . I have given my opinions (in the *Spectator*). Those who read them may receive or reject or find fault. I have nothing to do with that. I shall let thee enjoy thy opinion, but I must wait and see

the issue before I conclude it was one of Satan's provi-
dences. . . . I know the opposition to our views arises
in part from the fact that women are habitually regarded
as inferior beings, but chiefly I believe from a desire to
keep them in unholy subjection to man, and one way of
doing this is to deprive us of the means of becoming
their equals by forbidding us the privileges of education
which would fit us for the performance of duty. I am
greatly mistaken if most men have not a desire that
women should be silly. . . . I have not said half I wanted,
but this must suffice for the present, as Angelina has concluded to try her hand at scolding. Farewell, dear
brother. May the Lord reward thee tenfold for thy
kindness, and keep thee in the hollow of His holy hand.
"Thy sister in Jesus,
"S. M. G."

Angelina's part of the letter is not written in the
sweet, Quaker spirit which prevails through Sarah's, but
shows a very interesting consciousness of her power over
the man she addressed.

"Sister," she writes, "seems very much afraid that my
pen will be transformed into a venomous serpent when I
employ it to address thee, my dear brother, and no
wonder, for I like to pay my debts, and, as I received
ten dollars' worth of scolding,[1] I should be guilty of
injustice did I not return the favor. Well! such a lecture I never before had from anyone. What is the
matter with thee? One would really suppose that we

---

[1] Angelina and Sarah had sent Mr. Weld ten dollars for some
supposed debts. He returned it, and said if any trifling sums fell
due, he would take them out in scolding, and pay himself thus.

had actually abandoned the anti-slavery cause, and were roving the country, preaching *nothing* but woman's rights, when, in fact, I can truly say that whenever I lecture, I forget *everything but the slave.* He is all in all for the time being. And what is the reason *I* am to be scolded because *sister* writes letters in the *Spectator?* Please let every woman bear *her own burdens.* Indeed, I should like to know what I have done yet? And dost thou really think in my answer to C. E. Beecher's absurd views of woman that I had better suppress my own? If so, I will do it, as thou makest such a monster out of the molehill, but my judgment is *not* convinced that in this incidental way it is wrong to throw light on the subject."

She speaks very gratefully of "Brother Lincoln, of Gardner," who rejoiced to have them speak in his pulpit, and says: —

"My *keen sense of justice* compels me to admire such nobility. He hoped sister would give her views on this branch of the subject in the *Spectator.* He thought they were needed, and *we* are well convinced they are, T. D. W. notwithstanding. So much for my bump of obstinacy which even thy sledge-hammer cannot beat down."

The subsequent correspondence, which I regret I have not room to insert, shows that the remonstrances of Whittier and Weld were effective in restraining, for the time being, the impatience of the sisters to urge in their public meetings what, however, they faithfully preached in private — their conviction that the wrongs of woman were the root of *all* oppression.

Sarah meekly writes to "brother Weld."

"After a struggle with my feelings, so severe that I

was almost tempted to turn back from the anti-slavery cause, I have given up to what seemed the inevitable, and have thought little of it since. Perhaps I have done wrong, and if so, I trust I shall see it and repent it. I do not intend to make any promises, because I may have reason to regret them, but I do not know that I shall scribble any more on the objectionable topic of woman."

This interesting controversy did not end until several more letters had passed back and forth, and various other topics had been brought in; but it was carried through with the same spirit of candor and love on all sides which marked the beginning. There was one subject introduced, a sort of side-question which I must notice, as it reveals in a very pleasant manner the religious principle and manly moral courage of Theodore D. Weld. At the close of one of her letters, Sarah says: —

"Now just as it has come into my head, please tell me whether thy clothing costs one hundred dollars per annum? I ask because it was insisted upon that Mr. Weld must spend that amount on his wardrobe, and I as strenuously insisted he did not. It was thought impossible a gentleman could spend less, but I think anti-slavery agents know better."

To this, he answered thus, at the end of one of *his* letters.

"Oh! I forgot the wardrobe! I suppose you are going to take me to task about my shag-overcoat, linsey-woolsey coat, and cowhide shoes; for you Quakers are as notional about *quality* as you are precise about *cut*. Well, now to the question. While I was travelling and lecturing, I think that *one* year my clothing must have cost me nearly one hundred dollars. It was the first year of my lecturing in the West, when one entire suit and part of another were destroyed or nearly so by mobs. Since I resigned my commission as agent, which is now nearly a year, my clothing has not cost me one third that amount. I don't think it *even* cost me fifty dollars a year, except the year I spoke of, when it was ruined by mobs, and the year 1832, when, in travelling, I lost it all with my other baggage in the Alum River. There, I believe I have answered your question as well as I can. However, I have always had to encounter the criticism and chidings of my acquaintances about my coarse dress. They will have it that I have always curtailed my influence and usefulness by such a John the Baptist attire as I have always been habited in. But I have remarked that those persons who have beset me on that score have shown in some way that they had their hearts set more or less on showing off their persons to advantage by their dress. Now I think of it, I believe you are in great danger of making a little god out of your caps and your drab color, and '*thee*' and '*thou.*' Besides, the tendency is quite questionable. The moment certain shades of color, or a certain combination of letters, or modulation of sounds, or arrangement of seams and angles, are made the *sine qua non* of religion and principle, that moment religion and principle are hurled from their vantage-ground and become *slaves* instead of *rulers.* I cannot get it out of my mind that these must be a fetter on the spirit that clings to such stereotyped forms and ceremonies that rustle and clatter the more because life and spirit and power do not inhabit them. Think about it, dear sisters."

In Sarah's next letter to him she says : —

"Now first about the wardrobe. Thou art greatly mistaken in supposing that I meant to quiz thee; no, not I, indeed. I wish from my heart more of us who take the profession of Jesus on our lips were willing to wear shag cloaks and linsey-woolsey garments. Now I may inform thee that, notwithstanding my prim caps, etc., I am as economical as thou art. I do many things in the way of dress to please my friends, but perhaps their watchfulness is needful."

Dear Aunt Sarah! these last words will make many smile who remember how scrupulously careful she was about spending more on her dress than was absolutely necessary to cleanliness and health. Every dollar beyond this she felt was taken from the poor or from some benevolent enterprise. The watchfulness of her friends was indeed needful!

It appears from the above correspondence that both Sarah and Angelina had become tinctured with the doctrines of "non-resistance," which, within a few years, had gained some credit with a few "perfectionists" and active reformers in and about Boston. They had been presented by Lydia Maria Child, a genial writer, under the guise of the Scriptural doctrine of love. This sentiment was held to be adequate to the regulation of social and political life: by it, ruffians were to be made to stand in awe of virtue; thieves, burglars, and murderers were to be made ashamed of themselves, and turned into honest and amiable citizens; children were to be governed without punishment; and the world was to be made a paradise. Rev. Henry C. Wright, a man of some ability, but tossed by every wind of doctrine, embraced the new gospel. He applied its principles to public matters. From the essential sinfulness of all forms of force, if used towards human beings, he inferred that penal laws, prisons, sheriffs, and criminal courts should be dispensed with; that governments, which, of necessity, execute their decrees by force, should be abolished; that Christians should not take part in politics, either by voting or holding office; that they should not employ force, even to resist encroachment or in the defence of their wives and children; and that although slavery, being a form of force, was wrong, no one should vote against it. The slave-holder was to be converted by love. The free States should show their grief and disapprobation by seceding from the slave States, and by nullifying within their limits any unjust laws passed by the nation. All governments, civil, ecclesiastical, and family, were to disappear, so that the divine law, interpreted by each one for himself, might have free course. To this fanciful, transcendental, and anarchical theory, Mr. Wright made sundry converts, more or less thorough, including Parker Pillsbury, Wm. L. Garrison, and Stephen S. Foster. That he took a good deal of pains to capture the subjects of our biography is evident. He attended their lectures, cultivated their acquaintance, extended to them his sympathy, and made them his guests. There are certain affinities of the non-resistance doctrines with Quakerism, which made them attractive to these two women who had little worldly knowledge, and who had been trained for years in the peace doctrines of the Philadelphia Friends.

It was fortunate for the anti-slavery cause that Sarah and Angelina were warned in time by their New York friends of the fatally dangerous character of the heresies they were inclined to accept. They went no further in that direction. In all their subsequent letters, journals, and papers there is not a word to show that either of them ever entertained no-government notions, or identified herself with persons who did. During the remaining months of their stay in Massachusetts, they devoted them-

selves to their true mission of anti-slavery work, accepting
the co-operation and friendship of all friends of the slave,
but avoiding compromising relations with those known as
"no human government" non-resistants.   This course
was continued in after years, and drew upon them the
disapprobation and strictures of the non-voting, non-fight-
ing faction.   In a letter from Sarah to Augustus Wattles,
dated May 11, 1854, about the time of the Kansas war,
she says : —

"We were fully aware of the severe criticisms passed upon us by many of those who showed their unfitness to be
in the judgment seat, by the unmerciful censure they have
pronounced against us when we were doing what to us
seemed positive duty.   They wanted us to live out Wm.
Lloyd Garrison, not the convictions of our own souls,
entirely unaware that they were exhibiting, in the high
places of moral reform, the genuine spirit of slave-holding
by wishing to curtail the sacred privilege of conscience.
But we have not allowed their unreasonableness to sever
us from them ; they have many noble traits, have acted
grandly for humanity, and it was perhaps a part of their
business to abuse us.   I do not think I love Garrison any
the less for what he has said.   His spirit of intolerance
towards those who did not draw in his traces, and his
adulation of those who surrendered themselves to his
guidance, have always been exceedingly repulsive to me,
weaknesses which marred the beauty and symmetry of
his character, and prevented its symmetrical development,
but nevertheless I know the stern principle which is the
basis of his action.   He is Garrison and nobody else, and
all I ask is that he would let others be themselves."

The feeling thus expressed was probably never changed
until after the sisters had taken up their residence in the

neighborhood of Boston, when visits were interchanged with Mr. Garrison, and friendly relations established, which ended only with death.   It is certain, however, that Sarah and Angelina sympathized with the stalwart freemen who used Sharp's rifles in the defence of free Kansas, who voted the Liberty, Free Soil, and Republican ticket, who elected Abraham Lincoln President, and who shouldered muskets against the rebels.

CHAPTER XV.

THE anti-slavery cause, and intimate association with so many of its enthusiastic advocates, had indeed done much for Sarah Grimké. Her mind was rapidly becoming purified from the dross that had clogged it so long; religious doubts and difficulties were fading away one by one, and the wide, warm sympathies of her nature now freed, expanded gladly to a new world of light and love and labor. As she expressed it, she was like one coming into a clear brisk atmosphere, after having been long shut up in a close room. Her drowsy faculties were all stirred and invigorated, and though her disappointments had left wounds whose pain must always remind her of them, she had no longer time to sit down and bemoan them. There was so much to do in the broad, fresh fields which stretched around her, and she had been idle so long! Is it any wonder that she tried to grasp too much at first?

The affection between her and Angelina was growing daily more tender — perhaps a little more maternal on her part. Drawn closer together by the now complete separation from every member of their own family, and by the disapproval and coldness of their Philadelphia friends, they were an inexpressible solace and help to each other. Identified in all their trials, as now in their labors, they worked together in a sweet unity of spirit, which lessened every difficulty and lightened every burden.

They continued to lecture almost uninterruptedly for five months, and though the prejudice against them as women appeared but slightly diminished, people were becoming familiarized to the idea of women speaking in public, and the way was gradually being cleared for the advance-guard of that noble army which has brought about so many changes favorable to the weak and down-trodden of its own sex.

Invitations to speak came to the sisters from all parts of the State, and not even by dividing their labors among the smaller towns could they begin to respond to all who wished to hear them. Sometimes the crowds around the place of meeting were so great that a second hall or church would have to be provided, and Sarah speak in one, while Angelina spoke in the other. At one place, where over a thousand people crowded into a church, one of the joists gave way; it was propped up, but soon others began to crack, and, although the people were warned to leave that part of the building, only a few obeyed, and it was found impossible to persuade them to go, or to consent to have the speaking stopped.

At another place ladders were put up at all the windows, and men crowded upon them, and tenaciously held their uncomfortable positions through the whole meeting. In one or two places they were refused a meeting-house, on account of strong sectarian feeling against them as Quakers. At Worcester they had to adjourn from a large Congregational church to a small Methodist one, because the clergyman of the former suddenly returned from an absence, and declared that if they spoke in his church he would never enter it again. At Bolton, notices of their meetings were torn down, but the town hall was packed notwithstanding, many going away, unable to get in. The church here had also been refused them. Angelina, in the course of her lecture, seized an opportunity to refer to their treatment, saying that if the people of her native city could see her lecturing in that hall because every church had been closed against the cause of God's down-trodden creatures, they would clap their hands for joy, and say, " See what slavery is doing for us in the town of Bolton!"

She describes very graphically going two miles to a meeting on a dark and rainy night, when Sarah was obliged to remain at home on account of a cold, and Abby Kelly drove her in a chaise, and how nearly they came to being upset, and how they met men in flocks along the road, all going to the meeting. She says:—

" It seemed as if I could not realize they were going to hear me," and adds:—

" This was the first large meeting I ever attended without dear sister, and I wonder I did not feel desolate, for I knew not a creature there. Nevertheless, the Lord strengthened me, and I spoke with ease for an hour and a quarter."

But the incessant strain upon her nervous system, together with the fatigue and exposure of almost constant travelling, began to tell seriously on her health. In October she frequently speaks of being "so tired," of being " so glad to rest a day," etc., until, all these warnings being unheeded, nature peremptorily called a halt. In the beginning of November, after a week of unusual fatigue, having lectured six times in as many different places, they reached Hingham quite worn out. Sarah, though still suffering with a cold, begged to lecture in her sister's place, but Angelina had been announced, and she knew the people would be disappointed if she failed to appear. When they entered the crowded hall, a lady seeing how unwell Angelina looked, seized both her hands and exclaimed : —

" Oh, if you will only hold out to-night, I will nurse you for a week ! "

She did hold out for an hour and a half, and then sank back exhausted, and was obliged to leave the lecture unfinished. This was the beginning of an illness which lasted, with its subsequent convalescence, through the remainder of the year. Their good friends, Samuel and Eliza Philbrick, brought the sisters to their beautiful home in Brookline, and surrounded them with every care and comfort kind hearts could suggest. Sarah then found how very weary she was also, and how opportune was this enforced rest.

" Thus," wrote Angelina some weeks afterwards to Jane Smith, " thus ended our summer campaign. Oh, how delightful it was to stretch my weary limbs on a bed of ease, and roll off from my mind all the heavy responsibilities which had so long pressed upon it, and, above all, to feel in my soul the language, ' Well done.' It was luxury indeed, well worth the toil of months."

Sarah, too, speaks of looking back upon the labors of the summer with feelings of unmixed satisfaction.

That the leaven prepared in Sarah Grimké's letters on the " Province of Woman " was beginning to work was evidenced by a public discussion on woman's rights which took place at the Boston Lyceum on the evening of Dec. 4, 1837. The amount of interest this first public debate on the subject excited was shown by the fact that an audience of fifteen hundred of the most intelligent and respectable people of Boston crowded the hall and listened attentively to the end. Sarah and Angelina, the latter now almost entirely recovered, were present, accompanied by Mr. Philbrick.

"A very noble view throughout," says Angelina, and adds: "The discussion has raised my hopes of the woman question. It was conducted with respect, delicacy, and dignity, and many minds no doubt were roused to reflection, though I must not forget to say it was decided against us by acclamation, our enemies themselves being judges. It was like a meeting of slave-holders deciding that the slaves are happier in their present condition than they would be freed."

Soon after this, Angelina writes that some Boston women, including Maria Chapman and Lydia M. Child, were about to start a woman's rights paper, and she adds: "We greatly hope dear Maria Chapman will soon commence lecturing, and that the spark we have been permitted to kindle on the woman question will never die out."

The annual meeting of the Massachusetts Anti-Slavery Society was held the latter part of January, 1838, and was notable in several respects. On the second day, the "great Texas meeting," as it was called, was held in Faneuil Hall, and the fact that this Cradle of Liberty was loaned to the abolitionists was bitterly commented upon by their opponents, while abolitionists themselves regarded it as strong evidence of the progress their cause had made. Angelina writes Jane Smith a graphic account of the speakers and speeches at this meeting, but especially mentions Henry B. Stanton, who made the most powerful speech of the whole session, and was so severe on Congress, that a representative who was present arose to object to the "hot thunderbolts and burning lava" that had been let loose on the heads of "the powers that be, of those whom we were commanded to honor and obey." These remarks were so ridiculous as to excite laughter, and the manner in which Stanton demolished the speaker by his own arguments called forth such repeated rounds of applause that the great orator was obliged to *insist* upon silence.

At this meeting, said to have been the largest ever held in Boston, several hundred women were present, a most encouraging sign to Sarah Grimké of the progress of *her* ideas.

After some parleying, the hall of the House of Representatives was granted the Society for their remaining meetings, and here Quincy, Colver, Phelps, and Wendell Phillips spoke and made a deep impression, so deep that a committee was appointed to take into consideration the petitions on the subject of slavery.

Stanton, half in jest, asked Angelina if she would not like to speak before that committee, as the names of some thousands of women were before it as signers of petitions. She had never thought of such a thing, but, after reflecting upon it a day, sent Stanton word that if the friends of the cause thought well of it, she *would* speak as he had proposed. He was surprised and troubled, for, though he was all right in the abstract on the woman question, he feared the consequences of such a manifest assertion of equality.

"It seems," Angelina writes, "even the stout-hearted tremble when the woman question is to be acted out in full. Jackson, Fuller, Phelps, and Quincy were consulted. The first is sound to the core, and went right up to the State House to inquire of the chairman of the committee whether I could be heard.   Wonderful to tell, he said Yes, without the least hesitation, and actually helped to remove the scruples of some of the timid-hearted abolitionists.   Perhaps it is best *I* should bear the responsibility *wholly* myself.   I feel willing to do it, and think I shall say nothing more about it, but just let Birney and Stanton make the speeches they expect to before the committee this week, and when they have done, make an independent application to the chairman as a woman, as a Southerner, as a moral being. . . . I feel that this is the most important step I have ever been called to take: important to woman, to the slave, to my country, and to the world."

This plan was carried out, thanks to James C. Alvord, the chairman of the committee; and the halls of the Massachusetts Legislature were opened for the first time to a woman.   Wendell Phillips says of that meeting: —

" It gave Miss Grimké the opportunity to speak to the best culture and character of Massachusetts; and the profound impression then made on a class not often found in our meetings was never wholly lost.   It was not only the testimony of one most competent to speak, but it was the profound religious experience of one who had broken out of the charmed circle, and whose intense earnestness melted all opposition.   The converts she made needed no after-training.   It was when you saw she was opening some secret record of her own experience that the painful silence and breathless interest told the deep effect and lasting impression her words were making."

We have not Angelina's account of this meeting, but referring to it in a letter to Sarah Douglass, she says: " My heart never quailed before, but it almost died within me at that tremendous hour."

But one hearing did not satisfy her, and the committee needed no urging to grant her another. At the second meeting, the hall was literally packed, and hundreds went away unable to obtain seats. When she arose to speak, there was some hissing from the doorways, but the most profound silence reigned through the crowd within. Angelina first stood in front of the Speaker's desk, then she was requested to occupy the Secretary's desk on one side, and soon after, that she might be seen as well as heard, she was invited to stand in the Speaker's place. And from that conspicuous position she spoke over two hours without the least interruption. She says to Sarah Douglass: —

"What the effect of these meetings is to be, I know not, nor do I feel that *I* have anything to do with it. This I know, that the chairman was in tears almost the whole time I was speaking," and she adds: "We abolition women are turning the world upside down, for during the whole meeting there was sister seated up in the Speaker's chair of state."

These meetings were followed by the six evening lectures at the Odeon, to which reference has already been made. Sarah delivered the first lecture, taking for her subject the history of the country in reference to slavery. She spoke for two hours, fearlessly, as she always did, and though she says Garrison told her he trembled with apprehension, the audience of fifteen hundred people listened respectfully and attentively, frequently applauding the utterance of some strongly expressed truth, and showing no excitement even under the rebukes she administered to Edward Everett, then Governor of Massachusetts, for his speech in Congress in 1826, and to ex-Governor Lincoln for his in 1831. Both these worthies had declared their willingness to go down South to suppress servile insurrection.

This was the last time Sarah spoke in public. Her throat, which had long troubled her, was now seriously affected, and entire rest was prescribed. She did not murmur, for she had increasingly felt that Angelina's speaking was more effective than hers, and now she believed the Lord was showing her that this part of the work must be left to her more gifted sister, and she gladly yielded to her the task of delivering the five succeeding lectures. In relation to these lectures, the son of Samuel Philbrick has kindly sent me the following extract from a diary kept by his father. Under date of April 23, 1838, he says : —

" In February Angelina addressed the committee of our legislature on the subject of slavery and the slave trade in the District of Columbia and Florida, and the inter-state slave trade, during three sittings of two hours each, in the Representatives' Hall in Boston, before a crowded audience, stowed as close as they could stand in every aisle and corner. Her addresses were listened to with profound attention and respect, without interruption to the last. More than five hundred people could not get seats, but stood quietly during two full hours, in profound silence.

"During the last few weeks she has delivered five lectures, and Sarah one at the Odeon, before an assembly of men and women from all parts of the city. Every part of the building was crowded, every aisle filled. Estimated number, two thousand to three thousand at each meeting. There was great attention and silence, and the addresses were intensely interesting."

These over, the sisters bade farewell to their most ex-

cellent Brookline friends, in whose family they had so
peacefully rested for six months, and returned to Philadelphia, Sarah accepting a temporary home with Jane
Smith, while Angelina went to stay with Mrs. Frost, at
whose house two weeks later, that is on the 14th of May,
she was united in marriage to Theodore D. Weld.

No marriage could have been more true, more fitting
in every respect. The solemn relation was never entered
upon in more holiness of purpose or in higher resolve to
hold themselves strictly to the best they were capable of.
It was a rededication of lives long consecrated to God
and humanity; of souls knowing no selfish ambition, seeking before all things the glory of their Creator in the elevation of His creatures everywhere. The entire unity of
spirit in which they afterwards lived and labored, the
tender affection which, through a companionship of more
than forty years, knew no diminution, made a family life
so perfect and beautiful that it brightened and inspired
all who were favored to witness it. No one could be
with them under the most ordinary circumstances without feeling the force and influence of their characters.

Invitations were sent to about eighty persons, mostly
abolitionists, of all colors, some jet black. Nearly all
came; representing Pennsylvania, New York, New Jersey, Connecticut, Rhode Island, and Massachusetts.
Among them were H. B. Stanton, C. C. Burleigh, William Lloyd Garrison, Amos Dresser, H. C. Wright, Maria
and Mary Chapman, Abby Kelly, Samuel Philbrick, Jane
Smith, and Sarah Douglass of course, and Mr. Weld's
older brother, the president of the asylum for deaf mutes.
Sarah Grimké's account of the wedding, written to a
friend in England, is most interesting; and one cannot
but wonder if another like it ever took place. The letter

was written while the then and ever after inseparable trio
was at Manlius, New York, visiting Mr. Weld's family.
After a slight mention of other matters, she says : —

"I must now give thee some account of my dear sister's marriage, which probably thou hast already heard of.
Her precious husband is emphatically a man of God, a
member of the Presbyterian Church. Of course Angelina will be disowned for forming this connection, and I
shall be for attending the marriage. We feel no regret
at this circumstance, believing that the discipline which
cuts us off from membership for an act so strictly in conformity with the will of God, and so sanctioned by His
word as is the marriage of the righteous, must be anti-
Christian, and I am thankful for an opportunity to testify
against it. The marriage was solemnized at the house of
our sister, Anna R. Frost, in Philadelphia, on the 14th
instant. By the law of Pennsylvania, a marriage is legal
if witnessed by twelve persons. Neither clergyman nor
magistrate is required to be present. Angelina could not
conscientiously consent to be married by a clergyman,
and Theodore D. Weld cheerfully consented to have the
marriage solemnized in such manner as comported with
her views. We all felt that the presence of a magistrate,
a stranger, would be unpleasant to us at such a time, and
we therefore concluded to invite such of our friends as
we desired, and have the marriage solemnized as a religious act, in a religious and social meeting. Neither
Theodore nor Angelina felt as if they could bind themselves to any preconceived form of words, and accordingly uttered such as the Lord gave them at the
moment. Theodore addressed Angelina in a solemn and
tender manner. He alluded to the unrighteous power
vested in a husband by the laws of the United States

over the person and property of his wife, and he abjured all authority, all government, save the influence which love would give to them over each other as moral and immortal beings. I would give much could I recall his words, but I cannot. Angelina's address to him was brief but comprehensive, containing a promise to honor him, to prefer him above herself, to love him with a pure heart fervently. Immediately after this we knelt, and dear Theodore poured out his soul in solemn supplication for the blessing of God on their union, that it might be productive of enlarged usefulness, and increased sympathy for the slave. Angelina followed in a melting appeal to our Heavenly Father, for a blessing on them, and that their union might glorify Him, and then asked His guidance and over-shadowing love through the rest of their pilgrimage. A colored Presbyterian minister then prayed, and was followed by a white one, and then I felt as if I could not restrain the language of praise and thanksgiving to Him who had condescended to be in the midst of this marriage feast, and to pour forth abundantly the oil and wine of consolation and rejoicing. The Lord Jesus was the first guest invited to be present, and He condescended to bless us with His presence, and to sanction and sanctify the union which was thus consummated. The certificate was then read by William Lloyd Garrison, and was signed by the company. The evening was spent in pleasant social intercourse. Several colored persons were present, among them two liberated slaves, who formerly belonged to our father, had come by inheritance to sister Anna, and had been freed by her. They were our invited guests, and we thus had an opportunity to bear our testimony against the horrible prejudice which prevails against colored persons, and the equally awful prejudice against the poor."

This unconventional but truly religious marriage ceremony was in perfect harmony with the loyal, noble natures of Theodore Weld and Angelina Grimké, exemplifying the simplicity of their lives and the strength of their principles. No grand preparations preceded the event; no wedding bells were rung on the occasion ; no rare gifts were displayed: but the blessing of the lowly and the despised, and the heart-felt wishes of co-workers and co-sufferers were the offerings which lent to the occasion its purest joy and brightest light.

But though so quietly and peacefully solemnized, this marriage was to have its celebration, — one little anticipated, but according well with the experiences which had preceded it, and serving to make it all the more impressive and its promises more sacred.

Refused the use of churches and lecture-rooms, and denied the privilege of hiring halls for their meetings, the abolitionists of Philadelphia, with other friends of free discussion, formed an association, and built, at an expense of forty thousand dollars, a beautiful hall, to be used for free speech on any and every subject not of an immoral character. Daniel Neall was the president of this association, and William Dorsey the secretary. The hall, one of the finest buildings in the city, was situated at the southwest corner of Delaware, Sixth, and Harris streets, between Cherry and Sassafras streets.

It was opened for the first time on Angelina Grimké's wedding-day, and was filled with one of the largest audiences ever assembled in Philadelphia.

As soon as the president of the association had taken his seat, the secretary arose and explained the uses and purposes the hall was expected to serve. He said : —

" A number of individuals of all sects, and those of no

sect, of all parties, and those of no party, being desirous that the citizens of Philadelphia should possess a room wherein the principles of *liberty* and *equality of civil rights* could be freely discussed, and the evils of slavery fearlessly portrayed, have erected this building, which we are now about to dedicate to liberty and the rights of man. . . . A majority of the stockholders are mechanics or working-men, and (as is the case in almost every other good work) a number are women."

The secretary then proceeded to read letters from John Quincy Adams, Thaddeus Stevens, Gerrit Smith, Theodore Weld, and others, who had been invited to deliver addresses, but who, from various causes, were obliged to decline. That from Weld was characteristic of the earnestness of the man. After stating that for a year and a half he had been prevented from speaking in public on account of an affection of the throat, and must therefore decline the invitation of the committee, he adds : —

" I exult in the erection of your 'temple of freedom,' and the more, as it is the first and only one, in a republic of fifteen millions, consecrated to free discussion and equal rights.

" For years they have been banished from our halls of legislation and of justice, from our churches and our pulpits. It is befitting that the city of Benezet and of Franklin should be the first to open an asylum where the hunted exiles may find a home. God grant that your Pennsylvania Hall may be *free, indeed!*

" The empty name is everywhere, —*free* government, *free* men, *free* speech, *free* people, *free* schools, and *free* churches. Hollow counterfeits all! *Free!* It is the climax of irony, and its million echoes are hisses and jeers, even from the earth's ends. *Free! Blot it out.* Words are the signs of *things*. The substance has gone! Let fools and madmen clutch at shadows. The husk must rustle the more when the kernel and the ear are gone. Rome's loudest shout for liberty was when she murdered it, and drowned its death shrieks in her hoarse huzzas. She never raised her hands so high to swear allegiance to freedom as when she gave the death-stab, and madly leaped upon its corpse; and her most delirious dance was among the clods her hands had cast upon its coffin. *Free!* The word and sound are omnipresent masks and mockers. An impious lie, unless they stand for free *lynch law* and free *murder*, for they *are* free.

"But I 'll hold. The times demand brief speech, but mighty deeds. On, my brethren! uprear your temple.

"Your brother in the sacred strife for all,

"THEODORE D. WELD."

David Paul Brown, of Philadelphia, was invited to deliver the dedicatory address, which, with other exercises, occupied the mornings and evening of three days, and included addresses by Garrison, Thomas P. Hunt, Arnold Buffum, Alanson St. Clair, and others, on slavery, temperance, the Indians, right of free discussion, and kindred topics. On the second day, an appropriate and soul-stirring poem by John G. Whittier was read by C. C. Burleigh. The first lines will give an idea of the spirit of the whole poem, one of the finest efforts Whittier ever made: —

"Not with the splendors of the days of old,
The spoil of nations and barbaric gold,
No weapons wrested from the fields of blood,
Where dark and stern the unyielding Roman stood,
And the proud eagles of his cohorts saw

A world war-wasted, crouching to his law;
Nor blazoned car, nor banners floating gay,
Like those which swept along the Appian Way,
When, to the welcome of imperial Rome,
The victor warrior came in triumph home,
And trumpet peal, and shoutings wild and high,
Stirred the blue quiet of th' Italian sky,
But calm and grateful, prayerful, and sincere,
As Christian freemen only, gathering here,
We dedicate our fair and lofty hall,
Pillar and arch, entablature and wall,
As Virtue's shrine, as Liberty's abode,
Sacred to Freedom, and to Freedom's God."

The Anti-Slavery Convention of American Women was then holding a session in the city, and among the members present were some of the brightest and noblest women of the day, women with courage as calm and high to dare, as with hearts tender to feel for human woe. The Convention occupied the lecture-room of Pennsylvania Hall, under the main saloon. A strong desire having been expressed by many citizens to hear some of these able pleaders for the slave, notice was given that there would be a meeting in the main saloon on the evening of the 16th, at which Angelina, E. G. Weld, Maria Chapman, and others would speak.

Up to the time of this announcement, no apprehension of any disturbance had been felt by the managers of the hall. So far all the meetings had been conducted without interruption; nor could anyone have supposed it possible that in a city renowned for its order and law, and possessing a large and efficient police force, a public outrage upon an assemblage of respectable citizens, many of them women, could be perpetrated. But it was soon to be shown how deeply the spirit of slavery had infused itself into the minds of the people of the free States, leading them to disregard the rights of individuals and to wantonly violate the sacred principles guaranteed by the Constitution of the country.

During the day some threats of violence were thrown out, and *written* placards were posted about the city inviting interference with the proposed meeting, *forcibly if necessary*. But this was regarded only as the expression of malice on the part of a few, or perhaps of an individual, and occasioned no alarm. Still, the precaution was taken to request the mayor to hold his police force in readiness to protect the meeting in case of need. The day passed quietly. Long before the time announced for the meeting, the hall, capable of containing three thousand people, was thronged, and, by the time the speakers arrived, every seat was filled, every inch of standing room was occupied, and thousands went away from the doors unable to obtain admittance. The audience was for the most part a highly respectable and intelligent one, and, notwithstanding the great crowd, was exceedingly quiet. William Lloyd Garrison opened the meeting with a short but characteristic speech, during which he was frequently interrupted by hisses and groans; and when he ended, some efforts were made to break up the meeting. In the midst of the confusion, Maria W. Chapman arose, calm, dignified, and, with a wave of her hand, as though to still the noise, began to speak, but, before she had gone far, yells from the outside proclaimed the arrival there of a disorderly rabble, and at once the confusion inside became so great, that, although the brave woman continued her speech, she was not heard except by those immediately around her.

Sarah Grimké thus wrote of Mrs. Chapman's appear-

ance on that occasion: "She is the most beautiful woman
I ever saw; the perfection of sweetness and intelligence
being blended in her speaking countenance. She arose
amid the yells and shouts of the infuriated mob, the
crash of windows and the hurling of stones. She looked
to me like an angelic being descended amid that tempest
of passion in all the dignity of conscious superiority."

Then Angelina Weld, the bride of three days, came
forward, and so great was the effect of her pure, beautiful
presence and quiet, graceful manner, that in a few moments the confusion within the hall had subsided. With
deep solemnity, and in words of burning eloquence, she
gave her testimony against the awful wickedness of an
institution which had no secrets from her. She was frequently interrupted by the mob, but their yells and
shouts only furnished her with metaphors which she
used with unshrinking power. More stones were thrown
at the windows, more glass crashed, but she only paused
to ask: —

"What is a mob? What would the breaking of every
window be? Any evidence that we are wrong, or that
slavery is a good and wholesome institution? What if
that mob should now burst in upon us, break up our meeting, and commit violence upon our persons — would this
be anything compared with what the slaves endure? No,
no : and we do not remember them 'as bound with them,'
if we shrink in the time of peril, or feel unwilling to sacrifice ourselves, if need be, for their sake. I thank the
Lord that there is yet life enough left to feel the truth,
even though it rages at it — that conscience is not so completely seared as to be unmoved by the truth of the living God."

Here a shower of stones was thrown through the windows, and there was some disturbance in the audience, but quiet was again restored, and Angelina proceeded, and spoke for over an hour, making no further reference to the noise without, and only showing that she noticed it by raising her own voice so that it could be heard throughout the hall.

Not once was a tremor or a change of color perceptible, and though the missiles continued to fly through the broken sashes, and the hootings and yellings increased outside, so powerfully did her words and tones hold that vast audience, that, imminent as seemed their peril, scarcely a man or woman moved to depart. She sat down amid applause that drowned all the noise outside.

Abby Kelly, then quite a young woman, next arose and said a few words, her first public utterances. She was followed by gentle Lucretia Mott in a short but most earnest speech, and then this memorable meeting, the first of the kind where men and women acted together as moral beings, closed.

There was a dense crowd in the streets around the hall as the immense audience streamed out, but though screams and all sorts of appalling noises were made, no violence was offered, and all reached their homes in safety.

But the mob remained, many of its wretched members staying all night, assaulting every belated colored man who came along. The next morning the dregs of the populace, and some respectable *looking* men again assembled around the doomed hall, but the usual meetings were held, and even the convention of women assembled in the lecture room to finish up their business. The evening was to have been occupied by a public meeting of the Wesleyan Anti-Slavery Society of Philadelphia, but as the day waned to its close, the indications of approaching disturbance became more and more alarming. The crowd around the building increased, and the secret agents of slavery were busy inflaming the passions of the rabble against the abolitionists, and inciting it to outrage. Seeing this, and realizing the danger which threatened, the managers of the hall gave the building over to the protection of the mayor of the city, *at his request*. Of course the proposed meeting was postponed. All the mayor did was to appear in front of the hall, and, in a friendly tone, express to the mob the hope that it would not do anything disorderly, saying that he relied upon the men he saw before him, as his *policemen*, and he wished them " good evening! " The mob gave " three cheers for the mayor," and, as soon as he was out of sight, extinguished the gas lights in front of the building. The rest is soon told. Doors and windows were broken through, and with wild yells the reckless horde dashed in, plundered the Repository, scattering the books in every direction, and, mounting the stairways and entering the beautiful hall, piled combustibles on the Speaker's forum, and applied the torch to them, shrieking like demons, — as they were, for the time. A moment more, and the flames roared and crackled through the building, and though it was estimated that fifteen thous. nd persons were present, and though the fire companies were early on the scene, not one effort was made to save the structure so recently erected, at such great cost, and consecrated to such Christian uses. In a few hours the smouldering walls alone were left.

Angelina Weld never again appeared in public. An accident soon after her marriage caused an injury of such a nature that her nervous system was permanently impaired, and she was ever after obliged to avoid all excitement or over-exertion. The period of her public labors was short, but how fruitful, how full of blessings to the cause of the slave and to the many who espoused it through her powerful appeals! Great was her grief; for, knowing now her capabilities, she had looked forward to renewed and still more successful work; but she accepted with sweet submission the cross laid upon her. Not a murmur arose to her lips. She was content to leave all to the Lord. He could find some new work for her to do. She would trust Him, and patiently wait.

The loss of the services of one so richly endowed, so devoted, and so successful, was deeply felt by the friends of emancipation, and especially as at this important epoch efficient speakers were sorely needed, and two of the most efficient, Weld and Burleigh, were already, from overwork, taken from the platform.

But though denied the privilege of again raising her voice in behalf of the oppressed, Angelina continued to plead for them through her pen. She could never forget the cause that could never forget her, and to her writings was transferred much of the force and eloquence of her speaking.

Immediately after the destruction of Pennsylvania Hall, Mr. and Mrs. Weld, accompanied by Sarah Grimké, paid a visit to Mr. Weld's parents in Manlius, from which place, Sarah, writing to Jane Smith, says: —

"O Jane, it looks like almost too great a blessing for us three to be together in some quiet, humble habitation, living to the glory of God, and promoting the happiness of those around us; to be spiritually united, and to be pursuing with increasing zeal the great work of the abolition of slavery."

The "quiet, humble habitation" was found at Fort Lee, on the Hudson, and there the happy trio settled down for their first housekeeping.

CHAPTER XVI.

They were scarcely settled amid their new surroundings before the sisters received a formal notice of their disownment by the Society of Friends because of Angelina's marriage. The notification, signed by two prominent women elders of the Society, expressed regret that Sarah and Angelina had not more highly prized their right of membership, and added an earnest desire that they might come to a sense of their real state, and manifest a disposition to condemn their deviations from the path of duty.

Angelina replied without delay that they wished the discipline of the Society to have free course with regard to them. "It is our joy," she wrote, "that we have committed no offence for which Christ Jesus will disown us as members of the household of faith. If you regret that we have valued our right of membership so little, we equally regret that our Society should have adopted a discipline which has no foundation in the Bible or in reason; and we earnestly hope the time may come when the simple Gospel rule with regard to marriage, 'Be not unequally yoked together with unbelievers,' will be as conscientiously enforced as that sectarian one which prohibits the union of the Lord's own people if their shibboleth be not exactly the same.

"We are very respectfully, in that love which knows no distinction in color, clime, or creed, your friends,

"A. E. G. WELD.
"SARAH M. GRIMKÉ."

It will be noticed that in this reply Angelina avoids the Quaker phraseology, and neither she nor Sarah ever after used it, except occasionally in correspondence with a Quaker friend.

Thus ended their connection with the Society of Friends. From that time they never attached themselves to any religious organization, but rested contentedly in the simple religion of Christ, illustrating by every act of their daily lives how near they were to the heart of all true religion.

As I am approaching the limits prescribed for this volume, I can, in the space remaining to me, only note with any detail the chief incidents of the years which followed Angelina's marriage. I would like to describe at length the beautiful family life the trio created, and which disproved so clearly the current assertion that interest in public matters disqualifies woman for home duties or make these distasteful to her. In the case of Sarah and Angelina those duties were entered upon with joy and gratitude, and with the same conscientious zeal that had characterized their public labors. The simplicity and frugality, too, which marked all their domestic arrangements, and which neither thought it necessary to apologize for at any time, recall to one's mind the sweet pictures of Arcadian life over which goodness, purity, and innocence presided, creating an atmosphere of perfect inward and outward peace.

Sarah's letters detail their every-day occupations, their

division of labor, their culinary experiments, often failures, — for of practical domestic economy they had little knowledge, though they enjoyed the new experience like happy children. She tells of rambles and picnics along the Hudson, climbing rocks to get a fine view, halting under the trees to read together for a while, taking their simple dinner in some shady nook, and returning weary but happy to their "dear little No. 3," as she designates their house.

"Oh, Jane," she writes, "words cannot tell the goodness of the Lord to us since we have sat down under the shadow of our own roof, and gathered around our humble board. Peace has flowed sweetly through our souls. The Lord has been in the midst, and blessed us with his presence, and the daily aspiration of our souls is: Lord, show us thy will concerning us." And in another letter she says, "We are delighted with our arrangement to do without a girl. Angelina boils potatoes to admiration, and says she finds cooking much easier than she expected."

During the summer they were gratified by a visit from their good friend Jane, who, it appears, gave them some useful and much-needed lessons in the art of cookery. But about this time Sarah became converted to the Graham system of diet, which Mr. Weld had adopted three, and Mrs. Weld two years before. Sarah thus writes of it: —

"We have heard Graham lectures, and read Alcott's 'Young Housekeeper,' and are truly thankful that the Lord has converted us to this mode of living, and that we are all of one heart and one mind. We believe it is the most conducive to health, and, besides, it is such an emancipation of woman from the toils of the kitchen, and

saves so much precious time for purposes of more importance than eating and drinking. We have a great variety
of dishes, and, to our taste, very savory. We can make
good bread, and this with milk is an excellent meal.
This week I am cook, and am writing this while my
beans are boiling and pears stewing for dinner. We use
no tea or coffee, and take our food cool."

She then tells of the arrival one day of two friends
from the city, just as they had sat down to their simple
meal of rice and molasses. "But," she says, "we were
very glad to see them, and with bread and milk, and pie
without shortening, and hominy, we contrived to give
them enough, and as they were pretty hungry they par-
took of it with tolerable appetite." Answering some inquiries from Jane Smith, Angelina writes : —

"As to how I have made out with cooking, it so
happens that labor (planting a garden) gives Theodore
such an appetite that everything is sweet to him, so that
my rice and asparagus, potatoes, mush, and Indian bread
all taste well, though some might think them not fit to
eat."

They had but one cooking day, when enough was generally prepared to last a week, so that very little time
and mind was given to creature comforts; in fact, no
more than was necessary to the preservation of health.
Their motto literally was "to eat to live," and this they
felt to be a part of that non-conformity to the world of
which the apostle speaks, and after which Sarah, at least,
felt she must still strive. Their furniture corresponded
with the simplicity of their table. Angelina writes
shortly after her marriage : —

"We ordered our furniture to be made of cherry, and
quite enjoy the cheapness of our outfit as well as our

manner of life; for the less we spend, the less the Anti-Slavery Society will have to pay my Theodore for his labors as editor of all the extra publications of the Society."

Thus some high or unselfish motive inspired all their conduct and influenced every arrangement. Nothing superfluous or merely ornamental found a place with these true and zealous followers of Him whose precepts guided their lives. Everything in doors and out served a special purpose of utility, or suggested some duty or great moral aim. Angelina was exceedingly fond of flowers, but refrained from cultivating them, because of the time required, which she thought could be better employed. She felt she had no right to use one moment for her own selfish gratification which could be given to some more necessary work. Therefore, though both sisters were peculiarly gifted with a love of the beautiful, as their frequent descriptions of natural scenery show, they contented themselves, from principle, with the enjoyment of "glorious sunsets," and with the flowers of the field and wayside. Later they learned a different appreciation of all the innocent pleasures of life; but at the time I am describing, they had just emerged from Quaker asceticism, and in the flush of their new religion, and looking upon their past years as almost wasted, they were eager only to make amends for them. In one of her letters to her English friend, Angelina acknowledges the present from her of a large picture of a *Kneeling Slave*, and adds: —

"We purpose pasting it on binder's boards, binding it with colored paper, and fixing it over our mantelpiece. It is just such a speaking monument of suffering as we want in our parlor, and suits my fireboard most admirably. I first covered this with plain paper, and then arranged as well as I could about forty anti-slavery pictures upon it. I never saw one like it, but we hope other abolitionists will make them when they see what an ornamental and impressive article of furniture can thus be manufactured. We want those who come into our house to see at a glance that we are on the side of the oppressed and the poor."

Sarah Douglass spent a day with them in September, and as I can have no more fitting place to show how conscientious were these rare spirits in their practical testimony against the color prejudice, I will quote a few passages from a letter written to Sarah Douglass after her departure from the circle where she had been treated as a most honored guest. Sarah Grimké begins as follows: —

" Thy letter, my beloved Sarah, was truly acceptable as an evidence of thy love for us, and because it told us one of our Lord's dear children had been comforted in being with us. It would have been truly grateful to have had thee a longer time with us, and we hope thy next visit may be less brief. By the way, dear, as I love frankness, I am going to tell thee what I have thought in reading thy note. It seemed to me thy proposal 'to spend a day' with us was made under a little feeling something like this: 'Well, after all, I am not quite certain I shall be an acceptable visitor.' I can only say that it is no surprise to me that thou shouldst be beset with such a temptation, but set a strong guard against this entrance to thy heart, lest the adversary poison all the springs of comfort. I want thee to rise above the suspicions which are so naturally aroused. They are among the subtle devices of Satan, by which he alienates us from Jesus, and makes

us go morning on our way with the language in our
hearts : ' Is there not a cause ? ' "

Angelina adds : —

" MY DEAR SARAH, — I can fully unite with my precious sister in all she has said relative to thy late visit to
us. Theodore and I both felt surprised and disappointed
that thou proposedst spending but one day with us when
we had expected a visit of a week. It was indeed a comfort to receive such a letter from thee, dear, and yet there
was much of pain mingled in the feeling. Thou thankest
us for our ' Christian conduct.' In what did it consist?
In receiving and treating thee as an equal, a sister beloved
in the Lord? Oh, how humbling to receive such thanks!
What a crowd of reflections throng the mind as we inquire, *Why* does her full heart thus overflow with gratitude? Yes, how irresistibly are we led to contemplate
the woes which iron-hearted prejudice inflicts on the oppressed of our land, the hidden sorrows they endure —
the full cup of bitterness which is wrung out to them by
the hands of professed followers of Him who is no respec-
ter of persons. And oh, how these reflections ought to
lead us to labor and to pray that the time may soon come
when thou canst no longer write *such* a letter! The Lord
in his mercy has made our little household *one* in sentiment on this subject, and we know we have been blessed
in the exercise of those Christian feelings which He hath
taught us to cherish, not only towards the outraged people of color, but towards that large class of individuals
who serve in families, and are, at the same time, almost
completely separated from human society and sympathy
so far as their employers are concerned.

" Let me tell thee, dear Sarah, how much good it did
me to find that thy visit had made thee love my precious

husband as a brother, and afforded thee an opportunity to *feel* what manner of spirit is his. Now I greatly want thy dear mother to know him too, and cannot but believe she will come and visit us next summer."

The gratitude of Sarah Douglass for the reception given her at Fort Lee was not surprising, considering how different such kindness was from the treatment she and her excellent mother had always received from the Society of Friends, of which they were members. Scarcely anything more damaging to the Christian spirit of the Society can be found than the testimony of this mother and daughter, which Sarah Grimké obtained and wrote out, but, I believe, never published.

Before his marriage, Mr. Weld lodged, on principle, in a colored family in New York, even submitting to the inconvenience of having no heat in his room in winter, and bearing with singular charity and patience what Sarah calls the sanctimonious pride and Pharisaical aristocracy of his hosts. He, also, and the sisters when they were in the city, attended a colored church, which, however, became to Sarah, at least, a place of such "spiritual famine" that she gave up going.

In the winter of 1839–40, when it became necessary to have more help in the household, a colored woman, Betsy Dawson by name, was sent for. She had been a slave in Colonel Grimké's family, and, falling to the share of Mrs. Frost when the estate was settled up, was by her emancipated. She was received into the family at Fort Lee as a friend, and so treated in every respect. Sarah expresses the pleasure it was to have one as a helper who knew and loved them all, and adds: " Besides I cannot tell thee how thankful we are that our heavenly Father has put it in our power to have one who was once a slave in our family to sit at our table and be with us as a sister cherished, to place her on an entire equality with us in social intercourse, and do all we can to show her we feel for her as we, under like circumstances, would desire her to feel for us. I don't know what M. C. [a friend from New York] thought of our having her at table and in our parlor just like one of ourselves."

Some time later, Angelina writes of another of the family slaves, Stephen, to whom they gave a home, putting him to do the cooking, lest, being unaccustomed to a Northern climate, he should suffer by exposure to out-door work. He proved an eyesore in every way, but they retained him as long as it was possible to do so, and bore with him patiently, as no one else would have him. Mrs. Weld frequently allowed him to hire out for four or five hours a day to husk corn, etc., and was glad to give him this opportunity to earn something extra while she did his work at home. In short, wherever and whenever they could testify to their convictions of duty on this point, it was done unhesitatingly and zealously, without fear or favor of any man. We might consider the incidents I have related, and a dozen similar ones I could give, as evidence only of a desire to perform a religious duty, to manifest obedience to the command to do as they would be done by, while beneath still lay the bias of early training sustained by the almost universal feeling concerning the inferiority of the negro race. With people of such pure religious dedication, and such exalted views, it was perhaps not difficult to treat their ex-slaves as human beings, and the fact that they did so may not excite much wonder. But there came a time, then far in their future, when the sincerity of their convictions upon this matter of prejudice was most triumphantly vindicated.

Such a vindication even they, with all their knowledge of the hidden evils of slavery, never dreamed could ever be required of *them*, but the manner in which they met the tremendous test was the crowning glory of their lives. In all the biographies I have read, such a manifestation of the spirit of Jesus Christ does not appear. This will be narrated in its proper place.

Happy as the sisters were in their home, it must not be supposed that they had settled down to a life of ease and contented privacy, abandoning altogether the great work of their lives. Far from it. The time economized from household duties was devoted chiefly to private labor for the cause, from the public advocacy of which they felt they had only stepped aside for a time. Neither had any idea that this public work was over. Angelina writes to her friend in England soon after her marriage: —

" I cannot tell thee how I love this private life — how I have thanked my heavenly Father for this respite from public labor, or how earnestly I have prayed that whilst I am thus dwelling at ease I may not forget the captives of my land, or be unwilling to go forth again on the high places of the field, to combat the giant sin of Slavery with the smooth stones of the river of Truth, if called to do so by Him who put me forth and went before me in days that are past. My dear Theodore entertains the noblest views of the rights and responsibilities of woman, and will never lay a straw in the way of my lecturing. He has many times strengthened my hands in the work, and often tenderly admonished me to keep my eye upon my great Leader, and my heart in a state of readiness to go forth whenever I am called out. I humbly trust I may, but as earnestly desire to be preserved from going before I hear a voice saying unto me, ' This is the way, walk in it, and I will be thy shield and thy buckler.' This was the promise which was given me before, and how faithfully it was fulfilled, my soul knoweth right well."

Sarah too, writes to Sarah Douglass : —

" I have thought much of my present situation, laid aside from active service, but I see no pointing of the divine finger to go forth, and I believe the present dispensation of rest has been granted to us not only as a reward for past faithfulness, but as a means of personal advancement in holiness, a time of deep searching of heart, when the soul may contemplate itself, and seek nearer and fuller and higher communion with its God."

And again she says : —

" It is true my nature shrinks from public work, but whenever the mandate goes forth to declare on the house-tops that which I have heard in the ear, I shall not dare to hold back. I conclude that whenever my Father needs my services, He will prepare me to obey the call by exercise of mind."

In the meanwhile Sarah finished and published a most important contribution to the arguments on the woman's rights subject. This was a small volume of letters on the " Equality of the Sexes," commenced during her lecturing tour, and addressed to Mary S. Parker, president of the Boston Female Anti-Slavery Society. Written in a gentle, reverent spirit, but clothed in Sarah's usual forcible language, they not only greatly aided the cause which lay so near her heart, but relieved and strengthened many tender consciences by their strong arguments.

An extract or two from a letter written to Sarah by Angelina and Theodore early in the autumn of 1838 will show the tender relations existing between these three, and which continued undisturbed by all the changes and trials of succeeding years.

In September, Sarah went to Philadelphia to attend the Annual Anti-Slavery Convention. Angelina writes to her a few days after her departure : —

"We have just come up from our evening meal, my beloved sister, and are sitting in our little study for a while before taking our moonlight ramble on the river bank. After thou left us, I cleared up the dishes, and then swept the house ; got down to the kitchen just in time for dinner, which, though eaten alone, was, I must confess, very much relished, for exercise gives a good appetite, thou knowest. I then set my beans to boil whilst I dusted, and was upstairs waiting, ready dressed, for the sound of the 'Echo's' piston. Soon I heard it, and blew my whistle, which was *not* responded to, and I began to fear my Theodore was not on board. But I blew again, and the glad response came merrily over the water, and I thought I saw him. In a little while he came, and gave me all your parting messages. On Second Day the weather was almost cold, and we were glad to take a run at noon up the Palisades and sun ourselves on the rock at the first opening. Returning, we gathered some field beans, and some apples for stewing, as our fruit was nearly out. In the evening it was so cool that we thought a fire would be more comfortable, so we sat in the kitchen, paring apples, shelling beans, and talking over the Bible argument ;[1] and, as we had a fire, I thought we had

---

[1] This was the argument which Angelina heard Mr. Weld make before the A. S. Convention in New York two years before, and which was afterwards published by the A. A. S. Society. He was now revising it for a new edition. It made many converts to emancipation. Among them was the Rev. Dr. Brisbane of South Caro-

better stew the apples at once. This was done to save
time the next day, but I burnt them sadly. However,
thou knowest they were just as nice to our Theodore, who
never complains of anything. Third Day evening we took
a walk up the Palisades. The moon shone most beautifully, throwing her mantle of light all abroad over the
blue arch of heaven, the gently flowing river, and the
woods and vales around us. I could not help thinking, if
earth was so lovely and bright, what must be the glories
of that upper Temple which needeth not the light of the
sun or of the moon. O sister, shall we ever wash our
robes so white in the blood of the Lamb as to be clean
enough to enter that pure and holy Temple of the Most
High? We returned to our dear little home, and went to
bed by the lamp of heaven; for we needed no other, so
brightly did she shine through our windows. We remembered thee, dear sister, in our little seasons of prayer at
the opening and closing of each day. We pray the Lord
to bring thee back to us in the fulness of the blessing of
the Gospel of peace, and to make our house a *home* to thy
weary, tossed, afflicted spirit. We feel it a great blessing
to have thee under our roof. Thy room looks very desolate; for, though the sun shines brightly in it, I find, after
all, *thou* art the light of it."

Theodore adds a postscript, addresses Sarah as " My
dearly loved sister," and says, " As dear Angy remarks,
your room does look so chill and desolate, and your place
at table, and your chair in our little morning and evening

lina, a slave-owner, who, after reading it, sat down to answer and
refute it; but, before proceeding half way, he became convinced
that he was wrong, and Weld right. Acting upon this conviction,
he freed his slaves, went to Cincinnati, joined the abolition ranks,
and became one of their most eloquent advocates.

circle, that we talk about it a dozen times a day. But we rejoice that the Master put it into your heart to go and give your testimony for our poor, suffering brothers and sisters, wailing under bonds, and we pray without ceasing that He who sent will teach, strengthen, and help you greatly to do for Him and the bleeding slave."

Debarred from lecturing by the condition of his throat, Mr. Weld was a most untiring worker in the Anti-Slavery office in New York, from which he received a small salary. His time out of office hours was employed in writing for the different anti-slavery papers, and in various editorial duties. Soon after his marriage he began the preparation of a book, which, when issued, produced perhaps a greater sensation throughout the country than anything that had yet been written or spoken. This was, "AMERICAN SLAVERY AS IT IS: TESTIMONY OF A THOUSAND WITNESSES," a book of two hundred and ten pages, and consisting of a collection of facts relating to the actual condition and treatment of slaves; facts drawn from slaveholders themselves, and from Southern publications. The design was to make the South condemn herself, and never was success more complete. Of all the lists of crimes, all the records of abominations, of moral depravity, of marvellous inhumanity, of utter insensibility to the commonest instincts of nature, the civilized world has never read anything equal to it. Placed by the side of Fox's "Book of Martyrs," it outrivals it in all its revolting characters, and calls up the burning blush of shame for our country and its boasted Christian civilization. Notwithstanding all that had been written on the subject, the public was still comparatively ignorant of the sufferings of the slaves, and the barbarities inflicted upon them. Mr. Weld thought the state of the abolition cause demanded a work which would not only prove by argument that slavery and cruelty were inseparable, but which would contain a mass of incontrovertible facts, that would exhibit the horrid brutality of the system. Nearly all the papers, most of them of recent date, from which the extracts were taken, were deposited at the office of the American Anti-Slavery Society in New York, and all who thought the atrocities described in Weld's book were incredible, were invited to call and examine for themselves.

This book was the most effective answer ever given to the appeal made against free discussion, based on the Southampton massacre. It was, in fact, an offset of the horrors of that bloody affair, giving, as it did, a picture of the deeper horrors of slavery. It was the first adequate disclosure of this "bloodiest picture in the book of time," which had yet been made, and all who read it felt that, fearful as was the Virginia tragedy, the system which provoked it included many things far worse, and demanded investigation and discussion. Issued in pamphlet form, the "Testimony of a Thousand Witnesses," was extensively circulated over the country, and most advantageously used by anti-slavery lecturers and advocates; and it is not too much to say that by awakening the humanity and pride of the people to end this national disgrace, it made much easier the formation of the anti-slavery political party.

In the preparation of this work, Mr. Weld received invaluable assistance from his wife and sister. Not only was the testimony of their personal observation and experience given over their own names, but many files of Southern papers were industriously examined for such facts as were needed, and which Mr. Weld arranged. Early in January, 1839, Sarah writes : —

"I do not think we ever labored more assiduously for the slave than we have done this fall and winter, and, although our work is of the kind that may be privately performed, yet we find the same holy peace in doing it which we found in the public advocacy of the cause."

Referring a little later to this work, she says: "We have been almost too busy to look out on the beautiful winter landscape, and have been wrought up by our daily researches almost to a frenzy of justice, intolerance, and enthusiasm to crush the viper that is eating out the vitals of the nation. Oh, what a blessed privilege to be engaged in labor for the oppressed! We often think, if the slaves are never emancipated, we are richly rewarded by the hallowed influence óf abolition principles on our own hearts."

In a recent letter to me, Mr. Weld makes some interesting statements respecting this work. I will give them in his own words: —

"The fact is, those dear souls spent six months, averaging more than six hours a day, in searching through thousands upon thousands of Southern newspapers, marking and cutting out facts of slave-holding disclosures for the book. I engaged of the Superintendent of the New York Commercial Reading-Room all his papers published in our Southern States and Territories. These, after remaining upon the files one month, were taken off and sold. Thus was gathered the raw material for the manufacture of 'Slavery As It Is.' After the work was finished, we were curious to know how many newspapers had been examined. So we went up to our attic and took an inventory of bundles, as they were packed heap upon heap. When our count had reached *twenty thousand* news-

papers, we said: 'There, let that suffice.' Though
the book had in it many thousand facts thus authenti-
cated by the slave-holders themselves, yet it contained
but a tiny fraction of the nameless atrocities gathered
from the papers examined."

Besides this absorbing occupation, the sisters busied
themselves that winter getting up a petition to Congress
for the abolition of slavery in the District of Columbia,
and walked many miles, day after day, to obtain signatures, meeting with patience, humility, and sweetness the
frequent rebuffs of the rude and the ignorant, feeling only
pity for them, and gratitude to God who had touched and
softened their own hearts and enlightened their minds.

They received repeated invitations from the different
anti-slavery organizations to again enter the lecture field,
and great disappointment was felt by all who had once
listened to them that they should have retired from public
work.

Sarah speaks of attending "meeting," as, from habit,
she called it, and doubtless they all went regularly, as
Mr. Weld was a communicant of the Presbyterian
Church, and Mrs. Weld and Sarah were still sound on all
the fundamental points of Christian doctrine. During
some portion of every Sunday, Mrs. Weld was in the
habit of visiting among the very poor, white and colored,
and preaching to them the Gospel of peace and good
will. In her peculiarly tender and persuasive way, she
opened to those unhappy and benighted souls the promises and hopes which supported her, and lavished upon
them the treasures of an eloquence that thousands had
and would still have crowded to listen to. There were
none to applaud in those sorrowful abodes, but her words
of courage and consolation lifted many a despondent

heart from the depths, while her own faith in the love and mercy of her heavenly Father brought confidence and comfort to many a benumbed and wavering soul.

In December, 1839, the happiness of the little household was increased by the birth of a son, who received the name of Charles Stuart, in loving remembrance of the eminent English philanthropist, with whom Mr. Weld had been as a brother, and whom he regarded as living as near the angels as mortal man could live. The advent of this child was not only an inexpressible blessing to the affectionate hearts of the father and mother, but to Sarah it seemed truly a mark of divine love to her, compensating her for the home ties and affections once so nearly within her grasp, and still often mourned for. She describes her feelings as she pressed the infant in her arms and folded him to her breast as a rhapsody of wild delight. "Oh, the ecstacy and the gratitude!" she exclaimed: "How I opened the little blanket and peeped in to gaze, with swimming eyes, at my treasure, and looked upon that face forever so dear!"

For months before the birth of her child, Mrs. Weld had read carefully different authors on the treatment of children, and felt herself prepared at every point with the best theories derived from Combes' "Physiological and Moral Management of Infancy," and kindred works. It is rather amusing to read how systematically this baby was trained, and how little he appreciated all the wise theories; how he protested against going to sleep by rule; how he would n't be bathed in cold water; how he was fed, a tablespoonful at a time, five times during the twenty-four hours, — at 8, 12, 4, 8, and 3 in the morning; how his fretting at last induced his Aunt Sarah to take the responsibility of giving him a little license with his bottle, when, horrified at his gluttony, she was, at the same time, convinced that the child had been slowly starving ever since his birth. Allowed more indulgence in food, he soon stopped fretting, and became a healthy, lively baby.

Angelina, writing to a friend, speaks of the blessed influence the child was exerting over them all. "The idea," she says, "of a baby exercising moral influence never came into my mind until I felt its power on my own heart. I used to think all a parent's reward for early care and anxiety was reaped in after-life, save the enjoyment of an infant as a pretty plaything. But the Lord has taught me differently, and woe be unto me if I do not profit by the instructions of this little teacher sent from God."

It was about this time that the injury referred to in the last chapter was received, which frustrated all Angelina's hopes and plans for continued public service for the slave, and condemned her, with all her rare intellectual gifts, to a quiet life. The sweet submission with which she bore this trial proved how great was the peace which possessed her soul, and kept her ready for whatever it seemed good for the Father to send her. Henceforth, shut out from the praises and plaudits of men, in her own home, among her neighbors and among the poor and afflicted, quietly and unobtrusively she fulfilled every law of love and duty. And though during the remainder of her life she was subject to frequent weakness and intense pain, all was borne with such fortitude and patience that only her husband and sister knew that she suffered.

In the latter part of February, 1840, Mr. Weld, having purchased a farm of fifty acres at Belleville, New Jersey, removed his family there. Angelina, announcing the change to Jane Smith, says: —

"Yes, we have left the sweet little village of Fort Lee, a spot never to be forgotten by me as the place where my Theodore and I first lived together, and the birthplace of my darling babe, the scene of my happiest days. There, too, my precious sister ministered with untiring faithfulness to my wants when sick, and there, too, I welcomed *thee* for the first time under my roof."

To their new home they brought the simplicity of living to which they had adhered in their old one, a simplicity which, with their more commodious house, enabled them to exercise the broad hospitality which they had been obliged to deny themselves in a measure at Fort Lee. All the good deeds done under this sacred name of hospitality during their fourteen years' residence at Belleville can never be known. Few ever so diligently sought, or so cheerfully accepted, opportunities for the exercise of every good word and work. Scarcely a day passed that they did not feel called upon to make some sacrifice of comfort or convenience for the comfort or convenience of others; and more than once the sacrifice involved the risk of health and life. But in true humility and with an unwavering trust in God, they looked away from themselves and beyond ordinary considerations.

One of their first acts, after their removal, was to take back to their service the incompetent Stephen whom they had been forced to discharge from Fort Lee, and who had lived a precarious life afterwards. They gave him work on the farm, paid him the usual wages, and patiently endeavored to correct his faults. A young nephew in delicate health was also added to their household; and, a few months later, Angelina having heard that an old friend and her daughter in Charleston were in pecuniary distress and feeble health, wrote and offered them a home with her for a year.

"They have no means of support, and are anxious to leave Carolina," wrote Angelina to Jane Smith; "we will keep them until their health is recruited, their minds rested, and some situation found for them where they can earn their own living. We know not," she adds, "whom else the Lord may send us, and only pray Him to help us to fulfil His will towards all whose lot may be cast among us."

The visitors to the Belleville farm — chiefly old and new anti-slavery friends — were numerous, and were always received with a cordiality which left no room to doubt its sincerity.

At one time they received into their family a poor young man from Jamaica, personally a stranger, but of whose labors as a self-appointed missionary among the recently emancipated slaves of the West Indies they had heard. He had labored for three years, supporting himself as he could, until he was utterly broken down in health, when he came back to die. His friendless situation appealed to the warmest sympathy of the Welds, and he was brought to their hospitable home. The pleasantest room in the house was given to him, and every attention bestowed upon him, until death came to his relief.

The people of their neighborhood soon learned to know where they could confidently turn for help in any kind of distress. It would be difficult to tell the number of times that one or the other of the great-hearted trio responded to the summons from a sick or dying bed, and gave without stint of their sympathy, their time, and their labor.

Once, following only her own conviction of duty, Angelina left her home to go and nurse a wretched colored man and his wife, ill with small-pox and abandoned by everyone. She stayed with them night and day until they were so far recovered as to be able to help themselves.

What a picture is this! That humble cabin with its miserable occupants — and they negroes — ill with a loathsome disease, suffering, praying for help, but deserted by neighbors and friends. Suddenly a fair, delicate face bends over them; a sweet, low voice bids them be comforted, and gentle hands lift the cooling draught to their parched lips, bathe their fevered brows, make comfortable their poor bed, and then, angel as she appears to them, stations herself beside them, to minister to them like the true sister of mercy she was.

In this action, we may well suppose, Angelina was not encouraged by her husband or sister, but it was a sacred principle with them never to oppose anything which she conscientiously saw it was her duty to do. When this appeared to her so plain that she felt she could not hold back from it, they committed her to the Lord, and left their doubts and anxieties with Him. She never shrank from the meanest offices to the sick and suffering, though their performance might be followed, as was often the case, by faintness and nausea. She would return home exhausted, but cheerful, and grateful that she had been able to help " one of God's suffering children."

In other ways the members of this united household were diligent in good works. If a neighbor required a few hundred dollars to save the foreclosure of a mortgage, the combined resources of the family were taxed to aid him; if a poor student needed a helping hand in his preparation for college, or for teaching, it was gladly extended to him —perhaps his board and lodging given him for six months or a year — with much valuable instruction thrown in. The instances of charity of this kind were many, and were performed with such a cheerful spirit that Sarah only incidentally alludes to the increase of their cares and work at such times. In fact, their roof was ever a shelter for the homeless, a home for the friendless; and it is pleasant to record that the return of ingratitude, so often made for benevolence of this kind, was never their portion. They always seem to have had the sweet satisfaction of knowing, sooner or later, that their kindness was not thrown away or under-estimated.

Besides the work of the farm, Mr. Weld interested himself in all the local affairs of his neighborhood. His energy, common sense, and enthusiasm pushed forward many a lagging improvement, while the influence of his moral and intellectual views was felt in every household. He taught the young men temperance, and the dignity of honest labor; to the young women he preached self-reliance, contempt for the frivolities of fashion, and the duty of making themselves independent. He became superintendent of the public schools of the township, and gave to them his warmest and most active services.

Sarah, although always ready to second Angelina in every charity, found her chief employment at home. She relieved her sister almost entirely of the care of the children, for in the course of years two more little ones were given to them, and she lessened the expenses by attending to household work, which would otherwise have called for another servant. After a short time, Mr. Weld's father, mother, sister, and brother, all invalids, came to live near them, claiming much of their sympathy and their care. Their niece also, the daughter of Mrs. Frost, now married, and the mother of children, took up her residence in the neighborhood, and Aunt Sai, as the children called her, and as almost every one else came, in time, to call her, found even fuller occupation for heart and hands. Her love for children was intense, and she had the rare faculty of being able to bring her intelligence down to theirs. Angelina's children were literally as her own, on whom she ever bestowed the tenderest care, and with whose welfare her holiest affections were intertwined. She often speaks of loving them with " all but a mother's love," of having them " enshrined in her heart of hearts," of " receiving through them the only cordial that could have raised a heart bowed by sorrow and crushing memories."

In one of her letters she says : " I live for Theodore and Angelina and the children, those blessed comforters to my poor, sad heart," and, during an absence from home, she writes to Angelina : —

" I have enjoyed being with my friends : still there is a longing, a yearning after my children. I miss the sight of those dear faces, the sound of those voices that comes like music to my ears."

In a letter to Sarah Douglass, written towards the close of their residence in Belleville, she says :'—

" In our precious children my desolate heart found a sweet response to its love. They have saved me from I know not what of horrible despair, or rushing into some new and untried and unsanctified effort to let off the fire that consumed me. Crushed, mutilated, torn, they comforted and cheered me, and furnished me with objects of interest which drew me from myself. I feel that they were the gift of a pitying Father, and that to love and cherish them is my highest manifestation of love to the Giver."

As the children grew, the parents began to feel the difficulty of educating them properly without other companions, and it was at last decided to take a few children into the family to be instructed with their own.

This was the beginning of another important chapter in their lives. As educators Mr. and Mrs. Weld very soon developed such rare ability, that although they had thought of limiting the number of pupils to two or three, so many were pressed upon them, with such good reasons for their acceptance, that the two or three became a dozen, and were with difficulty kept at that figure. In this new life their trials were many, their labor great, and the pecuniary compensation exceedingly moderate; but it is inspiring to read from Sarah the accounts of Theodore's courage — " always ready to take the heaviest end of every burden," and of Angelina's cheerfulness; and from Angelina the frequent testimony to Sarah's patience and fidelity. It took this dear Aunt Sai many years to learn to like teaching, especially as she never had any talent for governing, save by love, and this method was not always appreciated.

With their new and exacting work, the farm, of course, had to be given up, and was finally sold.

In 1852 the Raritan Bay Association, consisting of thirty or forty educated and cultured families of congenial tastes, was formed at Eagleswood, near Perth Amboy, New Jersey; and a year later Mr. and Mrs. Weld were invited to join the Association, and take charge of its educational department. They accepted in the hope of finding in the change greater social advantages for themselves and their children, with less responsibility and less labor; for of these last the husband, wife, and sister, in their Belleville school, had had more than they were physically able to endure longer. Their desire and plan was to establish, with the children of the residents at Eagleswood, a school also for others, and to charge such a moderate compensation only as would enable the middle classes to profit by it. In this project, as with every other, no selfish ambition found a place.

They removed to Eagleswood in the autumn of 1854.

And now, as I am nearing the end of my narrative, this seems to be the place to say a few words relative to the religious views into which the two sisters finally settled. We have followed them through their various conflicts from early youth to mature age, and have seen in their several changes of belief that there was no fickleness, no real inconsistency. They sought the truth, and at different times thought they had found it. But it was the truth as taught in Christ Jesus, the simple doctrine of the Cross they wanted, the preaching and practice of love for God, and for the meanest, the weakest, the lowest of His children. The spiritual conflicts through which they passed, prepared them to see the nothingness of all outward forms, and they came at last to reject the so-called orthodox creed, and to look only to God for help and comfort.

During the entire period of Sarah's connection with religious organizations, and even from her very first religious impressions, she found it difficult to accept the doctrine of the Atonement; and yet she professed and tried to think she believed it, but only because the Bible, which she accepted as a revelation from God, taught it. That her reason rebelled against it is shown in her frequent prayers to be delivered from this great temptation of the arch enemy, and her deep repentance whenever she lapsed into a state of doubt. The fear that she might come to reject this fundamental dogma was — at least up to the time when she was driven from the Quaker Church — one of her most terrible trials, causing her at intervals more agony than all else put together. But the worshipful element was so strong in Sarah that she could not, even after her reason had satisfied her conscience on this point, give up this Christ at whose feet she had learned her most precious lessons of faith and meekness and gentleness and long-suffering, and whom she had accepted and adored as her intermediary before an awful Jehovah. In her whole life there appears to me nothing more beautiful than this full, tender, abiding love of Jesus, and I believe it to have been the inspiration always of all that was loveliest and grandest in her character. In one of her letters, written while at Belleville, she says : —

"I cannot grasp the idea of an Infinite Being; but, without perplexing myself with questions which I cannot solve, everything around me proclaims the presence and the government of an intelligent, law-abiding Law-giver, and I believe implicitly in his power and his love. But I must have the Friend of sinners to rest in."

And again : "In one sense, as Creator and Benefactor, I feel this Infinite Being to be my Father, but I want a Jesus whom I can approach as a fellow creature, yet who is so nearly allied to God that I can look up to Him with reverence, and love Him and lie in His bosom."

And later, in a letter to Gerrit Smith, she says : —

"God is love, and whoso dwelleth in love dwelleth in God and God in him. O friends, but for this faith, this anchor to the soul both sure and steadfast, I know not what would have become of us in the sweep which there has been of what we called the doctrines of Christianity from our minds. They have passed away like the shadows of night, but the glorious truth remains that the Lord of love and mercy reigns, and great peace have they who do His will."

Their increasingly liberal views, and their growing indifference to most of the established forms in religion, drew upon them the severe censure of their Charleston relatives, and finally, when, about 1847, it came to be known that they no longer considered the Sabbath in a sacred light, their sister Eliza wrote to them that all personal intercourse must end between them and her, and that her doors would be forever closed against them. Angelina's answer, covering four full pages of foolscap, was most affectionate; but, while she expressed her sorrow at the feeling excited against them, she could not regret that they had been brought from error to truth. She argued the point fully, patiently giving all the best authorities concerning the substitution of the Christian for the Jewish Sabbath, and against their sister's assertion that the former was a divine institution.

"When I began to understand," she says, "what the gift of the Holy Spirit really was, then all outwardisms fell off. I did not throw them off through force of argument or example of others, but all reverence for them died in my heart. I could not help it; it was unexpected to me, and I wondered to find even the Sabbath gone. And now, to give to God alone the ceaseless worship of my life is all my creed, all my desire. Oh, for this pure, exalted state, how my soul pants after it! In my nursery and kitchen and parlor, when ministering to the common little wants of my family, and encountering the fretfulness and waywardness of my children, oh, for the pure worship of the soul which can enable me to meet and bear all the *little* trials of life in quietness and love and patience. This is the religion of Christ, and I feel that no other can satisfy me or meet the wants of human nature. I cannot sanction any other, and I dare not teach any other to my precious children."

Thus it came to pass with them and with Theodore also, that to love Jesus more, and to follow more and more after him, became the sum of their religion. With increasing years and wider experiences, their views broadened into the most comprehensive liberality, but the high worship of an infinite God, and the sweet reverence for his purest disciple never left them.

CHAPTER XVII.

In a letter to Dr. Harriot Hunt, Sarah Grimké thus describes Eagleswood : —

" It was a most enchanting spot. Situated on the Raritan Bay and River, just twenty-five miles from New York, and sixty miles from Philadelphia, in sight of the beautiful lower bay and of the dark Neversink Hills, all its surroundings appeal to my sense of the beautiful. In rambles through the woods or along the shore, new charms are constantly presented. The ever-varying face of the bay alone is a source of ceaseless enjoyment, and with the sound of its waves, sometimes dashing impetuously, sometimes murmuring softly, the eye, the ear, and the soul are filled with wonder and delight."

In this beautiful spot a commodious stone building was erected, suitable for association purposes. One end was divided into flats for a limited number of families; the other into school-rooms, dormitories, and parlors for social uses, while the centre contained the refectory for pupils and teachers, of whom there was an efficient corps, and dining-rooms for the other residents and their visitors. Several families of intelligence and culture resided in the immediate neighborhood, adding much to the social life of the place. All who were so fortunate as to be members of the Eagleswood family during Mr. Weld's administration must often look back with the keenest pleasure to the days passed there. It seems to me there can never be such a centre to such a circle as the Welds drew around them. Here gathered, at different times, many of the best, the brightest, the broadest minds of the day. Here came James G. Birney, Wm. H. Channing, Henry W. Bellows, O. B. Frothingham, Dr. Chapin, Wm. H. Furness, Wm. Cullen Bryant, the Collyers, Horace Greeley, Gerrit Smith, Moncure D. Conway, James Freeman Clarke, Joshua R. Giddings, Youmans, and a host of others whose names were known throughout the land. Here, too, came artists and poets for a few days' inspiration, and weary men of business for a little rest and intellectual refreshment, and leaders of reform movements, attracted by the liberal atmosphere of the place. Nearly all of these, invited by Mr. Weld, gave to the pupils and their families and friends, assembled in the parlors, something of themselves, — some personal experience, perhaps, or a lecture or short essay, or an insight into their own especial work and how it was done. The amount of pleasant and profitable instruction thus imparted was incalculable; while the after discussions and conversation were as enjoyable as might be expected from the friction of such minds. Seldom, if ever, in the famous *salons* of Europe were better things said or higher topics treated than in the Eagleswood parlors. All the rights and wrongs of humanity received here earnest consideration; while questions of general interest, politics, religion, the arts and sciences, even the last new novel or poem, had each its turn. Thoreau, also, spent many days at Eagleswood, and spoke often to the pupils; and A. Bronson Alcott gave them a series of his familiar lectures.

Here, on Sundays, Theodore D. Weld delivered lay sermons, so full of divine light and love, of precious lessons of contempt for all littleness, of patience with the weaknesses of our fellow-men, that few could listen without being inspired with higher and holier purposes in life.

Here James G. Birney died, in 1857, and was buried in the beautiful little cemetery on the crest of the hill.

Here were brought and interred the bodies of Stevens and Hazlitt, two of John Brown's mistaken but faithful apostles.

Here stirring lessons of patriotism were learned in 1860 –61, and from this place went forth, at the first call, some of the truest defenders of the liberties of the nation.

At Eagleswood, Mr. Weld and his faithful wife and sister passed some of their most laborious as well as some of their most pleasant and satisfactory years. They did not find the association all or even the half of what they had expected. "We had indulged the delightful hope," writes Sarah, "that Theodore would have no cares outside of the schoolroom, and Angelina would have leisure to pursue her studies and aid in the cause of woman. Her heart is in it, and her talents qualify her for enlarged usefulness. She was no more designed to serve tables than Theodore to dig potatoes. But verily, to use a homely phrase, we have jumped out of the frying-pan into the fire in point of leisure, for there are innumerable sponges here to suck up every spare moment; but dear Nina is a miracle of hope, faith, and endurance."

In the new school Angelina taught history, for which she was admirably qualified, while Sarah taught French, and was also book-keeper, both of which offices were distasteful to her because of her conscious incompetency. She did herself great injustice, as the results of her work showed, but it required a great mental struggle to reconcile herself to it in the beginning.

"I am driven to it," she says, "by a stern sense of duty. I feel its responsibilities and my own insufficiency so deeply, that I never hear the school bell with pleasure, and seldom enter the schoolroom without a sinking of the heart, a dread as of some approaching catastrophe. Oh, if I had only been developed into usefulness in early life, how much happier I should have been and would be now. From want of training, I am all slip-shod, and all I do, whether learning or teaching, is done slip-shod fashion. However, I must try and use the fag-end of me that is left, to the most advantage."

In order to do this, although sixty-one years old, she set earnestly to work to brush up her intellectual powers and qualify herself as far as possible for her position. She took French lessons daily, that she might improve her accent and learn the modern methods of teaching, and for months after she entered the Eagleswood school her reading was confined to such books as could enlighten her most on her especial work. She was rewarded by finding her interest in it constantly increasing, and she would doubtless have learned to love it, if, as she expressed it, her heart, soul, and mind had not been so nearly absorbed by the woman movement. Age and reflection had not only modified her views somewhat on this subject, but had given her a more just appreciation of the real obstacles in the way of the enfranchisement of her sex. Speaking of Horace Mann, she says : —

"He will not help the cause of woman greatly, but his efforts to educate her will do a greater work than he anticipates. Prepare woman for duty and usefulness, and she will laugh at any boundaries man may set for her.

She will as naturally fall into her right position as the feather floats in the air, or the pebble sinks in the water."

And at another time she writes: "I feel more and more that woman's work is inside, that the great battle must first be fought within, and the conquest obtained over her love of admiration, her vanity, her want of moral courage, her littleness, ere she is prepared to use her rights without abusing them. Women must come into the arena with men, not to increase the number of potsherds, but to elevate the standard of right."

Her ideal of womanhood was very high, and comprehended an education so different from the usual one, that she seldom ventured to unfold it. But she longed to do something towards it, and there is no doubt that but for home duties, which she felt were paramount, she would have undertaken a true missionary work of regeneration among women, especially of the lower classes. Many sleepless nights were passed pondering upon the subject. At one time she thought of editing a paper, then of studying law, that she might sometimes be able to advise and protect the weak and defenceless of her sex. She went so far in this as to consult an eminent lawyer in Philadelphia, but was discouraged by him. Then she considered the medical profession as opening to her a door of influence and usefulness among poor women. Sarah Douglass, who was a successful medical lecturer among the colored women of Philadelphia and New York, encouraged her friend in this idea, and urged her to take a course of lectures.

"I would dearly like to do as you say," Sarah Grimké answered, "but it must not be in Philadelphia. I cannot draw a long breath there, intellectual or moral. Freedom to live as my conscience dictates, to give free utterance to my thoughts, to have contact with those who are pressing after progress and whose watchword is onward, is needful to me. In Philadelphia there is an atmosphere of repression that would destroy me. Ground to powder as I was, in the mill of bigotry and superstition, I shudder at the thought of encountering again the same suffering I went through there. Indeed, I wonder I was not altogether stultified and dried up beyond the power of revivification, when the spring came to my darkened soul after that long, long winter. . . . There must be something in this wide, progressive world for me to do, but I must wait patiently to see what the future has in store for me."

All this, from a woman in her sixty-second year, shows how fresh was still her interest in humanity, and how little her desires for usefulness and improvement were dampened by age. But Angelina's continued delicate health kept her from carrying out any of her plans. She could see no way of escape consistent with duty and her devotion to the children, and she cheerfully submitted to the inevitable. But she could never bring herself to be satisfied with the Association life. She had had no ideal about it, no golden dreams, but joined it because she could not be separated from those she loved, and, with singular reasoning, she put one thousand dollars into it, because, if there was to be a failure and loss, she wished to share it with her sister and brother. But she had no affinity for living together in a great hotel, and it fretted her much, also, to see Mr. and Mrs. Weld taking constantly increasing burdens upon themselves as the school increased. Her longings, for their sake, for a little quiet home, are very pathetic. But she never allowed her anxieties to affect her intercourse in the household; on the contrary, no one was more full of life and good humor than she. Her favorite maxim was: "Bravely to meet our trials is true heroism; to bear them cheerfully, an exhibition of strength and fortitude infinitely beyond trying to get rid of them."

But it is doubtful, after all, if everything else had been favorable to it, that Sarah could have brought herself to leave Angelina and the children. She says herself: —

"A separation from the darling children who have brightened a few years of my lonely and sorrowful life overwhelms me when I think of it as the probable result of any change. They seem to be the links that bind me to life, the stars that shed light on my path, the beings in whom past, present, and future enjoyments are centred, without whom existence would have no charms."

All through her letters we see that, though generally cheerful, and often even merry, there were bitter moments in this devoted woman's life, moments when all the affection with which she was surrounded failed to fill the measure of her content. The old wounds would still sometimes bleed and the heart ache for home joys all her own. Writing to Jane Smith in 1852, she says: "I chide myself that I am not happier than I am, surrounded by so many blessings, but there are times when I feel as though the sun of earthly bliss had set for me. I know not what would have become of me but for Angelina's children. They have strewed my solitary path with flowers, and gemmed my sky with stars. My heart has brooded o'er sorrows untold, until life has seemed an awful blank, humanity a cheat, and myself an outcast. Then have come the soft accents of my children's voices, and they have spoken to me so lovingly, that I have turned from my bitter thoughts and have said: 'Forgive thy poor, weak servant, Lord.'"

All through Sarah's life, children had a great attraction for her. Even amid her cares and doubts at Eagleswood she writes: "Surrounded by all these dear young people, and drinking in from their exuberance, and scarcely living my own life, I cannot but be cheerful."

And describing an evening in the school parlor, when she joined in the Virginia reel, she says: "The children make one feel young if we will only be children with them. I owe them so much that I shall try to be cheerful to the end of my days."

And in this school, where boys and girls of all ages and all temperaments mingled, "Aunt Sai" was the great comforter and counsellor. Her inexhaustible tenderness and mother-love blessed all who came near her and soothed all who had a heartache. The weak and erring found in her a frank but pitying rebuker; the earnest and good, a kind friend and wise helper, and a child never feared to go to her either to ask a favor or to confess a fault.

At Eagleswood the Welds kept up as far as practicable their frugal habits, though, soon after their establishment, they all modified their Graham diet so far as to take meat once a day. Sarah's economy, especially in trifles, was remarkable, almost as much so as the untiring, almost painful industry of herself and Mrs. Weld. A penny was never knowingly wasted, a minute never willingly lost. Among other thrifty devices, she generally wrote to her friends on the backs of circulars, on blank pages of notes she received, on almost any clean scrap, in fact. Angelina often remonstrated with her, but to no avail.

"It gives me a few more pennies for my love purse, and my friends won't mind," she would say.

This " love purse " was well named. Into it were cast all her small economies : a car-fare when she walked instead of riding; a few pennies saved by taking a simpler lunch than she had planned, when in New York on business; the ten cents difference in the quality of a cap, ribbon, or a handkerchief, — all these savings were dropped into the love purse, to be drawn out again to buy a new book for some friend too poor to get it herself; to subscribe to a paper for another; to purchase some little gift for a sick child, or a young girl trying to keep up a neat appearance. It was a pair of cuffs to one, mittens or slippers of her own knitting to another, a collar or a ribbon to a third. All through the letters written during the last twenty years of her life, the references to such little gifts are innumerable, and show that her generosity was only equalled by her thoughtfulness, and only limited by her means. Nothing was spent unnecessarily, in the strictest sense of the word, on herself; not a dollar of her narrow income laid by. All went for kindly or charitable objects, and was gladly given without a single selfish twinge.

It is scarcely necessary to say that few schools have ever been established upon such a basis of conscientiousness and love, and with such adaptability in its conductors as that at Eagleswood; few have ever held before the pupils so high a moral standard, or urged them on to such noble purposes in life. Children entered there spoiled by indulgence, selfish, uncontrolled, sometimes vicious. Their teachers studied them carefully; confidence was gained, weaknesses sounded, elevation measured. Very slowly often, and with infinite patience and perseverance, but successfully in nearly every case, these children were redeemed. The idle became industrious, the selfish considerate, the disobedient and wayward repentant and gentle. Sometimes the fruits of all this labor and forbearance did not show themselves immediately, and in a few instances the seed sown did not ripen until the boy or girl had left school and mingled with the world. Then the contrast between the common, every-day aims they encountered, and the teachings of their Eagleswood mentors, was forced upon them. Forgotten lessons of truth and honesty and purity were remembered, and the wavering resolve was stayed and strengthened; worldly expediency gave way before the magnanimous purpose, cringing subserviency before independent manliness. The letters of affection, gratitude, and appreciation of what had been done to make true men and women of them, which were received by the Welds, in many cases, years after they had parted from the writers, were treasured as their most precious souvenirs, and quite reconciled them to the trials through which such results were reached.

A short time before leaving Belleville, Mrs. Weld and Sarah adopted the Bloomer costume on account of its convenience, and the greater freedom it permitted in taking long rambles, but neither of them ever admired it or urged its adoption on others. Mrs. Weld, it is true, wrote a long and eloquent letter to the Dress Reform Convention which met in Syracuse in the summer of 1857, but it was not to advocate the Bloomer, but to show the need of some dress more suitable than the fashionable one, for work and exercise. She also urged that as woman was no longer in her minority, no longer " man's pretty idol before whom he bowed in chivalric gallantry," or " his petted slave whom he coaxed and gulled with sugar-plum privileges, whilst robbing her of intrinsic rights," but was emerging into her majority and claiming her rights as a human being, and waking up to a higher destiny: as she was beginning to answer the call to a life of useful exertion and honorable independence, it was time that she dressed herself in accordance with the change. " I regard the Bloomer costume," she says, " as only an approach to that true womanly attire which will in due time be inaugurated. We must experiment before we find a dress altogether suitable. . . . Man has long enough borne the burden of supporting the women of the civilized world. When woman's temple of liberty is finished — when freedom for the world is achieved — when she has educated herself into useful and lucrative occupations, then may she fitly expend upon her person *her own earnings*, not man's. Such women will have an indefeasible right to dress elegantly if they wish, but they will discard cumbersomeness and a useless and absurd circumference and length."

Sarah says, in a letter to a friend, that the Bloomer dress violated her taste, and was so opposed to her sense of modesty that she could hardly endure it. During the residence at Eagleswood, both sisters discarded it altogether.

The John Brown tragedy was of course deeply felt by Sarah and Angelina, and the bitter and desperate feelings which inspired it fully sympathized with. Angelina was made quite ill by it, while Sarah felt her soul bowed with reverence for the deluded but grand old man. " O Sarah ! " she writes to Sarah Douglass, " what a glorious spectacle is now before us. The Jerome of Prague of our country, the John Huss of the United States, now stands ready, as they were, to seal his testimony with his life's blood. Last night I went in spirit to the martyr. It was my privilege to enter into sympathy with him ; to go down, according to my measure, into the depths where he has travailed, and feel his past exercises, his present sublime position."

As mentioned a few pages back, two of John Brown's men, who died with him at Harper's Ferry, were brought to Eagleswood and there quietly interred. The proslavery people of Perth Amboy threatened to dig up the bodies, but the men and boys of Eagleswood showed such a brave front, and guarded the graves so faithfully, that the threat could not be accomplished.

The breaking out of the war found the Welds in deep family sorrow, watching anxiously by the sick bed of a dear son, with scarcely a hope of his recovery. Of Sarah's absolute devotion, of her ceaseless care by day, and her tireless watching by night, during the many long and weary months through which that precious life flickered, it is needless to speak. She took the delicate mother's place beside that bed of suffering, and, strong in her faith and hope, gave strength and hope to the heart-stricken parents, sustaining them when they were ready to sink beneath the avalanche of their woe. And when at last, though life was spared, it was evident that the invalid must remain an invalid for a long time, perhaps forever, Sarah's sublime courage stood steadfast. There was no sign of faltering. With a resignation almost cheerful, she took up her fresh burden, and, intent only on cheering her dear patient and comforting the sorrow of her sister and brother, she forgot her seventy-one years and every grief of the past. " I try," she writes, " to accept this, the most grinding and bitter dispensation of my checkered life, as what it must be, educational and disciplinary, working towards a better preparation for a higher life."

Chiefly on account of this son and the quiet which was necessary for him, Mr. and Mrs. Weld gave up their position at Eagleswood, to the deep regret of all who knew them and had children to educate. They settled themselves temporarily in a pleasant house in Perth Amboy. Here, between nursing their sick, and working for the soldiers, they watched the progress of events which they had long foreseen were inevitable.

Sarah speaks of the war as a retribution. "Hitherto," she says, "we have never been a republic, but one of the blackest tyrannies that ever disgraced the earth."

She calls attention to the fact that the South, by starting out with a definite and declared purpose, added much to its strength. "In great revolutions," she says, "confusion in popular ideas is fatal. The South avoided this. She set up one idea as paramount; she seized a great principle and uttered it. She shouted the talismanic words, 'Oppression and Liberty,' and said, 'Let us achieve our purpose or die!' The masses, blinded by falsehood, caught the spirit of the leaders, and verily believe they are struggling for freedom. We have never enunciated any great truth as the cause of our uprising. We have no great idea to rally around, and know not what we are fighting for.

Later she expresses herself very strongly concerning the selfishness of the politicians, North and South.

"It is true there are some," she writes, "who are waging this war to make our Declaration of Independence a fact; there is a glorious band who are fighting for human rights, but the government, with Lincoln at its head, has not a heart-throb for the slave. I want the South to do her own work of emancipation. She would do it only from dire necessity, but the North will do it from no

higher motive, and the South will feel less exasperation
if she does it herself."

In another letter in 1862, she writes : —

"The negro has generously come forward, in spite of
his multiplied wrongs, and offered to help to defend the
country against those who are trying to fasten the chains
on the white as well as the black. We have impiously
denied him the right of citizenship, and have virtually
said, ' Stand back ; I am holier than thou.' I pray that
victory may not crown our arms until the negro stands
in his acknowledged manhood side by side in this conflict
with the white man, until we have the nobility to say
that this war is a war of abolition, and that no concession
on the part of the South shall save slavery from destruction. Whatever Lincoln and his Cabinet are carrying on
the war to accomplish, God's design is to deliver from
bondage his innocent people."

About this time Mrs. Weld published one of the most
powerful things she ever wrote, " A Declaration of War
on Slavery." She and Sarah also drew up a petition to
the government for the entire abolition of slavery, and
took it around themselves for signatures. Very few
refused to sign it ; and they were proposing to canvass, by
means of agents, the entire North, when the Emancipation Proclamation was issued.

With their Charleston relatives, Mrs. Weld and Sarah
had always kept up a rather irregular, but, on one side, at
least, an affectionate correspondence. Their mother died
in 1839, retaining, to the never-ceasing grief of her
Northern daughters, her slave-holding principles to the
last. The few remaining members of the family were
settled in and around Charleston, and were, with one exception, in comfortable circumstances at the beginning of

the war. This exception was their brother John, who was infirm, and had outlived his resources and the ability to make a living. For years before the war, Sarah and Angelina sent him from their slender incomes a small annuity, sufficient to keep him from want, and it was continued, at much inconvenience during the war, until his death, which occurred in the latter part of 1863. Their sisters, Mary and Eliza, wrote very proud and defiant letters during the first two years of hostilities, and declared they were secure and happy in their dear old city. But gradually their tone changed, and they did not refuse to receive, through blockade-runners, a variety of necessary articles from their abolition sisters. As their slaves deserted them, and one piece of property after another lost its value or was destroyed, they saw poverty staring them in the face; but their pride sustained them, and it was not until they had lived for nearly a year on little else but hominy and water that they allowed their sisters to know of their condition. But in informing them of it, they still declared their willingness to die " for slavery and the Confederacy."

" Blind to the truth," writes Sarah, " they religiously believe that slavery is a divine institution, and say they hope never to be guilty of disbelieving the Bible, and thus rendering themselves amenable to the wrath of God. I am glad," she adds, " to have this lesson of honest blindness. It shows me that thousands like themselves are worshipping a false god of their own creation."

Of course relief was sent to these unhappy women as soon as possible ; and when hostilities ceased, more than two hundred dollars' worth of necessaries of every kind was despatched to them, with an urgent invitation to come and accept a home at the North. Some time before this, however, the Welds had moved to Hyde Park, near Boston, and were delightfully located, owning their house, and surrounded by kind and congenial neighbors. But much as they all needed entire rest, and well as they had earned it, they could not afford to be idle. Sarah became housekeeper and general manager, while Mr. and Mrs. Weld accepted positions, in Dr. Dio Lewis's famous school at Lexington. They were obliged to leave home every Monday and return on Friday.

The Charleston sisters refused for some time to accept the invitation given them; but so delicately and affectionately was it urged, that, goaded by necessity, they finally consented. They made their preparations to leave Charleston; but in the midst of them, the older sister, Mary, who had been very feeble for some time, was taken suddenly ill, and died. Eliza, then, a most sad and desolate woman, as we may well suppose, made the voyage to New York alone. There Sarah met her, and accompanied her to Hyde Park, where she was received with every consideration affection could devise. She seems to have soon made up her mind to make the best of her altered circumstances, and thus show her gratitude to those who had so readily overlooked her past abuse of them. Sarah writes of her in 1866: —

" My sister Eliza is well and so cheerful. She is a sunbeam in the family, but the failure of the Confederacy and the triumph of the ' Yankees ' is hard to bear, — the wrong having crushed the right."

This sister was tenderly cared for until arrangements were made for her return to Charleston with Mrs. Frost. There she died in 1867. This was only one of the many minor cases of retribution brought about by the Nemesis of the civil war. Sarah mentions another. The sale of lands for government taxes at Beaufort, S. C., was made from the verandah of the Edmond Rhett House, where, more than ten years before, the rebellion was concocted by the very men whose estates then (1866) were passing under the hammer. And the chairman of the tax committee was Dr. Wm. H. Brisbane, who, twenty-five years before, was driven from the State because he would liberate his slaves.

Quietly settled in what she felt was a permanent home, and with no cares outside of her family, Sarah found time not only to read, but to indulge her taste for scribbling, as she called it. She sent, from time to time, articles to the New York *Tribune*, the *Independent*, the *Woman's Journal*, and other papers, all marked by remarkable freshness as well as vigor. She also translated from the French several stories illustrative of various social reforms, and in 1867, being then seventy-five years old, she made a somewhat abridged translation of Lamartine's poetical biography of Joan of Arc. This was Sarah's most finished literary work, and aroused in her great enthusiasm. "Sometimes," she writes, "it seems to infuse into my soul a mite of that divinity which filled hers. Joan of Arc stands pre-eminent in my mind above all other mortals save the Christ."

When the book was finished, Sarah was most anxious to get it published, "in order," she writes, "to revive the memory in this country of the extraordinary woman who was an embodiment of faith, courage, fortitude, and love rarely equalled and never excelled."

But she had many more pressing demands on her income at that time, and had nearly given up the project, when a gentleman from Lynn called to see her, to whom she read a few pages of the narrative. He was so much pleased with it that he undertook to have it published. It was brought out in a few weeks by Adams & Co., of Boston, in a prettily bound volume of one hundred and six pages, and had, I believe, a large sale. Several long and many short notices of it appeared in papers all over the country, all highly complimentary to the venerable translator. These notices surprised Sarah as much as they delighted her, and she expressed herself as deeply thankful that she had translated the work.

A letter from Sarah Grimké to Jane Smith, written in 1850, contains the following paragraph : " We have just heard of the death of our brother Henry, a planter and a kind master. His slaves will feel his loss deeply. They haunt me day and night. Sleeplessness is my portion, thinking what will become of them. Oh, the horrors of slavery ! "

When she penned those lines, Sarah little imagined how great a mockery was the title, " kind master," she gave her brother. She little suspected that three of those slaves whose uncertain destiny haunted her pillow were that brother's own children, and that he died leaving the shackles on them — slaves to his heir, their white brother, though he *did* stipulate that they and their mother should never be sold. Well might Sarah exclaim : " Oh, the horrors of slavery ! " but in deepest humiliation and anguish of spirit would the words have been uttered had she known the truth. Montague Grimké inherited his brothers with the rest of the human chattels. He knew they were his brothers, and he never thought of freeing them. They were his to use and to abuse, — to treat them kindly if it suited his mood ; to whip them if he fancied ; to sell them if he should happen to need money, — and they could not raise voice or hand to prevent it. There was no law to which they could appeal, no refuge they could seek from the very worst with which their brother might threaten them. Was ever any creature — brute or human — in the wide world so defenceless as the plantation slave ! The forlorn case of these Grimké boys was that of thousands of others born as they were, and inheriting the intelligence and spirit of independence of their white parent.

I have little space to give to their pitiful story. Many have doubtless heard it. The younger brother, John, was, at least as a child, more fortunate. When Charleston was at last occupied by the Union army, the two oldest, Francis and Archibald, attracted the attention of some members of the Sanitary Commission by their intelligence and good behavior, and were by them sent to Massachusetts, where some temporary work was found for them. Two vacancies happening to occur in Lincoln University, Oxford, Pennsylvania, they were recommended to fill them. Thither they went in 1866, and, eager and determined to profit by their advantages, they studied so well during the winter months, and worked so diligently to help themselves in the summer, that, in spite of the drawbacks of their past life, they rose to honorable positions in the University, and won the regard of all connected with it. Some time in February, 1868, Mrs. Weld read in the *Anti-Slavery Standard* a notice of a meeting of a literary society at Lincoln University, at which an address was delivered by one of the students, named Francis Grimké. She was surprised, and as she had never before heard of the university, she made some inquiries about it, and was much interested in what she learned of its object and character. She knew that the name of Grimké was confined to the Charleston family, and naturally came to the conclusion, at first, that this student who had attracted her attention was an ex-slave of one of her brothers, and had, as was frequently done, adopted his master's name. But the circumstance worried her. She could not drive it from her mind. She knew so well that blackest page of slavery on which was written the wrongs of its women, that, dreadful as was the suspicion, it slowly grew upon her that the blood of the Grimkés, the proud descendants of the Huguenots, flowed in the veins of this poor colored student. The agitation into which further reflection on the subject threw her came very near making her ill and finally decided her to learn the truth if possible. She addressed a note to Mr. Francis Grimké. The answer she received confirmed her worst fears. He and his brothers were her nephews. Her nerves already unstrung by the dread of this cruel blow, Angelina fainted when it came, and was completely prostrated for several days. Her husband and sister refrained from disturbing her by a question or a suggestion. Physically stronger than she, they felt the superiority of her spiritual strength, and uncertain, on this most momentous occasion, of their own convictions of duty, they looked to her for the initiative.

The silent conflict in the soul of this tender, conscientious woman during those days of prostration was known only to her God. The question of prejudice had no place in it, — that had long and long ago been cast to the winds. It was the fair name of a loved brother that was at stake, and which must be sustained or blighted by her action. "Ask me not," she once wrote to a young person, "if it is expedient to do what you propose: ask yourself if it is *right*." This question now came to her in a shape it had never assumed before, and it was hard to answer. But it was no surprise to her family when she came forth from that chamber of suffering and announced her decision. She would acknowledge those nephews. She would not deepen the brand of shame that had been set upon their brows: hers, rather, the privilege to efface it. Her brother had wronged these, his children; his sisters must right them. No doubt of the duty lingered in her mind. Those youths were her own flesh and blood, and, though the whole world should scoff, she would not deny them.

Her decision was accepted by her husband and sister without a murmur of dissent. If either had any doubts of its wisdom, they were never uttered; and, as was always the case with them, having once decided in their own minds a question of duty, they acted upon it in no half-way spirit, and with no stinted measures. In the long letter which Angelina wrote to Francis and Archibald Grimké, and which Theodore Weld and Sarah Grimké fully indorsed, there appeared no trace of doubt or indecision. The general tone was just such in which she might have addressed newly-found legitimate nephews. After telling them that if she had not suspected their relationship to herself, she should probably not have written them, she questions them on various points, showing her desire to be useful to them, and adds, "I want to talk to you face to face, and am thinking seriously of going on to your Commencement in June." A few lines further on she says:—

"I will not dwell on the past: let all that go. It cannot be altered. Our work is in the present, and duty calls upon us now so to use the past as to convert its curse into a blessing. I am glad you have taken the name of Grimké. It was once one of the noblest names of Carolina. You, my young friends, now bear this *once* honored name. I charge you most solemnly, by your upright conduct and your life-long devotion to the eternal principles of justice and humanity and religion, to lift this name out of the dust where it now lies, and set it once more among the princes of our land."

Other letters passed between them until the youths had told all their history, so painful in its details that Angelina, after glancing at it, put it aside, and for months had not the courage to read it. When June came, though far from well, she summoned up strength and resolution to do as she had proposed in the spring. Accompanied by her oldest son, she attended the Lincoln University Commencement, and made the personal acquaintance of Francis and Archibald Grimké. She found them good-looking, intelligent, and gentlemanly young men; and she took them by the hand, and, to president and professors, acknowledged their claim upon her. She also invited them to visit her at her home, assuring them of a kind reception from every member of her family. She remained a week at Lincoln University, going over with these young men all the details of their treatment by their brother Montague, and of the treatment of the slaves in all the Grimké families. These details brought back freshly to her mind the horrors which had haunted her life in Charleston, and she lived them all over again, even in her dreams. She had been miserably weak and worn for some time before going to Lincoln; and the mental distress she now went through affected her nervous system to such an extent that there is no doubt her life was shortened by it.

The hearty concurrence of every member of the family in the course resolved on towards the nephews shows how united they were in moral sentiment as well as in affection. There was not the slightest hesitancy exhibited. The point touching her brother's shame thrust in the background by the conviction of a higher duty, Mrs. Weld allowed it to trouble her no more, but, with her husband and sister, expressed a feeling of exultation in acknowledging the relationship of the youths, as a testimony and protest against the wickedness of that hate which had always trampled down the people of color because they were as God made them.

On Angelina's return journey, Sarah, ever anxious about her, met her at Newark and accompanied her home. A few weeks later, writing to Sarah Douglass an account of the Grimké boys, she says : —

"They are very promising young men. We all feel deeply interested in them, and I hope to be able to get together money enough to pay the college expenses of the younger. I would rejoice to meet these entirely myself, but, not having the means, I intend to try and collect it somehow. Angelina has not yet recovered from the effects of her journey and the excitement of seeing and talking to those boys, the president, etc. When I met her she was so exhausted and excited that I felt very anxious, and when I found her brain and sight were so disordered that she could not see distinctly, even striking her head several times severely, and that she could not read, I was indeed alarmed. But, notwithstanding all she had suffered, she has not for a moment regretted that she went. She feels that a sacred duty has been performed, and rejoices that she had strength for it."

A few weeks later, she writes: "Nina is about and always busy, often working when she seems ready to drop, sustained by her nervous energy and irresistible will. She has kept up wonderfully under our last painful trial, and has borne it so beautifully that I am afraid she is getting too good to live."

I have no right to say that Angelina Weld suffered martyrdom in every fibre of her proud, sensitive nature during all the first months at least of this trial; but I cannot but believe it. She never spoke of her own feelings to any one but her husband; but Sarah writes to Sarah Douglass in August, 1869: —

"My cheerful spirit has been sorely tested for some months. Nina has been sick all summer, is a mere skeleton and looks ten or fifteen years older than she did before that fatal visit to Lincoln University. I do not think that she will ever be the same woman she was before and sometimes I feel sure her toilsome journey on this earth must be near its close. The tears will come whenever I think of it."

But not so! the sisters were to work hand in hand a few years longer; the younger, in her patient suffering, leaning with filial love on the stronger arm of the older, both now gray-haired and beginning to feel the infirmities of age, but still devoted to each other and united in sympathy with every good and progressive movement. The duty, as they conceived it, to their colored nephews was as generously as conscientiously performed. They received them into the family, treated them in every respect as relatives, and exerted themselves to aid them in finishing their education. Francis studied for the ministry, and is now pastor of the 15th Street Presbyterian Church of Washington city. Archibald, through Sarah's exertions and self-denial, took the law course at Harvard, graduated, and has since practised law successfully in Boston. Both are respected by the communities in which they reside. John, the younger brother, remained in the South with his mother.

Mrs. Weld and Sarah still took a warm, and, as far as

it was possible, an active interest in the woman suffrage movement; and when, in February, 1870, after an eloquent lecture from Lucy Stone, a number of the most intelligent and respectable women of Hyde Park determined to try the experiment of voting at the approaching town election, Mrs. Weld and Sarah Grimké united cordially with them. A few days before the election, a large caucus was held, made up of about equal numbers of men and women, among them many of the best and leading people of the place. A ticket for the different offices was made up, voted for, and elected. At this caucus Theodore Weld made one of his old-time stirring speeches, encouraging the women to assert themselves, and persist in demanding their political rights.

The 7th of March, the day of the election, a terrific snowstorm prevailed, but did not prevent the women from assembling in the hotel near the place of voting, where each one was presented, on the part of their gentlemen friends, with a beautiful bouquet of flowers. At the proper time, a number of these gentlemen came over to the hotel and escorted the ladies to the polls, where a convenient place for them to vote had been arranged. There was a great crowd inside the hall, eager to see the joke of women voting, and many were ready to jeer and hiss. But when, through the door, the women filed, led by Sarah Grimké and Angelina Weld, the laugh was checked, the intended jeer unuttered, and deafening applause was given instead. The crowd fell back respectfully, nearly every man removing his hat and remaining uncovered while the women passed freely down the hall, deposited their votes, and departed.

Of course these votes were not counted. There was no expectation that they would be (though the ticket was elected), but the women had given a practical proof of their earnestness, and though one man said, in consequence of this movement, he would sell his house two thousand dollars cheaper than he would have done before, and another declared he would give his away if the thing was done again, and still another wished he might *die* if the women were going to vote, the women themselves were satisfied with their first step, and more than ever determined to march courageously on until the citadel of man's prejudices was conquered.

The following summer, Sarah Grimké, believing that much good might be accomplished by the circulation of John Stuart Mill's "Subjection of Women," made herself an agent for the sale of the book, and traversed hill and dale, walking miles daily to accomplish her purpose. She thus succeeded in placing more than one hundred and fifty copies in the hands of the women of Hyde Park and the vicinity, in spite of the ignorance, narrowness, heartlessness, and slavery which, she says, she had ample opportunity to deplore. The profits of her sales were given to the *Woman's Journal*.

Under date of May 25, 1871, she writes : —

"I have been travelling all through our town and vicinity on foot, to get signers to a petition to Congress for woman suffrage. It is not a pleasant work, often subjecting me to rudeness and coldness; but we are so frequently taunted with : ' Women don't want the ballot,' that we are trying to get one hundred thousand names of women who do want it, to reply to this taunt."

But the work which enlisted this indefatigable woman's warmest sympathies, and which was the last active charity in which she engaged, was that of begging cast-off clothing for the destitute freedmen of Charleston and

Florida. Accounts reaching her of their wretched condition through successive failures of crops, she set to work with her old-time energy to do what she could for their relief. She literally went from house to house, and from store to store, presenting her plea so touchingly that few could refuse her. Many barrels of clothing were in this way gathered, and she often returned home staggering beneath the weight of bundles she had carried perhaps for a mile. She also wrote to friends at a distance, on whose generosity she felt she could depend, and collected from them a considerable sum of money, which went far to keep the suffering from starvation until new crops could be gathered. Writing to Sarah Douglass, she says : —

"I have been so happy this winter, going about to beg old clothing for the unfortunate freedmen in Florida. I have sent off several barrels of clothes already. Alas! there is no Christ to multiply the garments, and what are those I send among so many? I think of these destitute ones night and day, and feel so glad to help them even a little."

This happiness in helping others was the secret of Sarah Grimké's unvarying contentment, and there was always some one needing the help she was so ready to give, some one whose trials made her feel, she says, ashamed to think of her own. But the infirmities of old age were creeping upon her, and though her mental faculties remained as bright as ever, she began to complain of her eyes and her hearing. In August, 1872, she writes to a friend : —

"My strength is failing. I cannot do a tithe of the walking I used to do, and am really almost good for nothing. But I don't know but I may learn to enjoy doing nothing; and if it is needful, I shall be thankful, as that has always appeared to me a great trial."

Notwithstanding this representation, however, she was seldom idle a moment. She was an untiring knitter, and made quite a traffic of the tidies, cushion-covers, and other fancy articles she knitted and netted. These were purchased by her friends, and the proceeds given to the poor. Soon after she had penned the above quoted paragraph, too, she copied for the Rev. Henry Giles, the once successful Unitarian preacher, a lecture of sixty-five pages, from which he hoped to make some money. His eyesight had failed, and his means were too narrow to permit of his paying a copyist. She also managed to keep up more or less, as her strength permitted, her usual visits to the poor and afflicted; and during the hot summer of 1872 she and Angelina went daily to read to an old, bed-ridden lady, who was dying of cancer, and living almost alone. During the following winter Sarah's strength continued to fail, and she had several fainting spells, of which, however, she was kept in ignorance. But as life's pulse beat less vigorously, her heart seemed to grow warmer, and her interest in all that concerned her friends rather to increase than to lessen. She still wrote occasional short letters, and enjoyed nothing so much as those she received, especially from young correspondents. In January, 1873, she writes to an old friend : —

"Yes, dear . . . . I esteem it a very choice blessing that, as the outer man decays, the heart seems enlarged in charity, and more and more drawn towards those I love. Oh, this love! it is as subtle as the fragrance of the flower, an indefinable essence pervading the soul. My eyesight and my hearing are both in a weakly condition; but I trust, as the material senses fail, the interior perception of the divine may be opened to a clearer knowledge of God, and that I may read the glorious book of nature with a more heavenly light, and apprehend with clearer insight the majesty and divinity and capabilities of my own being."

A few months later, she writes : " My days of active usefulness are over; but there is a passive work to be done, far harder than actual work, — namely, to exercise patience and study humble resignation to the will of God, whatever that may be. Thanks be to Him, I have not yet felt like complaining; nay, verily, the song of my heart is, Who so blest as I ? In years gone by, I used to rejoice as every year sped its course and brought me nearer to the grave. Bnt now, though the grave has no terrors for me, and death looks like a pleasant transition to another and a better condition, I am content to wait the Father's own time for my removal. I rejoice that my ideal is still in advance of my actual, though I can only look for realization in another life. I know of a truth that my immortal spirit must progress; not into a state of perfect happiness, — that would have no attractions for me; there must be deficiencies in my heaven, to leave room for progression. A realm of unqualified *rest* were a stagnant pool of being, and the circle of absolute perfection a waveless calm, the abstract cipher of indolence. But I believe I shall be gifted with higher faculties, greater powers, and therefore be capable of higher aspirations, better achievements, and a nobler appreciation of God and His works."

The sweet tranquillity expressed in this letter, and which was the greatest blessing that could have been given to Sarah Grimké's last years, grew day by day, and shed its benign influence on all about her. She had long ceased to look back, and had long been satisfied that though she had had an ample share of sorrows and perplexities, her life had passed, after all, with more of good than evil in it, more of enjoyment than sorrow. Her experience had been rich and varied; and, while she could see, in the past, sins committed, errors of judgment, idiosyncracies to which she had too readily yielded, she felt that all had been blest to her in enlarging her knowledge of herself, in widening her sphere of usefulness, and uniting her more closely to Him who had always been her guide, and whose promises sustained and blessed her, and crowned her latter days with joy supreme.

CHAPTER XVIII.

SARAH GRIMKÉ had always enjoyed such good health, and was so unaccustomed to even small ailments, that when a slight attack came in the beginning of August, 1873, in the shape of a fainting-fit in the night, she did not understand what it meant. For two or three years she had had an occasional attack of the same kind, but was never before conscious of it, and as she had frequently expressed a desire to be alone when she died, to have no human presence between her and her God, she thought, as the faintness came over her, that this desire was about to be gratified. But not so: she returned to consciousness, somewhat to her disappointment, and seemed to quite recover her health in a few days. The weather, however, was extremely warm, and she felt its prostrating effects. On the 27th of August another fainting-spell came over her, also in the night, and she felt so unwell on coming out of it that she was obliged to call assistance. For several weeks she was very ill, and scarcely a hope of her recovery was entertained; but again she rallied and tried to mingle with the family as usual, though feeling very weak. Writing to Sarah Douglass of this illness, she says:—

" The first two weeks are nearly a blank. I only remember a sense of intense suffering, and that the second day I thought I was dying, and felt calm with that sweet peace which our heavenly Father gives to those who lay their heads on His bosom and breathe out their souls to Him. Death is so beautiful a transition to another and a higher sphere of usefulness and happiness, that it no longer looks to me like passing through a dark valley, but rather like merging into sunlight and joy. When consciousness returned to me, I was floating in an ocean of divine love. Oh, dear Sarah, the unspeakable peace that I enjoyed! Of course I was to come down from the mount, but not into the valley of despondency. My mind has been calm, my faith steadfast, my continual prayer that I may fulfil the design of my Father in thus restoring me to life and finish the work he must have for me to do, either active or passive. I am lost in wonder, love, and praise at the vast outlay of affection and means used for my restoration. Stuart was like a tender daughter, and all have been so loving, so patient."

She continued very feeble, but insisted upon joining the family at meals, though she frequently had to be carried back to her room. Still her lively interest in every one about her showed no diminution, and she still wrote, as strength permitted, short letters to old friends. A few passages may be quoted from these letters to show how clear her intellect remained, and with what a holy calm her soul was clothed. To one nearly her own age, she says : —

" You and I and all who are on the passage to redemption know that Gethsemane has done more for us than the Mount of Transfiguration. I am sure I have advanced more in the right way through my sins than through my righteousness, and for nothing am I more fervently grateful than for the lessons of humility I have learned in this way."

To another who was mourning the death of a dear child, she writes : "My whole heart goes out in unspeakable yearnings for you; not, dearest, that you may be delivered from your present trials; not only that you may be blessed with returning health, but that you may find something better, holier, stronger than philosophy to sustain you. Philosophy may enable us to *endure ;* this is its highest mission ; it cannot give the peace of God which passeth all understanding. This is what I covet for you. And how can you doubt of immortality when you look on your beloved's face? Can you believe that the soul which looked out of those eyes can be quenched in endless night? No; never! As soon doubt existence itself. It is this — these central truths, the existence and the love of God, and the immortality of the soul, which rob death of its terrors and shed upon it the blessed light of a hope which triumphs over death itself. Oh that you could make Christ your friend! He is so near and dear to me that more than ever does he seem to be my link to the Father and to the life everlasting."

As she complained only of weakness, Sarah's friends hoped that, when the cool weather came on, she would regain her strength and be as well as usual. But though she continued to move about the house, trying to make herself useful, there was very little perceptible change in her condition as the autumn passed and winter came on. Thus she continued until the 12th of December, when she took a violent cold. She was in the habit of airing her bed every night just before retiring, turning back the cover, and opening wide her window. On that day it had rained, and the air was very damp, but she had her bed and window opened as usual, insisting that Florence Nightingale asserted that damp air never hurt anyone. That night she coughed a great deal, but in answer to Angelina's expressions of anxiety, said she felt no worse than usual. But though she still went down to her meals, it was evident that she was weaker than she had been. On Sunday, the 14th, company coming to tea, she preferred to remain in her room. She never went down again. Her breathing was much oppressed on Monday and her cough worse, but it was not until Tuesday evening, after having passed a distressing day, that she would consent to have a physician called. Everything was done for her that could be thought of, and, as she grew worse, two other physicians were sent for. But all in vain: it was evident that the summons to "come up higher" had reached her yearning soul, and that a bright New Year was dawning for her in that unseen world which she was so well prepared to enter.

She lingered, suffering at times great agony from suffocation, until the afternoon of the 23d, when she was seized with the most severe paroxysm she had yet had. Her family gathered about her bed, relieved her as far as it was possible, and saw her sink exhausted into an unconscious state, from which, two hours later, she crossed the threshold of Eternity. Her "precious Nina" bent over her, caught the last breath, and exclaimed: "Well done, good and faithful servant, enter thou into the joy of thy Lord!"

The gates of heaven swung wide to admit that great soul, and the form of clay that was left lying there seemed touched with the glory that streamed forth. All traces of suffering vanished, and the placid face wore —

" The look of one who bore away
Glad tidings from the hills of day."

Every sorrow brings a peace with it, and Angelina's sorrow was swallowed up in joy that the beloved sister had escaped from pain and infirmity, and entered into fuller and closer communion with her heavenly Father.

She and Sarah had promised each other that no stranger hands should perform the last offices to their mortal remains. How lovingly this promise was now kept by Angelina, we must all understand.

The weather was very cold, and in order to give her friends at a distance opportunity to attend the funer:[1] it did not take place until the 27th. One of the last requests of this woman, whose life had been an embodiment of the most tender charity and the truest humility, was that she might be laid in a plain pine coffin, and the difference in price between it and the usual costly one be given as her last gift to the poor. She knew — divine soul! — that her cold form would sleep just as quietly, be guarded by the angels just as faithfully, and as certainly go to its resurrection glory from a pine box as from the richest rosewood casket. And it was like the sweet simplicity of her whole life, — nothing for show, all for God and his poor.

Her request was complied with, but loving hands covered every inch of that plain stained coffin with fragrant flowers, making it rich and beautiful with those sincere tributes of affection and gratitude to one whose memory was a benediction.

The funeral services were conducted by the Rev. Francis Williams, pastor of the Unitarian Church of Hyde Park, and eloquent remarks were made by him and by Wm. Lloyd Garrison.

Mr. Williams could only testify to Sarah's life as he had known it since she came to live in the village.

"To the last," he said, "while her mind could plan, her pen could move, and her heart could prompt, she was busy in the service of humanity, — with her might and beyond her strength, in constant nameless deeds of kindness to those in need in our own neighborhood, and far to the south, deeds which were wise and beautiful, — help to the poor, sympathy with the suffering, consolation to the dying. She has fought the good fight of right and love; she has finished her course of duty; she has kept the faith of friendship and sacrifice.

"We will more truly live because she has lived among us. May her hope and peace be ours."

Mr. Garrison gave a brief summary of her life, and ended by saying: "In view of such a life as hers, consecrated to suffering humanity in its manifold needs, embracing all goodness, animated by the broadest catholicity of spirit, and adorned with every excellent attribute, any attempt at panegyric here seems as needless as it must be inadequate. Here there is nothing to depress or deplore, nothing premature or startling, nothing to be supplemented or finished. It is the consummation of a long life, well rounded with charitable deeds, active sympathies, toils, loving ministrations, grand testimonies, and nobly self-sacrificing endeavors. She lived only to do good, neither seeking nor desiring to be known, ever unselfish, unobtrusive, compassionate, and loving, dwelling in God and God in her."

The last look was then taken, the last kiss given, and the coffin, lifted by those who loved and honored the form it enclosed, was borne to its resting-place in Mount Hope Cemetery.

"Dear friend," wrote Angelina to me, before yet the last rites had been performed, "you know what I have lost, not *a sister only*, but a mother, friend, counsellor, — everything I could lose in a woman."

The longer our loved ones are spared to us, the closer becomes the tie by which we are bound to them, and the deeper the pain of separation. It was thus with Angelina. She could rejoice at her sister's blessed translation, but she keenly felt the bereavement notwithstanding. Their lives had been so bound together; they had walked so many years side by side; they had so shared each other's burdens, cares, and sorrows, that she who was left scarcely knew how to live the daily life without that dear twin-soul. And so tender, so true and sacred was the communion which had grown between them, that they could not be separated long.

Angelina continued, as her feeble health permitted, to do alone the work Sarah had shared with her. The sick, the poor, the sorrowing, were looked after and cared for as usual; but as she was already weighed down by declining years, the burdens she tried to bear were too heavy. Sarah used to say: "Angelina's creed is, for herself, work till you drop; for others, spare yourself." Now, with no anxiously watchful sister to restrain her, she overtaxed every power, and brought on the result which had been long feared, — the paralysis which finally ended her life.

Those who have read Mr. Weld's beautiful memorial of his wife, with the touching account of her last days, will find no fault, I am sure, if I reproduce a portion of it here, while to those who have not been so fortunate, it will show her sweet Christian spirit, mighty in its gentleness, as no words of mine could do. In vain may we look back through the centuries for a higher example of divine love and patience and heroic fortitude; and, as a friend observed, her expressions of gratitude for the long and perfect use of her faculties at the very moment when she felt the fatal touch which was to deprive her of them, was the sublimity of sweet and grateful trust.

The early shattering of Angelina's nervous system rendered her always exceedingly sensitive to outward impressions. She could not look upon any form of suffering without, in a measure, feeling it herself; nor could she read or listen to an account of great physical agony without a sensation of faintness which frequently obliged her, at such times, to leave the room and seek relief in the open air. The first stroke of paralysis occurred the summer after Sarah's death, and was brought on in a singular manner. Mr. Weld's account of the incident and its consequences is thus given : —

" For weeks she had visited almost daily a distant neighbor, far gone in consumption, whose wife was her dear friend. One day, over-heated and tired out by work and a long walk in the sun, she passed their house in returning home, too much overdone to call, as she thought to do, and had gone a quarter of a mile toward home, when it occurred to her, Mr. W. may be dying now! She turned back, and, as she feared, found him dying. As she sat by his bedside, holding his hand, a sensation never felt before seized her so strongly that she at once attempted to withdraw her hand, but saw that she could not without disturbing the dying man's last moments. She sat thus, in exceeding discomfort, half an hour, with that strange feeling creeping up her arm and down her side.

" At last his grasp relaxed, and she left, only able to totter, and upon getting home, she hardly knew how, declined supper, and went at once to bed, saying only, 'Tired, tired.' In the morning, when her husband rose, she said, 'I 've something to tell you.' Her tone alarmed him. 'Don't be alarmed,' she said. To his anxious question, 'Pray, what is it?' she said again, 'Now you must n't be troubled, I 'm not; it 's all for the best. Something ails my right side, I can't move hand or foot. It must be paralysis. Well, how thankful I should be that I have had the perfect use of all my faculties, limbs, and senses for sixty-eight years! And now, if they are to be taken from me, I shall have it always to be grateful for that I have had them so long. Why, I do think I am grateful for *this*, too. Come, let us be grateful together.' Her half-palsied husband could respond only in weakest words to the appeal of his unpalsied wife. While exulting in the sublime triumph of her spirit over the stroke that felled her, well might he feel abashed, as he did, to find that, in such a strait, he was so poor a help to her who, in all his straits, had been such a help to him. After a pause she added: 'Oh, possibly it is only the effect of my being so tired out last night. Why, it seems to me I was never half so tired. I wonder if a hard rubbing of your strong hands might n't throw it off.' Long and strongly he plied with friction the parts affected, but no muscle responded. All seemed dead to volition and motion. Though thus crippled in a moment, she insisted upon rising, that she might be ready for breakfast at the usual hour. As the process of dressing went on, she playfully enlivened it thus: 'Well, here I am a baby again; have to be dressed and fed, perhaps lugged round in arms or trundled in a wheel-chair, taught to walk on one foot, and sew and darn stockings with my left hand. Plenty of new lessons to learn that will keep me busy.

See what a chance I have to learn patience! The dear Father knew just what I needed,' etc.

" Soon after breakfast she gave herself a lesson in writing with her left hand, stopping often, as she slowly scrawled on, to laugh at her 'quail tracks.' After three months of tireless persistence, she partially recovered the use of her paralyzed muscles, so that she could write, sew, knit, wipe dishes, and sweep, and do 'very shabbily,' as she insisted, almost everything that she had done before.

During the six years that remained of her life here, she had what seemed to be two other slight shocks of paralysis, — one about three years after the first, and the other only three weeks before her death. This last was manifest in the sudden sinking of her bodily powers, preeminently those of speech. During all those years she looked upon herself as 'a soldier hourly awaiting orders,' often saying with her good-night kiss, 'May be this will be the last *here*,' or, 'Perhaps I shall send back my next from the other shore;' or, 'The dear Father may call me from you before morning;' or, 'Perhaps when I wake, it may be in a morning that has no night; then I can help you more than I can now.'

" Many letters received asked for her latest views and feelings about death and the life beyond, — as one expressed it, 'when she was entering the dark valley.' The 'valley' she saw, but no darkness, neither night nor shadow; all was light and peace. On the future life she had pondered much, but ever with a trust absolute and an abounding cheer. Fear, doubt, anxiety, suspense, she knew nothing of; none of them had power to mar her peace or jostle her conviction. While she could speak, she expressed the utmost gratitude that the dear

Father was loosening the cords of life so gently that she had no pain.

"When her speech failed, after a sinking in which she seemed dying, she strove to let us know that *she knew it* by trying to speak the word 'death.' Divining her thought, I said, 'Is it death?' Then in a kind of convulsive outburst came, 'Death, death!' Thinking that she was right, that it was indeed to her death *begun*, of what *could* die, thus *dating* her life immortal, I said, 'No, oh no! not death, but life immortal.' She instantly caught my meaning, and cried out, 'Life eternal! E — ter — nal life.' She soon sank into a gentle sleep for hours. When she awoke, what seemed that fatal sinking had passed.

"One night, while watching with her, after she had been a long time quietly sleeping, she seemed to be in pain, and began to toss excitedly. It was soon plain that what seemed bodily pain was mental anguish. She began to talk earnestly in mingled tones of pathos and strong remonstrance. She was back again among the scenes of childhood, talking upon slavery. At first, only words could be caught here and there, but enough to show that she was living over again the old horrors, and remonstrating with slave-holders upon the wrongs of slavery. Then came passages of Scripture, their most telling words given with strong emphasis, the others indistinctly; some in tones of solemn rebuke, others in those of heart-broken pathos, but most distinctly audible in detached fragments. There was one exception, — a few words uttered brokenly, with a half-explosive force, from James 5 : 4: 'The — hire — of — the — laborers, — kept — back — by — fraud, — crieth : — and — the — cries — are — in — the — ears — of — the — Lord.' . . .

"As we stood around her, straining to catch again some

fragmentary word, she would turn her eyes upon our faces, one by one, as though lovingly piercing our inmost; but though all speech failed, the intense longing of that look outspoke all words. . . .

"Then there was again a vain struggle to speak, but no words came! Only abortive sounds painfully shattered! How precious those unborn words! Oh, that we knew them!"

Thus quietly, peacefully, almost joyfully, the life forces of the worn and weary toiler weakened day by day, until, on the 26th of October, 1879, the great Husbandman called her from her labors at last. She lived the life and died the death of a saint.

Who shall dare to say when and where the echoes of her soul died away? Not in vain such lives as hers and her beloved sister's. They take their place with those of the heroes of the world, great among the greatest.

One last thing I must mention, as strongly illustrative of Angelina's modesty, and that shrinking from any praise of man which was such a marked trait in her character. She never voluntarily alluded to any act of hers which would be likely to draw upon her commendatory notice, even from the members of her own family, and in her charities she followed out as far as possible the Bible injunction: "When thou doest alms, let not thy left hand know what thy right hand doeth."

Her husband relates the following: —

"In November, 1839, in making provision for the *then* to her not improbable contingency of sudden death, Angelina prepared a communication to her husband, filled with details concerning themselves alone. This was enclosed in a sealed envelope, with directions that it should be opened only after her death. When, a few days after her decease, he broke the seal, he found, among many details, this item: 'I also leave to thee the *liability* of being called upon eventually to support in part four emancipated slaves in Charleston, S. C., whose freedom I have been instrumental in obtaining.'"

It is plain from the wording of the letter that she had never stated the fact to him. She lived forty years after writing it and putting it under seal; and yet, during all those years, she never gave him the least intimation of her having freed those four slaves and contributed to their support, as she had done. Even Sarah could not have known anything of it. Her brother Henry, to whom the bill of sale was made out, as they could not be legally emancipated, was probably the only person who was aware of her generous act. He became technically their owner, responsible for them to the State, but left them free to live and work for themselves as they pleased.

Angelina's funeral took place on the 29th of October, and to it came many old friends and veteran co-workers in the anti-slavery cause. The services were in keeping with the record of the life they commemorated. They were opened by that beautiful chant, "Thy will be done," followed by a touching prayer from the Rev. Mr. Morrison, who then briefly sketched the life of her who lay so still and beautiful before them. He was followed by Elizur Wright, who, overcome by the memories with which she was identified, memories of struggles, trials, perils, and triumphs, that he stood for a moment unable to speak. Then, only partially conquering his emotion, he told of what she did and what she was in those times which tried the souls of the stoutest. "There is," said he, "the courage of the mariner who buffets the angry waves. There is the courage of the warrior who marches

up to the cannon's mouth, coolly pressing forward amid
engines of destruction on every side. But hers was a
courage greater than theirs. She not only faced death at
the hands of stealthy assassins and howling mobs, in her
loyalty to truth, duty, and humanity, but she encountered
unflinchingly the awful frowns of the mighty consecrated
leaders of society, the scoffs and sneers of the multitude,
the outstretched finger of scorn, and the whispered mockery of pity, standing up for the lowest of the low. Nur-
tured in the very bosom of slavery, by her own observation
and thought, of one thing she became certain, — that it
was a false, cruel, accursed relation between human
beings. And to this conviction, from the very budding
of her womanhood, she was true; not the fear of poverty,
obloquy, or death could induce her to smother it. Neither wealth, nor fame, nor tyrant fashion, nor all that the
high position of her birth had to offer, could bribe her to
abate one syllable of her testimony against the seductive
system. . . . Let us hope that South Carolina will yet
count this noble, brave, excellent woman above all her
past heroes. She it was, more than all the rest of us put
together, who called out what was good and humane in
the Christian church to take the part of the slave, and
deliver the proud State of her birth from the monster
that had preyed on its vitals for a century. I have no
fitting words for a life like hers. With a mind high and
deep and broad enough to grasp the relations of justice
and mercy, and a heart warm enough to sympathize with
and cherish all that live, what a home she made! Words
cannot paint it. I saw it in that old stone house, surrounded with its beautiful garden, at Belleville, on the
banks of the Passaic. I saw it in that busy, bright, and
cheery palace of true education at Eagleswood, New

Jersey.   I have seen it here, in this Mecca of the wise.
Well done!   Oh, well done!"

Mr. Wright was followed by Robert F. Walcutt, Lucy
Stone, and Wendell Phillips.

"The women of to-day," said Lucy Stone, " owe more
than they will ever know to the high courage, the rare
insight, and fidelity to principle of this woman, by whose
suffering easy paths have been made for them.   Her example was a bugle-call to all other women.   Who can
tell how many have been quickened in a great life purpose by the heroism and self-forgetting devotion of her
whose voice we shall never hear again, but who, ' being
dead, yet speaketh.' "

The remarks of Wendell Phillips were peculiarly affecting, and were spoken with a tenderness which, for once
at least, disproved the assertion that his eloquence was
wanting in pathos.

" Friends," he said, " this life carries us back to the
first chapter of that great movement with which her
name is associated, — to 1835, ' 36, ' 37, ' 38, when our
cities roared with riot, when William Lloyd Garrison was
dragged through the streets, when Dresser was mobbed
in Nashville, and Macintosh burned in St. Louis.   At
that time, the hatred toward abolitionists was so bitter
and merciless that the friends of Lovejoy left his grave
long time unmarked; and at last ventured to put, with
his name, on his tombstone, only this piteous entreaty:
Jam Parce Sepulto, ' Spare him now in his grave.'

" As Friend Wright has said, we were but a handful,
and our words beat against the stony public as powerless
as if against the north wind.   We got no sympathy from
most northern men: their consciences were seared as
with a hot iron.   At this time a young woman came from

the proudest State in the slave-holding section. She came to lay on the altar of this despised cause, this seemingly hopeless crusade, both family and friends, the best social position, a high place in the church, genius, and many gifts. No man at this day can know the gratitude we felt for this help from such an unexpected source. After this [1] came James G. Birney from the South, and many able and influential men and women joined us. At last John Brown laid his life, the crowning sacrifice, on the altar of the cause. But no man who remembers 1837 and its lowering clouds will deny that there was hardly any contribution to the anti-slavery movement greater or more impressive than the crusade of these Grimké sisters through the New England States.

"When I think of Angelina, there comes to me the picture of the spotless dove in the tempest, as she battles with the storm, seeking for some place to rest her foot. She reminds me of innocence personified in Spenser's poem. In her girlhood, alone, heart-led, she comforts the slave in his quarters, mentally struggling with the problems his position wakes her to. Alone, not confused, but seeking something to lean on, she grasps the Church, which proves a broken reed. No whit disheartened, she turns from one sect to another, trying each by the infallible touchstone of that clear, child-like conscience. The two old, lonely Quakers rest her foot awhile. But the eager soul must work, not rest in testimony. Coming North at last, she makes her own religion one of sacrifice and toil. Breaking away from, rising above, all forms, the dove floats at last in the blue sky where no clouds

---

[1] A mistake. James G. Birney was one of the most widely known and influential leaders in the abolition cause at the time Angelina came into it.

reach. . . . This is no place for tears. Graciously, in loving kindness and tenderly, God broke the shackles and freed her soul. It was not the dust which surrounded her that we loved. It was not the form which encompassed her that we revere; but it was the soul. We linger a very little while, her old comrades. The hour comes, it is even now at the door, that God will open our eyes to see her as she is: the white-souled child of twelve years old ministering to want and sorrow; the ripe life, full of great influences; the serene old age, example and inspiration whose light will not soon go out. Farewell for a very little while. God keep us fit to join thee in that broader service on which thou hast entered."

At the close of Mr. Phillips' remarks a hymn was read and sung, followed by a fervent prayer from Mr. Morrison, when the services closed with the reading and singing of "Nearer, my God to Thee." Then, after the last look had been taken, the coffin-lid was softly closed over the placidly sleeping presence beneath, and the precious form was borne to Mount Hope, and tenderly lowered to its final resting-place. There the sisters, inseparable in life, lie side by side next the "Evergreen Path," in that "dreamless realm of silence."

A friend, describing the funeral, says:—

"The funeral services throughout wore no air of gloom. That sombre crape shrouded no one with its dismal tokens. The light of a glorious autumn day streamed in through uncurtained windows. It was not a house of mourning, — no sad word said, no look of sorrow worn. The tears that freely fell were not of grief, but tears of yearning love, of sympathy, of solemn joy and gratitude to God for such a life in its rounded completeness, such an example and testimony, such fidelity to conscience, such recoil from all self-seeking, such unswerving devotion to duty, come what might of peril or loss, even unto death."

Florence Nightingale, writing of a woman whose life, like the lives of Sarah and Angelina Grimké, had been devoted to the service of the poor, the weak, the oppressed, says at the close: —

"This is not an *in memoriam*, it is a war-cry such as she would have bid me write, — a cry for others to fill her place, to fill up the ranks, and fight the good fight against sin and vice and misery and wretchedness as she did, — the call to arms such as she was ever ready to obey."

Date Due